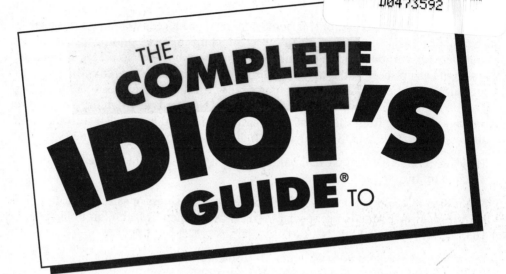

THE

COMPLETE IDIOT'S GUIDE® TO

Managing Your Time

by Jeff Davidson, MBA, CMC

alpha books

A Division of Macmillan General Reference
1633 Broadway, New York, NY 10019-6785

Macmillan Publishing books may be purchased for business or sales promotional use. For information please write: Special Markets Department, Macmillan Publishing USA, 1633 Broadway, New York, NY 10019.

International Standard Book Number: 0-02862943-4
Library of Congress Catalog Card Number: 98-89982

01 00 99   8 7 6 5 4 3 2 1

Interpretation of the printing code: the rightmost number of the first series of numbers is the year of the book's printing; the rightmost number of the second series of numbers is the number of the book's printing. For example, a printing code of 99-1 shows that the first printing occurred in 1999.

Printed in the United States of America

Alpha Development Team

Publisher
Kathy Nebenhaus

Editorial Director
Gary M. Krebs

Managing Editor
Bob Shuman

Marketing Brand Manager
Felice Primeau

Editor
Jessica Faust

Development Editors
Phil Kitchel
Amy Zavatto

Production Team

Development Editor
Nancy Gratton

Production Editor
Suzanne Snyder

Copy Editor
Krista Hansing

Cover Designer
Mike Freeland

Photo Editor
Richard H. Fox

Illustrator
Mark Hasselberger

Designer
Glenn Larsen

Indexer
John Jefferson

Layout/Proofreading
Carrie Allen
Jerry Cole

Contents at a Glance

Contents

Part 2: Appointing Yourself in Charge 67

7 Money Comes and Goes—Time Just Goes 69

8 To Sleep, Perchance to Not Wake Up Exhausted 81

Part 3: Communicating at All Speeds   125

12 Neat and Uncomplicated Tools to Manage Your Time   127

Appendices

Foreword

A funny thing happened on the way to the 21st century: It seems that all of society began marching to a faster drum beat. Despite all the books written on time management, all the software, all the gadgets, and all the tools designed to make your life simpler and easier, the sad reality is that, for most people, there still seems to be too much to do—and too little time in which to do it.

Author Jeff Davidson maintains—and it's hard to find fault with his observation—that no matter what tools or technologies are developed, your life will not change until you adhere to the simple realization that the *number* of items in competition for your time and attention is increasing—in some aspects, exponentially. At the same time, while you may live longer than you currently suppose (that is, if you think you'll hit 75 years of age, you may indeed hit 85 or 90), there still isn't enough time in your life on a daily, weekly, or yearly basis for you to ingest and absorb the array of necessary, scintillating, titillating, compelling, worthy, and downright fun items and issues that find their way into your personal kingdom. Jeff contends, and rightly so, that less can indeed be more. Enjoy that video that you chose, the meal you're eating, the spouse or significant other sitting on the couch with you, the car you're driving, the home you're living in, the book you're reading, and so on.

In this remarkable book, Jeff offers a plan that will help you consistently stay in control of your time, whether you are a college student, a sales executive, or the head of a sovereign nation. He does this by first leading you through a friendly but thorough discussion of the realities each of us faces on a daily basis. Then he gives you fresh perspectives and practical solutions to the time-crunching situations you encounter in all aspects of your life, whether at work, at home, while traveling, while on vacation, in a conference, or elsewhere. He's crafted this book so that you gain top-level advice offered with a touch of mirth and alarming honesty, in a down-to-earth style that will win you over in seconds flat.

One of the first notions that Jeff splendidly drives home is that to maintain control of your time, you have to begin leaving your place of work at the "normal" closing time, even if you can manage to do this for only one day a week for openers. With Jeff's plan, one day per week can expand to two, and then perhaps even three. You actually find yourself home while there's still daylight—and, if you're particularly careful and follow what else he has to say in this book, with an evening free on occasion. The twenty-six additional chapters that follow focus on a wide variety of ways to manage your time in every other situation you can imagine.

Jeff mercilessly abandons antiquated maxims about time management and instead offers real world, hands-on suggestions that you'll know and feel are right for you—and, most of the time, that work from the first moment you try them. His goal is nothing short of helping you to improve the quality of your life, for the rest of your life, and his central theme is that this is entirely achievable, based on how you approach each day—particularly, this day. Sometimes the changes Jeff suggests are subtle. He does this intentionally because it's his core belief that by asking you to change too much, too fast, you won't change at all. If you bite off more than you can chew, you'll all too often end up reverting back to where you were. Or, you'll resist the change altogether. So he treads carefully, acknowledging that you're already a very busy person, that your plate is already full, and that any suggestions he may offer to help you manage your time must be done so within that context.

If you're like me, you keep your favorite books nearby. This is one you'll want to keep close at hand. Even after you finish reading in its entirety, you'll want to refer back to it again and again. When you feel yourself slipping, break open this book to the chapter or passage that has immediate applicability for you. If you do, you'll be reinvigorated by the power and practicality of the suggestion, if not the wit and empathy inherent in Jeff's writing style.

As you conclude each chapter, you'll notice a neat bonus. Part and parcel with *The Complete Idiot's Guide* series by Macmillan, Jeff offers tips called "The Least You Need to Know" that quickly summarize chapter highlights. If you do nothing else but take these tips to heart, you'll gain great benefit from this book.

I, for one, am confident that you will be among the many thousands of readers who have successfully gleaned information and advice from this book that they put to use in their lives immediately. Let's face it: Time isn't money—time is life. By following the principles in this book, you effectively add to the length and quality of your life.

Yours truly,

Bob Losure

Former CNN headline news anchor and author of *Five Seconds to Air.*

Introduction: Get in Control of Time (Or Someone Else Will)

You're holding a book about winning back and managing your time. The chances are astronomical-to-nearly-100 percent that you lost it during the last decade. The quest to *win back* your time is a noble pursuit, but it's a fast-paced and frenzied existence you're enduring. With all that competes for your time and attention, how do you alter the pace of your career and life so *you* are in control of your time? How can you enjoy what your career and life have to offer, and once again have time to reflect, to ponder, to muse? Keep readin'.

We will examine how to improve the quality of your life *for the rest of your life*—a tall order to be sure. To achieve all this, first understand that whatever changes you make have to come *without* too much pain. I know this is contrary to what you've been led to believe about change, but bear with me. If the changes needed to win back your time are too difficult—too many rules, too many things to remember or do—then you're not going to stay with them.

What will work, then? Simple steps—a moderate shift here, an adjustment there. Gradual, subtle, natural changes in what you're already doing yield far greater long-term results. Changes that are radical or anxiety-provoking have much less chance of taking hold. Why? Well, if you've been alive for 25, 35, 45 years or more, it took that long to become who you are—just the way you are. You're clearly perfect at it! You're probably not going to change suddenly in 35 minutes or 35 hours, and in many cases not in 35 days.

Whenever you embark upon making changes that are too big a leap from *your current ways of doing things,* they won't last—or be effective. Therefore, *ignore* anything in this book that represents too much of a stretch for you right now. Proceed with the suggestions you can undertake most readily. As you initiate more changes, others will fall into place from the momentum of your actions. Such a deal! Gradually, with the proper perspective, a few specific techniques, and some built-in follow-up, you'll be able to win back your time naturally and easily.

I've structured the book to ease you into each topic as you reclaim your time. We'll move from broad-based to nitty-gritty workday issues; in the last few chapters, we tackle personal perspectives.

Part 1, "The Clock of Your (Current) Life Is Ticking," looks at the broad context of why you feel mounting time pressure, and offers specific strategies for winning back your time—starting with the fundamental notion of leaving work at a semi-decent hour *and feeling good about it!* You'll get a look at some specific ways your time is depleted, why many others face the same predicament you do, and how to exert more control over where your time goes. I'll discuss how you can determine what's most important to you and what will be required (realistically) to support your priorities.

Part 2, "Appointing Yourself in Charge," focuses on specific areas of your life—including how much sleep you're getting (versus how much you *need*), responding to the requests others make for your time, keeping your office organized, mastering your own files, and handling correspondence efficiently. You'll find tools and technologies that can help you be more efficient or (if you don't use them) slide farther into the morass of the overwhelmed.

Part 3, "Communicating at All Speeds," examines fundamental problems people face when coming face to face with technology and options for potentially staying in touch with others around the clock. This may sound enticing but is actually a great hindrance both to managing your time and feeling in control of your life.

Part 4, "Springing Yourself from Time Traps," discusses key areas for saving time—making decisions more quickly, honing the ability to focus on *one thing at a time*, and the importance of *constantly reducing what you hold on to* (it'll keep your own systems uncomplicated).

Part 5, "Managing Your Time in Special Situations," highlights how to carve out time for yourself and for others in your life. After all, if managing your time only applies to the functional aspects of your work and life, your life could seem quite empty.

Part 6, "Own a Peace of the Mental Rock," delves into higher-order notions such as undertaking a quest to live in "Real Time," catching up with today, and occasionally withdrawing from the maddening crowd.

I conclude with an observation about why the future is bright for you—assuming, of course, that you *follow* the sage advice offered throughout! I suggest pausing after each chapter and *acting on some of what you've taken in*—otherwise you're unlikely to act on anything in the book.

Extras

Keep an eye open for the helpful hints, tips, warnings, and definitions that are sprinkled throughout this book—they're there to ease you on your way to taking control of your time. Here's what to look for:

A Stitch in Time

Tips and advice that will make improving your time-management skills a snap.

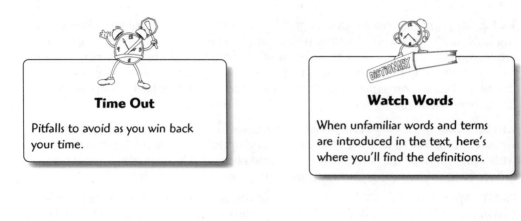

Time Out

Pitfalls to avoid as you win back your time.

Watch Words

When unfamiliar words and terms are introduced in the text, here's where you'll find the definitions.

Chronos Says

Longer anecdotes that explain, clarify, or elaborate on points raised in the chapter. Look here for background info, insights, and helpful recommendations for further techniques you'll find useful in reaching your goal of managing your time.

Acknowledgments

Thanks to all the wonderful folks at Macmillan General Reference for picking me to write this book and giving me the support that would make it the winner that it is! Thanks to Kathy Nebenhaus, Bob Shuman, Gary Krebs, Nancy Gratton, Suzanne Snyder, and Krista Hansing for their careful editing, insights, and guidance.

Thanks to Jennifer Hayes, Christine Ramos, Rachelle Schifter, Julie Sanders, Grace Sullivan, Margaret Durantee, Guardi Wilks, and all the other marketing, sales, special markets, and promotion specialists for ensuring that people throughout the world will by this book.

Thanks to Seth Kotch, Kate Simpson, and R. J. Beatty for proofing, Sandy Knudsen for her fingers that fly over the keyboard like quicksilver, and Valerie Davidson, age 8, my daily inspiration.

Special Thanks to the Technical Reviewers

The Complete Idiot's Guide to Managing Your Time was reviewed by experts who not only checked the technical accuracy of what you'll learn here, but also provided insight and guidance to help us ensure that this book gives you everything you need to know to begin making better decisions about how you spend your time. We extend our special thanks to these folks:

Claire Conway is a freelance writer who served as features editor for *Psychology Today* in New York City. Prior to that, she was managing editor of *Stanford Medicine* magazine, a publication of the Stanford University Medical School Alumni Association. Born and raised in California, she received an M.S.J. from Northwestern's Medill School of Journalism.

Carol Krucoff writes a health and fitness column for the *Washington Post*, where she was founding editor of the weekly Health Section. A freelance writer based in Chapel Hill, North Carolina, she contributes to a variety of publications, including *Reader's Digest*, *Self*, *Parents*, and *The Saturday Evening Post*. She also teaches Creative Nonfiction for Duke University's Continuing Education Department. She has two school-age children, is married to a cardiologist, and holds a brown belt in karate.

Part 1
The Clock of Your (Current) Life is Ticking

For all that's been written about life, it is still finite. Your life, in particular, had a distinct beginning and will have a distinct ending—at least the part that occurs on earth—unless, of course, you believe you're coming back as someone else or in some other form. In that case (cosmically speaking), you're not facing any time pressure and might not need this book; whatever you don't take care of in this life, you can always address in your next life—or in the second or third life after this one. Of course, advances in human technology are making the future more complex all the time; you'll have a whole new set of challenges if you come back as a human being. (You know, come to think of it, maybe you are better off continuing with this book now. If you learn to win back your time in this life, you'll have a head start in future lives.)

Ahem…back in the here-and-now, I'll gently present seven hard-hitting chapters that explore mysteries of the ages. Among these revelations: why staying at work longer can be self-defeating, what really happens to your time, quality (versus quantity) of life, whose fault the present mess isn't, getting real and getting what you want, identifying and going after your priorities, and why time and money are not the same thing. You know, the basics…

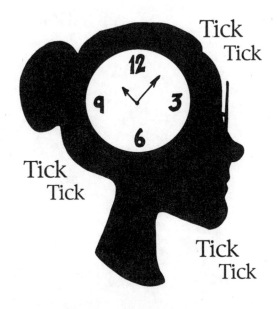

I Know I Can Finish Most of This (If I Stay Late)

> ### In This Chapter
>
> ➤ Designing a campaign to win back your time
>
> ➤ Making subtle changes that you can stick to
>
> ➤ Feeling good about leaving work on time
>
> ➤ Establishing a plan—and following it

For the heck of it, let's begin this book at the beginning. One of the most insidious time traps you can possibly fall into is believing that by working a little longer (or taking work home on the weekend) you can finally "catch up." This is a fallacy that will keep you perpetually chasing the clock for at least the rest of your career—and maybe the rest of your life.

Hey, I sympathize with you if you've found yourself staying at the office later, or toting a bulging briefcase home with you. At face value, these maneuvers probably seem to be the logical response to the pressures you face. For too many people, however, they are also a trap.

Staying Longer Ain't the Answer

If you find yourself perpetually taking work home or working a little longer at the office, putting in overtime becomes the norm. Soon you're taking another 30 i(40 pages of reading material home at night as if this habit were *simply the way it is*.

Chronos Says

Now and then it makes sense to take work home from the office. All career achievers do. During specific campaigns (such as the launch of a new business, product, or service), when you change jobs, or when you're approaching a significant event, it makes sense to bone up and spend a few extra hours at work. But this should be the *exception*, not the rule.

When you consistently work longer hours or take work home from the office, you begin to forget what it's like to have a free weeknight—and eventually a free weekend. I've observed the working styles of some of the most successful people in Eastern and Western society: multimillionaires, best-selling authors, high-powered corporate executives, association leaders, top-level government officials, educators, people from all walks of life. The most successful people in any endeavor maintain a healthy balance between their work and non-work lives.

Americans *are* working longer hours, but not everybody puts in marathon work days. The typical German worker, by comparison, works 320–400 *fewer* hours per year than his American counterpart. A journalist for *U.S. News and World Report* observed that Europeans are shocked to discover that most Americans get only two weeks of annual vacation time. The norm in Germany (as well as France and Great Britain) is five weeks off annually. American entrepreneurs, as a whole, work the longest: an average of 54 hours a week, if you believe they're reporting their true work time (they probably work many *more* hours than they reported).

Time Out!

U. S. Department of Labor statistics reveal that in the past quarter century, the amount of time Americans have spent at their jobs has risen steadily.

Americans, in general, also are sleeping less (the subject of Chapter 8, "To Sleep, Perchance to Not Wake Up Exhausted"), which significantly affects work performance. In fact, all aspects of life are becoming more complex. As a result, you may be enjoying your life a bit less these days (Chapter 3, "With Decades to Go, You Can't Keep Playing Beat the Clock," discusses five mega-realities that may tell you why).

People aren't just working more and scurrying more because they feel like it: Our society as a whole has become more competitive and demanding. Employers require more. Kids seem to have to be part of more activities. There are kabillions of entertainment options. So we work more hours, try to keep up, quietly go nuts, and consider it normal.

Part-timers, Students, and Homemakers Are Not Exempt

Doesn't anybody get a break in this world? Nearly all the time-pressure problems that plague the denizens of the full-time working world will visit you as well. While you may have extra moments to yourself here and there, *everyone* who holds any position of responsibility today—and those responsibilities include studying, managing a home, caring for others, and nearly any other pursuit you can think of— faces pressures unknown to previous generations (as you'll learn in Chapter 3).

Your key to reducing the time pressure you feel is not to stay longer at work. Indeed, to reclaim your day you *cannot* stay longer. This will become clear shortly.

A Stitch in Time

Your quest becomes accomplishing that which you seek to accomplish *within* the eight or nine hours you call the workday.

The Workday Does End, Just Like Careers and Lives

Suppose your workday is 8:00 a.m. to 5:00 p.m., with an hour for lunch, yielding a total working time of eight hours. Studies show that most people are working only about 60 percent of those eight hours for which they were hired. Even in downsizing times, most people work a daily average of only four hours and 48 minutes on the tasks, assignments, and activities for which they were hired. Notable exceptions include the self-employed and the fanatically driven. When everyone around you is fanatically driven, whoa boy, that can seem normal!

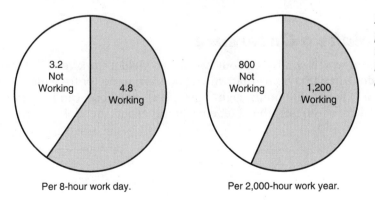

3.2 Not Working — 4.8 Working

Per 8-hour work day.

800 Not Working — 1,200 Working

Per 2,000-hour work year.

Many people don't work a full eight hours a day, even though they spend eight hours on the job, as these charts illustrate.

Excuse me! So maybe you're not among those who dawdle—and you certainly don't goof off for 40 percent of your day. Still, it's unlikely that you're working the full eight hours. Among the many factors that inhibit your inclination to work a solid eight hours every day are these:

1. *Too many domestic tasks*. See Chapter 7, "Money Comes and Goes—Time Just Goes," to learn how easy it is to get *stuck* thinking that if you spend a few minutes here and a few minutes there taking care of domestic tasks yourself, you can 1) stay on top of it all, 2) save a little money, *and* 3) cruise into work in high gear.

2. *Not getting enough sleep*. Zzzz. See Chapter 8, "To Sleep, Perchance to Not Wake Up Exhausted," which discusses why you're probably not getting enough sleep, and how this leads to lack of efficiency and effectiveness.

3. *Overcommitting*. See Chapter 9, "Volunteering a Little Less—and Liking It," about how widely available technology gives managers and businesses the opportunity to get more done—and also to expect more from their employees. Much more.

4. *Not being sufficiently organized*. See Chapter 10, "Making Your Office Work for You," which explains that a desk is not a filing cabinet, and that window sills and the corners of your room are not permanent storage locations. You can rule an empire from a desk if you know how to do it correctly.

5. *Lacking effective tools*. See Chapter 12, "Neat and Uncomplicated Tools to Manage Your Time," on how you can put new technology to work for you—and how to avoid being overwhelmed by what you acquire.

Beyond these factors, over-socializing is the norm in many offices. Some professionals develop elaborate rituals, such as sharpening three pencils, refilling the coffee cup, making a personal call, or waiting until the clock on the wall is at the top of the hour before they get down to work. (I know, that's not something you would ever do, but some people do this.)

2,000 Hours to Make a Difference

Eight-hour workdays, of which you have about 250 a year, yield a work year of 2,000 hours. Can you get done in 2,000 hours that which you want to do (or for which you were hired)? Yes—2,000 hours, 200 hours, eight hours, even one hour, can be a great deal of time if you have the mindset, the quiet environment, and the tools you need to be productive.

Leaving and Feeling Good About it Takes Discipline (...at First)

To sustain the habit of leaving work on time, start with a small step. For example, decide that on every Tuesday you will stop working on time and take no extra work home with you. After freeing up Tuesdays for an entire month, perhaps add Thursdays. In another month, add Mondays; in the fourth month, add Wednesdays. I'm assuming there's no way you work late on Friday! (Or *do* you? If you do, then start with Fridays!)

What transpires in the first month when you've decided that each Tuesday will be a normal eight- or nine-hour workday and nothing more? Automatically you begin to be more focused about what you want to get done on Tuesdays. Almost imperceptibly, you begin to parcel out your time during the day more judiciously.

By midday, stop and assess what you've done and what else you'd like to get done. Near the end of the day, assess what more you can (realistically) get done and what's best to leave for tomorrow.

You begin to set a natural, internal alignment in motion. (Sounds exciting, doesn't it?) Your internal cylinders fire in harmony to give you a vibrant, productive workday on Tuesday so you can leave on time.

> **Time Out!**
>
> If you deplete yourself of crucial elements to high productivity by coming to work feeling exhausted or mentally unprepared—or if you keep getting interrupted—one hour, eight hours, 200 hours, 2,000 hours, or more won't be sufficient for you to do your work. (See Chapter 18 for a simple system to minimize interruptions.)

> **Chronos Says**
>
> For some reason that only the gods of Mount Olympus can explain, once you've solidly made the decision to leave on time on Tuesdays, every cell in your body works in unison to help you accomplish your goal.

Preparing for the Unforeseen: Marking Out Boundaries

Okay, so you're thinking that these resolutions look good on paper, but what about when the boss comes in and hands you a 4-inch stack of reports at 3:45 in the afternoon? Or what about when you get a fax, an e-mail message, or a memo that upsets the applecart? These things *do* happen—and not just to you!

Take a real-world approach to your time, your life, and what you're likely to face during the typical workday. Consider how to approach the predictable impediments to leaving on time on Tuesday.

Rather than treat an unexpected project that gets dumped in your lap late in the day as an intrusion, stretch a tad to view it as something else. You got the project because you were trusted, accomplished, or, in some cases, simply there.

Many government workers have no trouble establishing their time boundaries at work. They leave on time because that's what their government policy manual says, right there in clause 92-513-ak7-1, subclause 8-PD 601-00 07, paragraph 6.12, line 8—*no overtime, pal.* If you're in the private sector, however, you may not have such regulations on your side. (See Chapter 9 for some options you *do* have.)

Overworked, Underproductive

If you're concerned that staying late and putting in ridiculous hours is *de rigueur* in your organizational culture, you need data and special strategies. First the data! Professor Carey Cooper, an American at Manchester University in England, is one of Europe's foremost stress specialists. He has found that performance declines by 25 percent after a 60-hour workweek. He also calculated that the annual cost of stress-related illnesses attributed to overwork topped $80 billion in the United States—more than $1,600 a year for every other worker in America. Other studies show that work output is growing faster in Germany than in the United States—even though (as you've seen) Germans work fewer hours than Americans.

Stated bluntly, excess work hours put in by already overtaxed employees are of negative value to an organization when viewed in the context of overall work performance, direct health-care costs, and productivity lost to absenteeism and general lethargy on the job.

Strategies for Survival

Now that you know the downside of overwork, it's time to learn the strategies for avoiding it:

1. Let it be known that you maintain a home office where you devote countless hours to the organization after 5:00 each evening. Then take most evenings off.

2. Invite bosses and coworkers to your home for some other reason, and conveniently give them a tour of your command-center-away-from-the-office.

3. When you discuss your work, focus on your results (as opposed to the hours you log after 5:00). It is exceedingly difficult for anyone to argue with results.

4. Find role-models—outstanding achievers within your organization who leave at (close to) normal closing time at least a few nights a week—and drop hints about those role-models' working styles in conversation with others in your organization.

5. Acquire whatever high-tech tools (see Chapter 12) you can find that will help you be more productive. If your organization won't foot the bill, do it yourself. Often your long-term output and advancement will more than offset the upfront cost.

6. On those evenings you *do* work late at the office, be conspicuous. Make the rounds; let yourself be seen. After all, if you've *got* to stay late, at least make sure it's noticed.

7. On those evenings when you take work home, use oversized containers or boxes to transport your projects. You may even choose to bring boxes back and forth to the office even when you have no intention of doing any work at home (this makes you look productive).

Watch Words

A **dynamic bargain** is an agreement you make with yourself to assess what you've accomplished (and what more you want to accomplish) from time to time throughout the day, adjusting to new conditions as they emerge.

8. If zipping out at 5:00 carries a particular stigma in your office, leave earlier. Huh? Yes, schedule an appointment across town for 3:30 p.m. and when it's completed, *don't* head back to the office. This is a tried-and-true strategy for laggards, but it can work as well for highly productive types like you. If you feel guilty, work for the last 30 or 45 minutes at home.

For now I'm only discussing ending work at a sane hour *one* night a week. If this represents too much of a leap for you, either stop reading this book and continue suffering the way you have been, or change jobs and try to find a more enlightened employer. Otherwise begin to plot your strategy now: It's your job and it's your life.

Bring on Da Crunch Time

On the way to developing Microsoft Windows 98 and getting it out the darn door on time, the elite Seattle nerd corps found themselves working progressively longer hours each day. For some, it became unbearable. Some went into a robot phase (you know, work, work, work, work...). Some quit. Some will be added to the ranks of the millionaires. All got the opportunity to chill out afterward. Yes, there are exceedingly tough campaigns, but they are always of *finite* duration.

Crunch times come and go, and they're often unavoidable. Still, you don't want to get into the bind of treating the typical workday like crunch time. When you do, you start to do foolish things—like throwing more and more of your time at challenges instead of devising less time-consuming ways to handle them—and that means not leaving work on time tonight, tomorrow, or any other night in the foreseeable future.

Make a Great Bargain with Yourself

A master stroke for winning back your time at any point in your day—Tuesdays or any other day—is to continually strike a *dynamic bargain* with yourself. It's a self-reinforcing tool for achieving a desired outcome that you've identified within a certain time frame, as in the end of the day! Suppose it's 2:15 and you'd like to accomplish three more items before the day is over. Here's the magic phrase I want you to begin using:

> *"What would it take for me to feel good about ending work on time today?"*

This is what I mean when I talk about a dynamic bargain. I have this powerful question as a poster on my wall in my office. It can give you the freedom to feel good about leaving the office on time because, when you answer it each morning, you're making that bargain with yourself—*you're stating exactly what you'll need to accomplish to feel good about leaving on time that day.*

Suppose that today your answer to the question is to finish three particular items on your desk, after which you can feel good about leaving on time. Now suppose that the boss drops a bomb on your desk late in the day. You automatically get to strike a *new* dynamic bargain with yourself, given the prevailing circumstances. Your new bargain may include simply making sufficient headway on the project that's been dropped in your lap, or accomplishing two of your previous three tasks and *x* percent of this new project.

Thank God It's Friday, and I Feel Good About What I've Done!

The same principle holds true for leaving the office on Friday: feeling good about what you accomplished during the work week. Here is the question to ask yourself (usually sometime around midday on Friday, but even as early as Thursday):

> *"By the end of work on Friday, what do I want to have accomplished so I can feel good about the weekend?"*

By employing such questions and striking these dynamic bargains with yourself, you get to avoid what too many professionals in society still confront: leaving, on most workdays, not feeling good about what they've accomplished, not having a sense of completion, and bringing work home. If you're like most of these people, you want to be more productive. You want to get raises and promotions, but you don't want to have a lousy life in the process!

Rather than striking dynamic bargains with themselves, most people frequently do the opposite. They'll have several things they wanted to accomplish that day—and actually manage to accomplish some of them, crossing them off the

A Stitch In Time

Regardless of projects, e-mail, faxes, phone calls, or other intrusions into your perfect world, continually strike a dynamic bargain with yourself so you get to leave the workplace on time, feeling good about what you accomplished.

list. Rather than feel good about their accomplishments and accept the reward of the freedom to leave on time, they add several *more* items to the list—a great way to guarantee that they'll still leave their offices feeling beleaguered. Here you have the perfect prescription for leaving the workplace every day *not* feeling good about what you've accomplished: If you always have a lengthy, running list of "stuff" you have to do, you never get a sense of getting things *done,* and you never get any sense of being in control of your time.

A Self-Reinforcing Process

When you've made the conscious decision to leave on time on Tuesday and strike the dynamic bargain with yourself, almost magically the small stuff drops off your list of things to do. You focus on bigger, more crucial tasks or responsibilities. On the first Tuesday—and certainly by the second or third—you begin to benefit from *a system of self-reinforcement,* whereby the rewards you enjoy (such as leaving the office on time and actually having an evening free of work-related thoughts) are so enticing that you structure your workday so as to achieve your rewards.

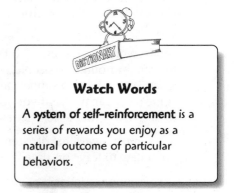

Watch Words

A **system of self-reinforcement** is a series of rewards you enjoy as a natural outcome of particular behaviors.

Eventually, when you add Thursdays, then Mondays, then Wednesdays to the roster of days that you leave work on time, you begin to reclaim your entire work week. A marvelous cycle is initiated. You actually

➤ leave the workplace with more zest.

➤ have more energy to pursue your non-work life.

➤ sleep better.

➤ arrive at work more rested.

➤ are more productive on the job.

And as you increase the probability of leaving another workday on time, you perpetuate the cycle and its benefits.

Choosing to Leave on Time at Will

How do you get this ball rolling? Declare that the following Tuesday will be an eight- or nine-hour workday and nothing more. You leave on time that day feeling good about what you've completed. That's it—no grandiose plan, no long-term commitment, no radical change, and 'nary any anxiety.

If you're having trouble giving yourself permission for this one-day, no-overtime treat, recall how long you've been in your profession, and remember that you're in your present position for a lengthy run. On no particular day and at no particular hour are you truly rooted to your desk. After all, you're a professional. You've gotten the job done before; you'll get it done now as well. Feel free to trust your own judgment about when it's okay for you to go home.

Now it may be that on a given day when you've decided you're going to leave on time, something happens to upset your workload so that you have more to do than you can get done that day (and when won't that happen?). The temptation will be to stay late and deal with the new task. Resist it! Instead, map out exactly what you're going to *begin* on the next morning to handle this addition to your workload. Preparing a plan for tomorrow will reduce any anxiety or guilt you feel about leaving on time *today*. Ultimately, you'll have little anxiety or guilt. After all, you have a right to a personal life, don't you?

Let everyone in your office know that you're leaving at five, or whatever closing time is for you. Announce to people, "I've got to be outta here at five today," or whatever it takes. People tend to support another's goal when that goal has been announced. Some people may resent you for leaving on time; fortunately, most will not. You have to decide whether to let the resentful attitudes of a few control your actions.

If you must have a list of "steps," here's what you can do on that first Tuesday, or any other day, to leave on time when you choose to:

1. Announce to everyone that you have a personal commitment at 5:30 that evening. If you have a child, you could say your child is in need of your assistance.

2. Mark on your calendar that you'll be leaving at five.

3. Get a good night's rest the night before, so you'll feel up for the effort of fulfilling your dynamic bargain with yourself.

4. Eat a light lunch; it keeps you from being sluggish in the afternoon.

5. Strike a dynamic bargain with yourself at the start of the day, in late morning, in early afternoon, and in late afternoon. (Remember, it's okay to modify the bargain to accommodate a changing situation.)

6. Regard any intrusion or upset as merely part of the workday, deal with it as you can, and plan tomorrow's strategy for coping. Do *not* let it change your plans about leaving on time today.

A Stitch in Time

Silently repeat to yourself, "I choose to easily leave at closing time today and feel good about it." Never mind if at first you think this mantra doesn't have any power. Do it. You'll find yourself leaving more often, more easily, and on time.

7. After striking the dynamic bargain with yourself, don't be tempted to add more items to your list at the last minute.

8. Envision how you'll feel when you leave right at closing time (but there is no reason for you to be staring at the clock for the last 45 minutes).

9. If you want support, ask a coworker to walk you out the door at closing time.

Chronos Says

This chapter is intentionally simple, if for no other reason than this: The more you have to do and have to remember, the less you'll do and the less you'll remember. Your only assignment, boiled down to four words: *Leave work on time.*

Ensuring that you leave the workplace on time may seem too involved to accomplish. If you engage in only two or three of these steps, however, you'll still get the reinforcement you need.

The Least You Need to Know

➤ You deserve to leave on time—*at least* occasionally—and to feel good about it.

➤ Depending on your organization's culture, you may have to use one or more of the strategies discussed in this chapter to leave on time.

➤ The changes you need to make have to be easy to follow. If they're too difficult, they won't hold. Winning back your time requires only small steps, but a progression of them.

➤ To leave on time, start with one day per week (such as Tuesday) and strive to leave on time every Tuesday for an entire month.

➤ You can strike a dynamic bargain with yourself to feel good about what you've done, choose what else you want to accomplish, and feel good about leaving.

➤ As you develop the habit of leaving on time, you develop a positive cycle of high productivity, even while leaving on time more often.

Chapter 2

Time Flies Whether You're Having Fun or Not

In This Chapter

➤ A cheerful subject: how much longer you're likely to be on the planet

➤ The number one activity that sucks the time out of your life

➤ The cumulative impact of spending time daily on what you don't enjoy doing

➤ Why simplifying things is important now—and will become ultra-important in the future

Have you ever considered how much time you have in your whole life, and how much time you've spent on various activities? Suppose you graduated from college at the age of 22, and in the course of your life expect to work about 48 years, bringing you to age 70. Over the course of those 48 years, how much time would you suppose you spend on routine activities such as working, sleeping, watching television, recreating, eating, and commuting?

Here's the typical breakdown, based on various demographic studies and my own calculations:

Working	16 years
Sleeping	15 years
Watching TV	5–7 years
Recreation	2–4 years
Eating	3 years
Commuting	2 years

It's amazing when you look at the cumulative total of the time you'll spend engaged in these activities during your productive work life, isn't it? Suppose that you're already 30-something and on average will live another 45 years. Thus, you have about 30 *waking* years left, and about 20 years to accomplish whatever you're seeking to accomplish. That realization alone may help you focus your time.

If you're thinking, "Hey, I'm 35 now, but I don't expect to reach age 80," think again. The Society of Actuaries estimates that if you're female and you're 40 years old, your life expectancy is age 85 (see Table 2.1). For males it's slightly less: age 80.3.

Table 2.1   Life Expectancy of Americans

FEMALE		MALE	
AGE NOW (Years)	EXPECTED LIFE (Years)	AGE NOW (Years)	EXPECTED LIFE (Years)
40	85.0	40	80.3
50	85.5	50	81.1
60	86.3	60	82.6
70	87.9	70	85.0

Data from the National Center for Health Statistics shows that every 25 years since 1900, the life expectancy of both men and women has increased by about five to seven years. The increase in life expectancy for people born between 1975 and the year 2000 may be as much as nine or 10 years (see Table 2.2).

Table 2.2   Life Expectancy of Americans (from Birth, by 25-Year Intervals)

FEMALE		MALE	
YEAR BORN	EXPECTED LIFE (Years)	YEAR BORN	EXPECTED LIFE (Years)
1900	48.3	1900	46.3
1925	57.6	1925	55.6
1950	71.1	1950	65.6
1975	76.5	1975	68.7
2000	85.0?	2000	79?

On average, most people are likely to live longer than they think they will. If you think you're going to reach 75, you may well reach 85. If you think you'll reach 85, you may hit 95!

The realization that you may live much longer than you think necessitates developing some longer-term perspectives about how you want to spend your life. (I'll cover these in greater detail in the last few chapters of the book.)

Do More Because of Limits

With decades to go, it's easy to get caught in the trap of delaying the activities and events you promised yourself you'd undertake. Whether life seems short and merry or long and boring, there's only so much of it. Architect Frank Lloyd Wright once observed that people build "most nobly when limitations are at their greatest." You can use the limits on your time or resources to achieve your most desired accomplishments.

Consider how productive you are, for example, before you leave for a vacation, or consider how well you do on a task when a deadline's been imposed (even though you might not enjoy *having* the deadline or like the person who imposed it). As the author of many books, I can testify about deadlines. Each time I signed a book contract, I had to deliver a specified number of manuscript pages in coherent order and accomplish what I said I would do by a certain date. These contracts with their deadlines imposed limits that actually helped me be productive.

Time Out!

Whether you have 30 or 60 years left, it will be to no avail if your days race by, you wake up thinking "I'm already behind," you stay late at work night after night, or you let stuff pile up and then feel exhausted because you can't get to it.

These limits may not always appear helpful or supportive, yet you undoubtedly have many of them confronting you. Here are some examples of limits you may be facing right now:

➤ You have to pick your kids up by 5:30 p.m. each weekday.

➤ You have to turn in a work log on Fridays.

➤ The author of this book said you need to leave the office most days by 5:00 p.m.

➤ You can work about nine hours daily before your mind turns to mush.

➤ Your hard disk is almost full, and you have no intention of spending more money for disk space.

➤ Your contract is ending in 11 weeks.

➤ You have only 24 minutes left on your lunch break.

➤ The post office closes weekdays at 5:00 p.m.

➤ The oil in your car needs changing after another 300 miles.

➤ A loved one is nearing the end of his or her life.

➤ You get paid every two weeks.

What limits do you face in your career or personal life that you could employ to propel yourself to higher productivity? When you learn to harness these for the benefit they provide, you begin to reclaim your time. I suggest that your daily, primary limit be finishing your day so that you leave work at the normal closing hour.

Wanted for Time Theft

After examining the problem for many years, sifting through extensive research, interviewing dozens (even hundreds) of people, collecting articles, and tapping the minds of many learned people, I found that the No. 1 element that robs people of their time can be boiled down to a single word. (Please be sure you are seated in a chair that can support your full weight in case you slump over when the answer is revealed to you.)

Okay, if you're ready, take a deep breath, because here's the revelation of the ages. The No. 1 activity in society, in your life, that steals your time is (here it is…I hope you're ready for this):

Television

Is there anything I can say in a couple of pages that will help you reduce the amount of TV you watch? Consider the findings of TV-Free America, a public service organization in Washington, D.C., that has compiled some rather startling data about television viewership in America.

The average American watches more than four hours of TV each day, equal to two months of non-stop TV-watching per year, and equal to more than 12 solid years of non-stop TV-watching in the life of a person who lives to age 72. African-Americans on average watch 50 percent more TV than that. (You, of course, watch less…or so everyone self proclaims!)

➤ 66 percent of Americans regularly watch TV while eating dinner.

➤ 49 percent of Americans say they watch too much television.

➤ 19 percent of Americans say they would like to read or visit friends but have no time!

Chronos Says

More than 90 million adults watch television at least two hours on any Monday and Tuesday night—that's at least 360 million viewer-hours. These viewer-hours, if applied elsewhere, could transform the nation. Ah, but you can choose to watch TV whenever you want, can't you? Or can you? Television is a drug, with many of the same side effects. And as the Internet becomes an even more dominating aspect of more people's lives, it will compete (or merge!) with TV, to claim your time.

The Road to Oblivion

In his book *Amusing Ourselves to Death*, Dr. Neil Postman says that entertainment is the dominant force in public discourse in society, affecting the arts, sciences, politics, religion, and education. Certainly entertainment has a necessary function in your life: It stimulates thinking. It can be liberating to your soul. It can give you a break from the monotony of daily living. Of note, entertainment can free you to explore new ways of thinking, new ideas, and new possibilities.

The harm in being over-entertained—which everyone now faces—is that your daily life seems to pale by comparison to what you view on the screen. What is the true cost of entertainment? Certainly your time, and usually your money. You're willing to trade these because entertainment expressly is not reality. It's designed to be "superior" to reality—it's more titillating and more engaging. Fantasy sells almost as much stuff on TV as sports, and a lot more stuff than reality ever could. In a 1978 lecture at Indiana University, the late Gene Roddenberry, creator of *Star Trek*, boldly stated: "TV does not exist to entertain you. TV exists to sell you things."

A Stitch in Time

Don't make the erroneous assumption that watching brain-drain TV or listening to shock-talkers on the radio has no impact on your time. They vacuum up time you could have used doing something worthwhile. Turn 'em off.

When compared to what you see on the screen, your own life may seem dull and plastic. Instead, it is real and holds great potential. Ultimately, the quality of your life and your memories will depend on what you actively did, not what you passively ingested (such as seeing *Titanic* for the fourth time). What will you do in the next month to enrich your life—*actually* enrich it? Who will you meet? Where will you go? What will you risk?

Consider how much time and energy you're willing to spend with your favorite TV personalities. Now contrast that figure with how much time you actually spend with any of your neighbors.

Neighbors. You know, those near-strangers next door. Do you even care about their lives? They are, in fact, flesh-and-blood people with real strengths, real weaknesses, and real lives. They could even become your lifelong friends. Do they offer as much pleasure to you, however, as the fantasy heroes on *Star Trek*, Nicolas Cage in his latest role, or Kate Moss simply posing in garments you'll never own? You might have a reason to like your neighbors: Consider all the expensive stuff they're not trying to sell you.

Hey, Bud, I Tune In to the News to Be Informed

I know people who habitually watch the nightly news believing that this will make them informed citizens. The problem is, most of what passes for news on television isn't news. It's merely a constant rehash of the same stories, over and over.

I'm sorry (and truly, who isn't?) that there's drug infestation in society and that too many teenagers get pregnant, or that there are homeless people roaming many cities. Unless you're going to take action on any of this stuff, however, watching another report about it doesn't count toward your status as an informed citizen. So the time you spend watching it is largely wasted.

I'm not saying you shouldn't watch *any* news. I'm saying you need to understand the context in which news is presented. News shows are designed to attract viewers so sponsors can sell things, the same as any other show; they heighten the emphasis on some stories and completely ignore others. As long as you understand the limitations of TV news, watch away! Just don't turn off your brain when the news comes on. And remember that there are probably many more productive ways you could be spending that time.

A Bad Mix: Kids and Too Much Television

Maybe you didn't watch as much television as kids today are watching, but you probably watched a lot, and the habit is ingrained. Kids today, however, are going to set some all-time records. Here's what TV-Free America found about children's television viewing:

➤ The number of minutes per week that parents spend in meaningful conversation with their children is 38.5.

➤ The number of minutes per week that the average child watches television is 1,680.

➤ 50 percent of children ages 6–17 have television sets in their bedrooms.

➤ 70 percent of day-care centers use TV sets during a typical day.

➤ 73 percent of parents would like to limit their children's TV viewing (but apparently they don't or they can't).

As if you're not watching enough television, what are the chances that you're turning on the radio, cluttering up your mind from that source as well? I know, I know, if you listen to the radio on the way to work, how can that possibly be stealing your time? Well, it is. Consider a friend of mine who liked to listen to a West Coast shock-jock in the morning. Year after year, my friend Bill was titillated on his way to work by the shock-talk.

In essence, he settled for an electronic fix, another type of drug, if you will, that briefly took him out of his own life and into some form of contemptuous humor that got him through the

Time Out!

Dr. James Twitchell, author of *The Carnival Culture*, notes that most American children begin watching television before they can talk. A child by age 6 will have invested more hours watching television than in speaking with his or her father over an entire lifetime.

So sad.

next 10 minutes (or however long) on his way to work. After all the years of listening, my friend is not empowered, energized, or any better able to face his day. Obviously, however, he isn't alone; this particular shock-jock has become a multimillion-dollar media franchise with strong ratings for more than a decade.

If you listen closely to the shock-jocks of the world, you can sometimes detect that they are angry people. They vent their anger through a form of broadcast that has (for whatever reason) become a socially tolerated route to riches.

Okay So What Would You Suggest?

Instead of listening to the radio on his drive to work, Bill could contemplate what he'd like to achieve for that day. If he has meetings, he could consider some of the points he would like to make. He might visualize having a pleasant lunch with a coworker. He might put on some classical music to ease his mind as he makes his way through the otherwise-unforgiving rush-hour traffic.

If he consciously chooses to play the radio, maybe he'll switch to a provocative newsmagazine-type show where important issues are covered with some depth and perspective. Perhaps he'll tune into something else that truly stimulates his intellect.

Of course, he has the option of playing CDs or cassettes. He can listen to famous speeches,

A Stitch In Time

Question: How many shock-jocks does it take to change a light bulb? Answer: Three...one to throw the bulb away, one to stick his finger in the socket, and one to yell about it on the air.

motivational programs, or entire books on cassette. He can play cassettes of famous old-time radio programs or listen to the Bible on cassette. By applying a modicum of creativity, he can turn his commuting time into something special. He can turn his use of the television into something special.

My friend has many different pockets of time available. He also has many options to determine how he spends them.

So do you.

Jeff Davidson's 10 Steps to Kick Electronic Addiction

Okay, I can hear you wailing, "I'm not giving up television. There are some worthwhile things on TV, and I can turn it off whenever I want." If that's so, then fine. If you're hooked and you can't admit it to me, however, perhaps you can admit it to yourself. Here are 10 techniques you can use to get yourself unplugged:

➤ Go a whole weekend without turning on a radio or television.

➤ Call your friends (both local and out-of-town) one evening per week instead of watching any television.

➤ Return to hobbies such as stamp collecting, playing a musical instrument, gardening, or playing word games one other weeknight instead of watching TV.

➤ Allow yourself to selectively watch two hours of programming each Saturday and Sunday for one month.

➤ Permit yourself one high-quality video per weekend during another month. The video has to inspire, inform, reflect history, be biographical, or be otherwise socially redeeming. Stop watching shoot-em-ups, chase scenes, and films that titillate but add little to your life.

➤ If you walk or jog with a Walkman, undertake these exercises three times in a row without such a device so you can experience another way to jog: naturally taking in what you pass on your trip.

➤ Look for others seeking to wean themselves from electronics. Is there a book discussion group? How about a bowling league, outing club, or biking group?

➤ Attend sporting events rather than viewing the same type of event on television. Watching a good high school baseball team or women's collegiate tennis match can be as rewarding as watching major-league baseball or Wimbledon, respectively. And you visibly support the athletes by being there.

➤ Recognize that the number of videos, CDs, computer games, and other electronic items competing for your attention exceeds the time you have in life to pay homage to them.

➤ Recognize that rightly or wrongly, you've been programmed since birth to tune in to electronic media for news, information, entertainment, and diversion. It's by no means your only option.

New Math for Reclaiming Your Time

While the cumulative impact of being hooked on electronic media is considerable, the cumulative impact of doing what you don't like to do, such as household tasks, is equally insidious.

Recall the example of your 48-year career—graduating college at age 22 and working until age 70. Here's a quick way to see that you need to delegate or cast off those things you don't like to do. Any activity in which you engage for only 30 minutes a day in the course of your 48-year productive work life will take one solid year of your life! Any activity in which you engage for only 60 minutes a day will take two solid years of your 48 years. How can this be so?

Think of it as a mini math lesson most of us never had in school: Numbers That Really Mean Something. One half-hour is to 24 hours as one hour is to 48 hours. That's true by the good old commutative principle of arithmetic. Likewise, one hour is to 48 hours as one year is to 48 years.

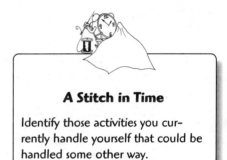

A Stitch in Time

Identify those activities you currently handle yourself that could be handled some other way.

For you math buffs, here it is in equation form:

1/2 hour is to 24 hours as 1 hour is to 48 hours, or .5/24 = 1/48

1 hour is to 48 hours as 1 year is to 48 years, or 1/48 = 1/48

When you consume one-forty-eighth of your day (only 30 minutes out of 24 hours) the cumulative effect over 48 years is to consume one year of your 48 years. There's no way around it. If you clean your house, on average, for 30 minutes a day, then in the course of 48 years you've spent the equivalent of one solid year, nonstop, cleaning your house.

This immediately tells you that if you can't stand cleaning your house (or something else you don't like) for an average of 30 minutes a day, stop doing it. I don't mean let your house get filthy; hire somebody to clean your house, clean it yourself less often, or find some other alternative. Why? Because the time in your life is being drained; the cumulative impact of doing what you don't like to do, as illustrated above, is that your precious years are being consumed—time you simply cannot reclaim under any scenario.

"Well," you say, "that's fine to pay somebody to clean the house, but ultimately I'll be paying people for all kinds of things I don't like to do, just so I can have more time." Yes! Exactly. In Chapter 6, "Supporting Your Priorities for Fun and Profit," I'll get into this in spades.

What can you list as those things that you know you need to stop doing because they are taking up valuable time in your life? For openers, here are some suggestions:

➤ Cleaning the house.

➤ Reading the newspaper every day. If it makes you late for work or prevents you from handling higher-priority activities, only do it now and then.

➤ Cutting the grass, or any other yard work. (See Chapter 7, "Money Comes and Goes—Time Just Goes," about when it makes sense to pay others to do it.)

➤ Fixing your car.

➤ Cooking.

➤ Reading junk mail because it's addressed to you. (Don't laugh. I know many people who feel compelled to read their junk mail: "Gee, somebody took the time to send me this.")

➤ Reading every godforsaken e-mail message zapped over to you.

➤ Answering the phone.

Cutting Through the Confusion

If you enjoy some of these activities, hey, by all means keep doing them. Perhaps you can do them a little less; perhaps there's another way to proceed. Your goal is to delegate or eliminate those tasks or activities which you can't *stand* doing. One author advises, "Don't manage something if you can eliminate it altogether." Not bad advice.

My contact-lens routine was becoming a bore—taking them off, cleaning them, lubricating them, and so forth. I was able to save several minutes per day by switching to a new type of contact lens that's thinner, requires little maintenance, can be worn 16 or 18 hours a day with no irritation, and after several days, can simply be chucked.

What have you been putting off that you could handle right now, knowing you would simplify your life? I won't be offended if you stop reading for a moment, close the book, and give this question the full consideration it merits in your life...unless, of course, a Seinfeld rerun is coming on.

The Least You Need to Know

➤ You're probably going to live longer than you think, but it will be to no avail if your days continue to race by full of frustration and the same old stuff.

➤ To the extent you can reduce your television viewing, you'll experience an abundance of extra time in your life.

➤ The cumulative impact of doing what you don't like to do is profound. A 30-minute, 20-minute, or even 10-minute savings per day is significant and increases the amount of discretionary time you have in your life.

➤ If drudgery sticks you up for either your life's time or your money, which would you rather hand over?

➤ Don't manage what you can eliminate altogether; simplify what you can't eliminate.

Chapter 3

With Decades to Go You Can't Keep Playing Beat the Clock

In This Chapter

➤ Why the time pressure you face is not a personal shortcoming ("Hey, I already knew that.")

➤ The time-pressure problems that others report they are experiencing ("You too?")

➤ Five converging factors that conspire to consume your time ("Gotcha!")

➤ The future: more choices competing for your time and attention than you ever imagined ("Where's it all going?")

You've been exposed to two major principles thus far. From Chapter 1, "I Know I Can Finish Most of This (If I Stay Late)," you learned that the key to winning back your time is to redevelop the habit of getting your work done within the course of a normal eight- or nine-hour workday. In Chapter 2, "Time Flies Whether You're Having Fun or Not," you saw that even small segments of time each day have a dramatic impact on the amount of time in your life over which you *have* control. The dilemma of this entire culture, however, is that everyone is feeling time-pressed—and feeling as if he or she is a poor time manager. As if somehow he or she is at fault. (Do you know the feeling?)

It may *not* be your fault, and you're not alone. The problem you face is a wide-sweeping phenomenon more than a personal one. Fortunately, there are various measures you can take in your career and life to win back more of your time, and that's what this book will examine.

Let's see how to live longer and enjoy it more.

Time Out!

Simply being born into this culture at this time all but guarantees that much of your day will be consumed if you're not careful.

An Entire Society in a Hurry

Suppose that all of society *was* in a hurry (which at most times seems to be the case). People having to do more all the time, in *less* time. Sound familiar? The evidence is mounting that time has become the most valuable commodity in society. A study entitled "Time Pressure in the '90s," conducted by Hilton Time Value Surveys, found that folks feel just plain rushed:

➤ 77 percent of people surveyed selected "spending time with family and friends" as their top goal in the '90s.

➤ 66 percent said they would put more emphasis on "having free time."

➤ 38 percent report cutting back on sleep to make more time.

➤ 33 percent said they are unlikely to be able to make time for their ideal weekend.

➤ 33 percent said they don't accomplish what they set out to do each day.

➤ 31 percent worry that they don't spend enough time with their families and friends.

➤ 29 percent constantly feel under stress.

➤ 21 percent said they don't have time for fun anymore.

➤ 20 percent reported calling in sick to work at least once in the past year when they simply needed time to relax.

So, You Feel it Too? We All Do!

In my book *Breathing Space: Living and Working at a Comfortable Pace in a Sped-Up Society*, I identify five mega-realities that have an unconditional impact on everybody all the time. The factors include the following:

➤ An expanding volume of knowledge

➤ Mass-media growth and electronic addiction

➤ The paper-trail culture

➤ An overabundance of choices

➤ Population growth

Does it seem as if these factors are ganging up on you? If so, it's time to divide and conquer: Examine them one by one and suggest some strategies.

Expanding Knowledge

Knowledge is power, or so it's been said, but how many people feel powerful? Do you? Many people fear that they are underinformed. The volume of new knowledge broadcast and published in every field is enormous; it exceeds anyone's ability to keep pace. All told, more words are published or broadcast *in an hour* than you could comfortably ingest in the rest of your life. By far, America leads the world in the sheer volume of information generated and disseminated.

This is why so many books designed to help readers be more effective in managing their time fall wide of the mark. They list dozens, if not hundreds, of rules. You already have more "rules for being effective" to follow in your career and life, however, than you can comfortably handle. I doubt that feels effective.

Chronos Says

The key to winning back your time is to be more effective at *being* rather than *doing*. If this sounds like mumbo-jumbo, let me say it another way: To win back your time ultimately means *having less to do*, not more. Doing the "less" I'm talking about means carefully identifying what's vitally important to you, which is the subject of Chapter 6, "Supporting Your Priorities for Fun and Profit."

Mass-Media Growth

As you may recall from Chapter 2 (and probably from personal experience), the negative effect of the mass media on people's lives continues unchecked. In America, more than five out of six households own VCRs. In 1972, three major television networks dominated television: ABC, NBC, and CBS. Now, there are more than 500 full-power independent television stations. Many cable TV subscribers receive up to 140 channels that offer more than 72,000 shows per month. (Bruce Springsteen understated it best: "Fifty-seven channels and nothin' on." It may soon be 5,700 channels. Same complaint.)

With its sensationalized trivia, the mass media overglut obscures fundamental issues that *do* merit concern, such as preserving the environment or feeding the starving.

Time Out!

Here's the impasse of this over-information era that confronts you: The time necessary to learn all the rules for effective living now exceeds your life expectancy.

Paper Trails to You

It's like being a computer overloaded with data or a detective swamped with too many eyewitness reports. Having too much paper to deal with makes you feel overwhelmed and overworked. We are consuming at least three times as much paper as 10 years ago. There are two basic reasons why American society in particular spews so much paper:

➤ We have nearly the lowest postal rates in the world.

➤ We have the most equipment that can generate paper.

The typical executive receives more than 225 pieces of *unsolicited* mail each month, or about 12 pieces daily. Annually the average family receives more than 200 catalogs they did not request—on top of those they *did* request, with an onslaught arriving between late August and Christmas.

Watch Words

In *Future Shock* (1970), Alvin Toffler used the term **overchoice** to describe the stress that comes from too many options, especially the so-what variety. In paperback, the book itself was a classic example: You could buy it with a blue, orange, or hot-pink cover.

Way too Many Choices

Choice is the blessing of a free market economy. Like too much of everything else, however, having too many choices is, well, overwhelming. Currently, more than 1,350 varieties of shampoo are on the market. More than 2,000 skin care products are currently selling. Some 100 different types of exercise shoes are now available, each with scores of variations in style, functions, and features. Every choice demands time; increased time expenditure means mounting exhaustion.

Population Unchecked

Not only are you not alone, but you're less alone all the time. From the dawn of creation to A.D. 1850, world population grew to one billion. It grew to two billion by 1930, three billion by 1960, four billion by 1979, five billion by 1987, and six billion by 1996, with seven billion en route. Every 33 months, 272 million people (the current population of America) are added to the planet.

Each *day*, world population (births minus deaths) increases by more than 275,000 people. Geometric growth in human population permeates and dominates every aspect of the planet: its resources, the environment, and all living things.

One could argue that having all these new people around makes the world more hectic, its people more competitive for fewer economic niches, and employers more apt to see the labor force as a cheap commodity whose personal time they can claim willy-nilly. The increasing effects of population pressure has a profound impact upon the reality of current human existence. I don't see how you can ignore it.

The Weight of the World

In the Philippines, the Manila Hotel now provides 5-minute helicopter rides for guests between the hotel and the downtown business district. Otherwise, the rush-hour trip would take an hour and a half by car.

Sixty Minutes reporter Morley Safer narrated a segment on the show, which discussed how mass tourism is "turning the world's places of beauty into swarming ant hills and rancid junk heaps." Among the worldwide treasures being laid to waste are these:

A Stitch In Time

If you feel better about your own life, it's easier to empathize and take action on behalf of those who need help. For one thing, you have a little more time to do so.

> ➤ Venice is sinking more rapidly than it would be otherwise because of the extreme number of pedestrian tourists.

> ➤ The Great Wall of China is crumbling under the weight of increasing numbers of tourists.

> ➤ The face of the Parthenon is slowly but surely being scratched to oblivion.

Undoubtedly, you've already heard about the number of endangered species throughout the globe. This is directly attributable to the increase in human population, increase in development, and clearing of rain forests.

While scientists debate whether global temperatures are irrevocably rising, the trend of the last 50 years is now becoming clear. In 1950, according to *Vital Signs,* the average global temperature was 58.75 degrees Fahrenheit. By 1970, this had risen to 59.07 degrees Fahrenheit—and by the mid '90s it had risen to 59.36 degrees Fahrenheit.

More People, Less Mobility

The effect of rapid increases in population alone has a dramatic impact on the pace of society and your life. Predictably, more densely packed urban areas have resulted in a gridlock of the nation's transportation systems.

It *is* taking you longer to drive merely a few blocks; it's not the day of the week or the season, and it's not going to subside soon. Our population and road use grow faster than government's ability to repair highways, bridges, and vital urban arteries.

Watch Words

What the words gridlock, airlock, camplock, shoplock, and cyberlock tell you is that it pays to be a **contrarian**, a word I like that means "somebody too stubbornly individual to do what everybody else is trying to do at once."

The roads aren't going to clear up soon; it would cost more than $2 trillion over the next 30 years to repair and maintain the nation's pipes, tunnels, cables, and roads. More than half of the heavily traveled roads in America that link urban and suburban areas are in fair to poor condition. Is it any wonder you lose a good chunk of your time getting to work and back?

Commuting snarls are increasing. City planners report there will be no clear solution to gridlock for decades, and population studies reveal that the nation's metropolitan areas will become home to an even greater percentage of the population.

Crowding makes urban space harder to traverse, which eats up more time; hence the less space there is, the less time there is. Even suburban areas will face unending traffic dilemmas. If only the gridlock were confined to commuter arteries. Not so. Shoppers, air travelers, vacationers, even campers—everyone in motion—is (or will be) feeling its effects. We'll get to counteracting them in a minute; for now, consider some of these "locks" on your time.

Airlock

If you haven't noticed, airline passenger traffic has more than tripled since 1980. Concurrently, there are fewer nonstop flights, particularly on cross-continental trips. Airport expansion trails the increased passenger loads. Worse, all airlines pad their scheduled departure and arrival times—extended more than 50 percent since 1980—to appear as if they're not late, while actual air time remains about the same. When you're scheduled to board at 10:10 a.m., that is simply when you're supposed to be seated in the plane. Rollout from the gate is always later. Consequently they're as slow and late as ever, but now they're within the promised limits.

If you're not already doing it, bring plenty of work (or another diversion) with you so you can remain productive (or at least calm) despite flight delays.

Camplock

On an average summer day, Yellowstone Park has more visitors than the population of Houston. Other national parks across the country are faced with swarms of visitors; campsites are in high demand. While the federal government is making good progress restoring the parks, in the meantime vacationers have to contend with traffic, lines for concessions, and waiting lists for campsites.

Hereafter it may make sense to do your camping Tuesday through Thursday—whenever the masses are not there—or find "undiscovered" parks closer to home.

Shoplock

If all 272 million Americans went shopping at the same time, each would have 20 square feet of retail space. There is more retail space in America today than ever. Despite the dramatic increase in catalog and TV shopping, shopping malls still always appear crowded. Waiting for a parking space can take 10 minutes, unless you're willing to park in the far reaches of some lots. Once inside, you have to jostle through crowds to get to shops, movie theaters, and restaurants—and that's on slow days. You get the worst during the holidays.

Maybe it's time to shop by catalog with more fervor.

Cyberlock

With the increasing number of people going online—combined with the inability of major online services to meet the increased demand—cyberlock is in full swing. Several-minute waits to be connected are common (to a computer, even one minute is an eon). Cyberlock could become a recurring phenomenon as even more people go online for longer periods of time, sending and downloading ever-larger volumes of information.

Are you willing to log on at 3:00 a.m.? It would help (as long as you don't make a habit of disrupting your sleep).

A Stitch In Time

To avoid the locks that so many others encounter, commute at different times, fly at different times, camp at other times, shop at different times, and get online at other times than the masses.

Avoiding Lines, or Time-Shifting 101

If you find yourself perpetually waiting in lines, practice time-shifting to avoid crowds. No, you don't need a time machine—just your good sense. Consider these suggestions:

➤ Go get your movie tickets early, take a walk, and then return three minutes before the picture starts (after everyone has already filed into the theater). There are always available seats, even for twosomes; theater management knows exactly how many tickets they're selling for each showing.

➤ A different approach to movies: Go to the theater early for the first showing, buy your tickets, go in and take a seat, and for the next 20 minutes or so listen to your favorite music with a Walkman headset.

➤ If you commute, rather than going earlier or later, explore not going in at all— by telecommuting. (I'll discuss this in detail in Chapter 6, "Supporting Your Priorities for Fun and Profit.")

➤ To avoid airlock, fly in the day before and fly out after everyone else has. Schedule vacation travel time, particularly around Thanksgiving and Christmas, as much as six months in advance. You might stay home during those times and travel when everyone else isn't—namely, the week after the holidays.

➤ To avoid camplock, patronize some of the less-traveled national and state parks. There are more than 200 national parks and thousands of state parks; most do not experience hordes of visitors.

➤ To avoid cyberlock, consider getting online later (say, after 10:00 p.m.) if you're on the West Coast; most East Coast users will have gone to bed. If you're on the East Coast, get online early (say, 6:00 or 7:00 a.m.); most West Coast users will still be asleep.

➤ To avoid shoplock, make more purchases by catalog—but be careful of how and when you give out your name. Otherwise you'll be inundated by dozens of other catalog vendors. You probably have a fax machine at work, and you may even have one at home. Shopping by fax has never been easier. It's actually a great time-saver because your name, address, phone, and fax number are accurately submitted to vendors, along with your order, order number, and the price.

Saving Shopping Time

"Shop 'til you drop" is often too true for too many people. Why do it? The list in this section contains a host of tips you can use to budget your time more effectively and feel less stressed when shopping (in general, and during the holidays):

➤ First, don't wait until the last days or hours before picking up a crucial item.

➤ Avoid going to huge shopping malls, if you can. Use the 800-numbers found in catalogs, or go online. Ask that your name be kept off the vendors' direct-mail lists. Receiving dozens of unwanted catalogs throughout the year diminishes your breathing space and contributes to landfills.

➤ Spend a few minutes at home or work contemplating what you are going to buy and for whom. Then draw up a list and bring it with you—this will help keep you focused and less prone to becoming overwhelmed once you're inside the stores.

➤ If you have to go to a super regional mall because of the choice or selections available, arrive near the opening or closing. Don't compete with the mad rush of shoppers during peak hours.

➤ Find a mall entrance that is less popular than the others. You're likely to find a parking space more easily.

➤ Reduce the strain of carrying large bundles by choosing smaller-sized gifts, such as jewelry, compact discs, cassettes, gloves, sunglasses, and so forth.

➤ Shop on Monday, Tuesday, or Wednesday evenings. Avoid weekend shopping!

➤ Give yourself frequent breaks while shopping. It's not a marathon event. There is no reason to make shopping for friends and loved ones anything but a joyful experience. Lighten up!

➤ Patronize establishments that have one long line, now used in banks or airports, where the person at the front of the line goes to the next available service attendant. Avoid stores that have parallel lines that prompt shoppers to guess which line will be the fastest.

Time Out!

Don't patronize stores that have one line for purchases and another line for pickup. You'll easily double your time in line. Such an arrangement is highly beneficial for the store, but not for you.

➤ If you find a gift that would please many of those on your gift list, such as chocolates or a book, buy multiple quantities in one transaction to reduce overall shopping time.

➤ When buying holiday gifts and cards, make your shopping count three and four times. Think: Is there someone having a wedding, birthday, or baby shower soon? It may mean doing a little more shopping now, but you'll avoid many more trips in the throes of January, February, and March.

➤ If you anticipate a long line, bring something that will help to make the time pass by more easily. This could be a bit of reading material, something to eat, a hand-gripper, or even a hand-held game.

➤ Vote with your feet. If a store consistently causes you to wait and has not figured out how to handle varying streams of customers throughout the day and week (because they've never plotted their own internal rush hours), decide to take your business elsewhere.

➤ Once you get the packages home, take them to your table, desk or wherever you're going to complete the shopping trip—you still have to remove tags and stickers, file the invoices, wrap items, mail some of them, and store others.

➤ Designate one evening for greeting cards—if you send out cards, send them all out the same evening; then they're out of the way and en route.

Chronos Says

From now on, you're likely to experience other forms of "lock" in whatever career or personal endeavors you undertake. Engaging in activities at times when the masses are not has never been a more useful option. Become a contrarian!

The simple reality of today and of your life (not to mention everyone else's) is that society will grow more complex every day for the rest of your life. (Wow, what an existence.) Who gets the blame? As we'll see in the next chapter, nobody.

The Least You Need to Know

➤ Simply being born into this society, at this time, all but guarantees that increasingly you will feel pressed for time.

➤ The time pressure you feel is largely not your fault.

➤ More choices mean more time spent choosing.

➤ Shop, travel, camp, and drive when others are not. Time-shift to avoid crowds whenever you can.

➤ Use store services when shopping, such as catalog ordering, delivery, and gift-wrapping.

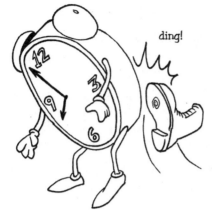

ding!

Chapter 4

Cooling Down the Feverish Pace

In This Chapter

➤ Social complexity happens!

➤ The basics for approaching a new task, learning a new procedure, or assimilating new information

➤ The virtue and wisdom of slowing down

➤ Your checkbook and your time are inextricably linked

➤ Abdicating low-level choices

As a professional speaker, I often address groups at annual conventions and conferences. I am no longer amazed at the ever-growing variety of professional associations that have not only been established, but that actually have thousands of members. For example, there is (whether you believe it or not) a National Association of Sewer Service Companies, a Cranial Academy, a Medieval Academy of America, a Society of Certified Kitchen and Bathroom Designers, a Society of Wine Educators, and even an International Concatenated (the spelling *is* correct) Order of Hoo-Hoo. Ho-ho.

More people, more groups, more information generated, where's it all leading? One result is that the amount of information that competes for your time on a daily basis is on the rise—and taking a staggering toll. You may have an M.B.A. degree, you may have 10 years of management experience under your belt, and you may have read every book on time management in creation. Nevertheless, you can't keep up. You are not alone—and you are probably not to blame.

How Your Feel About Yourself Is *Not* the Issue

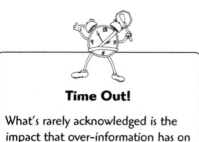

Time Out!

What's rarely acknowledged is the impact that over-information has on your own sense of adequacy. More and more professionals feel inadequate, as if somehow they're supposed to be on top of it all.

If you feel any diminished sense of self-worth or self-esteem, ease up. This is a characteristic response when human beings are overexposed to stimuli.

Feeling time-pressed today is not connected to how you were raised, it's not a question of where you went to school, where you live, your profession, or who you married. Even individuals who display high self-worth and high self-esteem often have too many concerns competing for their time and attention; they feel extreme time pressure. Even people who set goals—and do it well—frequently feel overwhelmed.

If you can accept the notion that the dissipation of your career and personal time is probably not your fault, you're already well on the road to winning back your time.

Rain Barrels Keep Falling on My Head

Suppose you were extremely parched and the only source of water was a huge, heavy rain barrel. One way to quench your thirst would be to lift it up and try to gulp a few sips at a time. This feat would require impressive strength and balance, but why waste so much effort on such a difficult way to drink? If you take a small cup, stick it in the rain barrel, and extract a couple of ounces at a time, you could far more easily quench your thirst. Now consider the daily information deluge. When you attempt to take in everything that's flung your way, the predictable response is that you drown in information (and still don't quench your thirst).

Tackling new information—such as navigating the Internet, integrating another technology into your work routine, or assimilating other changes—is smoother when you employ the *basics*.

What are the basics? It's simple:

1. Follow directions.
2. Take one step at a time.
3. Assess where you are every couple of steps.
4. After each assessment, having determined that you are on the right path, continue.

Information comes to you at a breakneck pace, and that pace will accelerate day after day for the rest of your life. How can you avoid being overwhelmed? Don't bite off more than you can chew; sometimes simply slowing down is the best response to "too much of too much" competing for your time and attention. Slow down so that you can figure out the best way to proceed.

Slowing Down Has Its Virtues

When I speak to audiences about the dilemma of coping with today's complexities and discuss potential solutions, I ask, "Do you want it fast, or do you want it to last?" Hereafter, I'd like you to begin practicing a new response when a lot is thrown at you: Take a momentary pause.

I saw a clever phrase that sums up the philosophy here: "Don't just do something, sit there." Too often, the reflex to take action only exacerbates your time-pressure problems. I'll tackle this issue head-on in Part 6.

Are You Deficit-Spending?

A Stitch in Time

Give up trying to stay on top of it all, which only ensures monumental frustration. Nobody today can keep on top of everything, nor is the attempt worthwhile. What you *can* do—and this is quite a lot—is make choices about where (and to what) you'll direct your time and attention.

One area of day-to-day living where most of us feel overwhelmed is in handling our debts and other financial obligations. The bills come in, and everybody needs to be paid. Staying in a positive cash-flow position can start to feel like a full-time job in itself. Running a deficit budget, if you're stuck there, is a full-scale time thief.

Has there ever been a nation in the history of the earth that accumulated huge deficits over a prolonged period of time, lacked a concerted effort toward reducing these deficits, and was able to sustain economic prosperity for its citizens?

No, this isn't a paid political announcement. What I'm basically asking you is this: Can a nation (or a person—*you*, in particular) run up huge deficits and expect no consequences? Chances are you have some financial deficits (lucky guess, huh?). For decades, millions of Americans have accumulated personal debt via credit cards, loans, and other forms of financing. Such sustained deficit-spending eventually erodes your ability to prepare for the future—and, worse, to capitalize on current opportunities.

What's all this got to do with winning back your time? Well, it's an exercise in fiendishly simple logic: The more you owe, the more enslaved you are! Chances are you've been taught to consume way past your needs. As time passes, I find (and you may have hit upon a similar insight) that the more material possessions I own, the less I feel in control of my time. (Not that there aren't some really neat things to buy). For example, during my college days and early 20s, when I had little, I felt the freest—freest from worry, and freest from the time-consuming task of juggling my bills.

Right now, how would it feel if all your credit cards were paid off? How would it feel if you paid your monthly rent or mortgage several for months in advance? How would it feel if your car loan was paid off? How would it feel if you were actually able to pay some of your utility bills for months down the road? For most people, it would feel wonderful. You'd feel in control of your time. I've experienced this first-hand, because I do this. More to the point, the time spent worrying is reduced to zip.

I know the arguments about losing the interest I could have earned on the money if I pay for the electric bill three months in advance. Ah, but wait. A month after I've paid my electric bill three months in advance, I get the next month's bill. Guess what? It shows that I have a huge credit and that *nothing* is due. I *smile* when I see bills like these. So will you. This approach frees you twice: Not only is the bill already paid (which robs the bill of its wet-blanket effect), but you've freed yourself from having to fight the reluctance to sit down and pay it now.

To reduce your personal financial deficits, I suggest placing a moratorium on spending—regardless of what items entice you—until your credit cards are paid off. Now, please, let's not confuse issues. In Chapter 2, "Time Flies Whether You're Having Fun or Not," I discuss briefly the value of paying others to do those things that you don't like to do—it's a way of investing in your freedom. This is a theme I'll return to in detail in Chapter 7, "Money Comes and Goes—Time Just Goes." That's not what I'm talking about here. Learning to rein in your tendency for overspending is different from buying back the time you would otherwise have to spend on unnecessary chores you actively dislike.

Chronos Says

Paying for something that frees up your time is a life benefit. Paying for material things that you don't need (and that certainly don't save you time) may be satisfying, but ultimately can be draining.

Here are some useful exercises for controlling your checkbook, simplifying your financial life, and winning back more of your time:

1. *Write checks to pay bills in advance of their due dates.* Then keep an advance file with a folder for each day of the month. Place the check in a sealed, addressed, stamped envelope. Then put the envelope in the folder of the day it's to be mailed. This way the money is allocated in advance in your checkbook, and your

bills are paid on time. If your checking account pays interest (for you "interest" buffs), it also means that you don't lose interest.

2. *Occasionally overpay the balance due on your continuing accounts, or pay early.* This provides you the aforementioned psychological boost when you see a credit on your next statement, and it gives you a good reputation with your creditors— which could come in handy in the future.

3. *Keep a stick-on note in your checkbook for an immediate reference that lists what's coming in this month and what needs to go out.* This provides you with a running mini-cash-flow list that you can refer to any time. Update it every couple of weeks, or days, if necessary.

4. *Look back through your old checks and carefully see what you paid to whom for what.* Do the same thing with your monthly credit card statements. Put a red mark next to all those expenditures that you didn't need to make, or that in retrospect you could have done without.

5. Now, considering expenditures on the horizon, which ones can you cut?

As author Roger Dawson says, it doesn't matter how much money you're making; if you're spending more than you take in each month, you're headed for trouble.

Enough Choices to Confound Anyone

One fundamental reason you might not be enjoying this time of your life as much as you did a year (or five years) ago is the number of choices you continually confront (one of the "mega-realities"). While flying from Denver to San Francisco and flipping through one of the airline magazines, I came upon an ad for jelly beans. You remember jelly beans, little bundles of mouth-size fun? When people in my age group were growing up, how many different colors of jelly beans where there? Six, maybe eight? Let's see: green, black, pink, red, yellow, blue, and orange.

A Stitch In Time

At all times, your goal is to scoop out information in amounts you can digest, and tackle activities in amounts you can do.

The ad I saw had names and pictures—if you can believe this—of 48 types of jelly beans. Banana mint swirl. Peppermint polka-dot patty. Lazy lime sublime. What's a kid to do? (I have tasted some of that company's product, including jalapeño. Weird, but fun. Of course, if you're going to habituate kids to overchoice, you've gotta start 'em early.)

And it's not merely in the candy world that choices have proliferated. Go into an athletic shoe store today and the clerk asks you, "What'll it be—air up, air out, pump up, pump down?" Go into a bike store, and the clerk asks you, "10-speed, 15-speed,

21-speed, men's, women's, mountain bike, trail bike, or racing bike?" The same phenomenon occurs when you go to buy a tennis racquet, an exercise machine, a whirlpool bath, or even a birdbath (no kidding, you have to shop for a birdbath to appreciate the overabundance of choices that can suddenly confront you. I wonder if all this choice matters to the birds.)

The *New York Times* ran a major feature saying that people are experiencing stress and anxiety today when shopping for (excuse me?) leisure goods. There are so many choices! Weighing such choices takes up your time. The problem is worse in the workplace.

Time Out!

At first blush, it wouldn't seem as if a plethora of choices is such a bad thing. After all, what can be the harm in having a wide variety of options available? The answer is that there is great harm in filling precious time with nagging-but-trivial decisions.

More Choices at Work than You Can Shake a Stick At

Consider all the vendor product catalogs you're retaining. How about all the flyers for management-training seminars? How about magazine and newsletter subscription offers at incredible savings? How about the coffee service options that await? Everywhere you turn, you see, you're confronted with more choices than you can comfortably respond to.

Using Up Your Life on too Many Choices

Every moment adds up. If you spend a lot of them contemplating which product or service to choose from among dozens or hundreds, you are consuming considerable amounts of your time to little or no good effect. Even when you choose, however wisely, it isn't once and for all. Next week, next month, next year, a new, better, faster, sleeker, less expensive, more powerful version of your product or service will be available. It will be that way for the rest of your life. (And these choices are only some of the small stuff. In Chapter 17, "Decision-Making: Step It Up and Go!", I'll discuss making *big* decisions in record time.)

Your unrelenting responsibility to keep choosing is another one of those mostly unacknowledged aspects of being born into this culture at this time. And, once again, its cumulative effect is to rob you of your time.

As often as possible, avoid making such low-level choices. If the same yardstick is available in red, blue, yellow, or white and it's all the same to you, grab the one that is closest—or take the one that the clerk hands to you.

Whenever you find yourself having to make a low-level decision, consider this: Does this make a difference? Get in the habit of making only a few decisions a day: the ones that count. For the low-level stuff, reclaim your right to say, "Who cares?" or "It doesn't matter."

You're in Charge of How You Spend Your Time— Honest

Many people proceed through their day and their lives as if others were in control of their time. Do you fall into this category? Right now, look at this list and put a check mark next to any party on the list that you believe is in control of your time.

❏ Your parents?   ❏ Spouse?

❏ Children?   ❏ Neighbors?

❏ Community?   ❏ Landlord or mortgagor?

❏ Company president?   ❏ Boss?

❏ Coworkers?   ❏ Peers?

❏ Your industry?   ❏ Opinion leaders?

❏ Government? The President?   ❏ Your PC?

❏ Governor, mayor?   ❏ The press?

❏ Television, radio?   ❏ Unknown forces?

When I ask people in seminars to complete this checklist, most catch on quickly and leave all the boxes unchecked. The one box that does get checked, if any, is Boss. There *are* bad bosses, unreasonable bosses, workaholic bosses, and even psychotic bosses. I've had them all! (See the section on "Managing Your Boss," in Chapter 9, "Volunteering a Little Less—and Liking It.") Your boss may pile on the assignments, but you're the one who determines how, largely when, and often with whom you'll tackle them.

The degree to which you believe that your boss or anyone else controls your time, however, is the degree to which you'll have to struggle to win back your time. Denis Waitely, author of *The Psychology of Winning*, says that you are in the control booth of your life (unless, of course, you relinquished control—or, worse, forgot you ever *were* in control).

Time Out!

Family and friends are important, of course, but their expectations should not dictate how you spend your time. "Being there" for them is not the same thing as being at their beck and call.

Consultant for Yourself

Perhaps you have no problem acknowledging intellectually that you are, in fact, in control of your time. Putting that knowledge into practice may be a bit more difficult. An article I once read taught me a technique for proceeding when confronted with too much stuff competing for my time and attention. It originated with none other than Richard Nixon, America's 37th president. Nixon practiced the notion of becoming a consultant to himself.

When you're faced with many choices (what decision to make, which road to take, which dish to bake), pretend that you are a highly paid consultant—to yourself. If your last name is Smith, your internal dialogue would begin as follows: "What does Smith need to do next?" You proceed as if you are able to separate yourself from your physical shell, moving to a corner of the room and observing yourself from the vantage point of an objective third party.

By referring to yourself in the third person ("What does Smith need to do next?"), you derive different answers from those you'd get if you simply thought, "What should *I* do next?"

How so? A semantic shift occurs when you refer to yourself as if you were an observer. A channel of discovery opens that is not readily available to you otherwise. (Maybe it has to do with whether you're seeing the forest or the trees.)

When can you use this technique? When *can't* you use it? Becoming a consultant to yourself works as well in crunch times as it does in milder times. A variation on this theme is to pretend a real-life trusted advisor or mentor is there with you. Ask yourself how he or she would advise you.

Look for that Inner Wisdom Hiding Somewhere

Whether it's becoming a contrarian, taking one step at a time, spending less and keeping your debts to zero, being more prudent about the information you ingest, remembering who's in control, avoiding low-level choices when possible, or becoming a consultant to yourself, you can always turn to yourself for the important task of safeguarding your time.

Chronos Says

You are more resourceful than you often acknowledge, and you always have more options than you know.

The Least You Need to Know

➤ Social complexity will continue and will make you feel less in control—and it has that effect on everybody; your ability to manage your affairs is not a self-worth or self-esteem issue.

➤ The health of your cash flow directly influences the control you have over your time. Spend more, work longer, and watch your control disappear.

➤ From now on, you'll face a mind-boggling array of choices competing for your time and attention; you can use up valuable time in your life on the less important choices. Avoid low-level decision-making, if possible.

➤ Take one step at a time. Don't be afraid to slow down temporarily.

➤ You get to decide where you spend the time in your life, not your boss, not your landlord, not your spouse, not the press, not the mayor, not the President. Become a consultant to yourself whenever you need to have third-party objectivity.

Chapter 5

Okay, So What Do You Want?

In This Chapter

➤ Why it's crucial to choose and support only a handful of priorities, not two dozen

➤ Health, wealth, or wisdom all accumulate gradually

➤ How to reinforce your priorities and support your goals

A major key to managing your time is deciding what is important to you. If you don't decide what's important to you, almost anything can (and will!) compete for your time and attention—and thereby dissipate your day, your week, your year, your career, and your life. Once you decide what's important to you, you can then become a consultant to yourself to determine what it actually takes to maintain or achieve what you've designated as important. (If it seems the pieces are starting to fit together, read on. If not, read on anyway; they will.)

> There is no inherent problem in our desire to escalate our goals, as
> long as we enjoy the struggle along the way.
> –Mihaly Csikszentmihalyi, *Flow: The Psychology of Optimal Experience*

Getting real about what you want means being honest with yourself. It also means taking the time and trouble to compose a list of priorities, and it means reviewing your list often until your priorities sink in. (I know you've encountered this type of advice before, but if you had followed it well, you probably wouldn't have bought this book! Call it a hunch....)

Chronos Says

If you don't know where you're going, any road will take you there. It's like the guy who jumped on his horse and ran off in all directions.

What Would Tom Say?

What was important to Thomas Jefferson? Here are Jefferson's *Ten Rules:*

➤ Never put off until tomorrow what you can do today.

➤ Never trouble another for what you can do yourself.

➤ Never spend your money before you have earned it.

➤ Never buy what you don't want because it is cheap.

➤ Pride costs more than hunger, thirst, and cold.

➤ We seldom repent of having eaten too little.

➤ Nothing is troublesome that we do willingly.

➤ How much pain the evils have cost us that never happened.

➤ Take things always by the smooth handle.

➤ When angry, count to 10 before you speak; if very angry, count 100.

What Makes Your Big List?

The great paradox about priorities is that if you have too many of them, then by definition they can't *all* be priorities. Do you have 15 or 18 things that you list as top priorities in your life? If so, you'd better look again, because no one has time to pay homage to 15–18 top priorities. Life doesn't work that way.

To help you identify what your priorities are, let's look at the concerns that traditionally have served as top priorities for many people. I'm not saying that your list has to match this one—it probably won't—but this is a starting point:

➤ Family

➤ Society

➤ Health and well-being

➤ Wealth

➤ Career growth

➤ Intellectual growth

➤ Spiritual growth

Let's tackle each of these (suggested) priority areas one by one, with some concrete examples. Keep in mind that you may have others, not listed here, that are appropriate for you.

Addams Family Values

For most people, the family is Numero Uno. If you're married and you love your spouse, being with your spouse is easily a top priority. If you have children and you love them, same situation. If you're single, your priority may be to find a spouse and to raise a family someday, or to treat the people closest to you like a chosen family. If you're in school, it may be to spend time with your nuclear family: your mom and dad, and your brothers and sisters.

A Stitch in Time

As with all the priorities to be discussed, you want to attach goals—specific, action-oriented steps with timelines—to your priorities to reinforce them. Write them down.

If family is a top priority, then one of your goals may be to listen to your spouse in earnest for at least 35 minutes three times per week. (Won't he or she be pleased as punch if you listen at all—never mind *three* times a week!)

Likewise, there are a variety of other goals you can choose to support this priority. Here is a quick list of other possible goals related to family:

➤ Take the children for a day-trip once every two weeks.

➤ Have a photo of the family taken *every other* December; as a shared family project every year, put some old photos in a family chronicle.

➤ Have or adopt one or more children within seven years. (There are a lot of kids already out there who need good homes.)

➤ Send flowers to your spouse, unannounced, once a month.

➤ Buy life insurance to ensure your family's prosperity in the event of your demise. (Maybe you'd better not announce this one.)

➤ Begin an annuity so you can more easily afford your child's college education by the time he or she is ready to enter college 12 (or however many) years hence.

Many of the goals that support your family priority are related to other priorities, such as wealth, intellectual growth, and so forth. Actually, that's understandable; it's wonderfully efficient when you set goals that address more than one priority.

Society and You

If you want to do something about society's woes (besides yelling at your TV set), participate in your community—help it be the best it can be. You might get involved with religious, social, fraternal, or community groups. You might choose to run for local office—not for purposes of ego gratification, but to give something of value back to the community. Here are some possible goals that may support your social priorities:

➤ Volunteer to serve on the Welcome Wagon Committee for new residents.

➤ Contribute to the XYZ campaign in the forthcoming election.

➤ Begin an environmental-awareness movement in your town by the first day of spring.

➤ Recycle your paper, plastic, glass, and other recyclable materials every week hereafter.

➤ Run for town council for the next term.

➤ Write, by the end of this summer, an article on the importance of nurturing America's youth.

➤ Be the host to a foreign exchange student during the next academic year.

➤ Chair this season's March of Dimes campaign in your region, or volunteer on a Habitat for Humanity project.

➤ Send one e-mail message per month to the major networks concerning the gratuitous violence on television.

➤ Coach a community-league sports team.

➤ Volunteer every two weeks at a local homeless shelter or kitchen.

➤ Tutor a student from your local elementary or high school.

➤ Participate in a community theater or choral production.

Jumpin' Jehoshaphat! You may have surmised that it takes time and energy to support your priorities. Hold that thought. If your goal is to win back your time, why would you want suggestions for *new* stuff that you're not currently undertaking? The answer: Tasks in support of your priorities do indeed help you win back your time. It's less of a mystery than it might seem.

Chronos Says

The few things that you'll do in support of your priorities will take far less time than all the things you do now in support of who-knows-what. And they'll have the added benefit of moving you closer to your goals. That's time well spent!

When you have 15–18 "priorities," you're involved in many tasks, some personally rewarding, some not. There is an inherent efficiency in identifying your priorities and establishing some goals to support those priorities.

Here's to Your Health (and Well-Being)

It's true. Even I, yours truly, have been duped. After a decade and a half of staying in top shape, surrounding myself with others who were doing the same, and reading articles that reinforced my beliefs about fitness, I thought all of society was also focused on health and well-being. Then I came across a report in the *Journal of the American Medical Association* that says the number of overweight Americans gained steadily in the past decade.

Depending on what study you read, between one-third and one-half of people over age 20 tip the scales in the wrong direction. "On average, adults weigh 8 pounds more than they did a decade ago," say Dr. Robert Kuczmarski and colleagues at the National Center for Health Statistics in Hyattsville, Maryland. "Comparisons...indicate dramatic increases in the prevalence of overweight people," Kuczmarski says. By some reports, America is the most obese nation on earth. Tsk, tsk.

Dr. F. Xavier Pi-Sunyer, of St. Lukes-Roosevelt Hospital Center in New York City, observes that "while our caloric intake increases, our caloric expenditure decreases." He also takes a dim view of duff-sitting: "Sedentariness has become a way of life." (Slow and short, but a way of life.)

Couch potatoes, beware! This area—you guessed it—is another gold mine of worthy places to put time and energy. There are dozens of possible goals you could have in support of your health and well-being priority. Here's a quick list; though not all will be for everyone, consider them in the light of your situation and lifestyle:

Time Out!

Check with your doctor before you start any exercise or diet program, of course—especially if you haven't been exerting yourself much. You'll get two benefits: (1) valuable (maybe life-saving) guidance, and (2) a kick out of the look on the doctor's face.

➤ Join a health club within a month and set a goal of working out four times per week for at least 30 minutes.

➤ Buy five healthy foods you've never tried.

➤ Take two health-and-fitness books out of the library, read them cover to cover, and gain at least five new ideas you'll put into practice within one month.

➤ Become a lifetime member of a local bicycle club, walking club, or exercise group.

➤ Begin going on walking and hiking dates rather than going to restaurants and movies.

➤ Hire a fitness trainer in February.

➤ Get a good night's sleep at least five times per week (more on sleep in Chapter 8, "To Sleep, Perchance to Not Wake Up Exhausted").

➤ Have an annual check-up every January (especially important if you live alone and don't cook).

➤ Take daily the vitamin supplements that meet your needs, as determined by a dietitian.

➤ Imbibe 50 percent less alcohol per week, starting this week.

➤ Make one weekend hike of at least 6 miles every weekend.

➤ Visit a nutritionist or dietitian this month to determine your nutritional needs.

The great thing about having well-being as a priority is that it gives you a license to engage in social and personal behaviors that you might not have otherwise. Picking up a piece of litter in a neighbor's yard, for example, is good for you, is good for the neighbor, and is good for the community. I know a man who carefully tucks a $5 bill into the last 50 pages of classic novels on the shelves at the local library. He wants to anonymously reward people, albeit in a small way, who read such books. If you're thinking, "Yeah right, five bucks down the drain…," perhaps you're simply not ready for this level of well-being.

The Millionaire Next Door

I'm guessing that accumulating outrageous wealth isn't one of your priorities, so I won't spend too much time on this one…just kidding. Far be it from me to say that accumulating wealth is evil. The Bible says "the *love* of money is the root of all evil." It doesn't say that *money* per se is the root of all evil. You can accumulate as much wealth as you want, as long as you don't love your money more than you love people or your country.

There are all kinds of wealth: intellectual wealth, spiritual wealth, and so forth. These are about to be covered in subsequent pages, so let's confine the focus to economic wealth. Here are examples of goals you could choose in support of this priority:

➤ I will call a certified financial planner this month and pay him or her to advise me about how to invest for the future.

➤ I will start an IRA by this Friday and contribute *x* amount of dollars each month until I reach the maximum contribution level.

➤ This week, I will redirect my employer to automatically invest *x* amount from my paycheck in a 401(k), mutual fund account, or other investment.

➤ By next quarter, I will lower the number of deductions on my paycheck so I get a larger refund from the IRS after filing taxes at the end of this year.

➤ I will join an investment club this month, meet with the members monthly, learn about investment opportunities, and participate in intelligently selected group investments.

➤ During my next performance review, I will ask for an immediate raise and offer irrefutable supporting evidence that spells out the merits of my request.

➤ (For sales professionals) I will earn $*x* in commissions for the fourth quarter of 200*X*.

➤ By September 30, 200*X*, I will launch the business venture of my dreams.

➤ By the end of this month, using the spreadsheet on my computer to calculate cash flow, I will trim monthly expenditures by $400.

➤ Within six months, I will live within my means.

➤ I will open a retirement account with my credit union next week.

➤ I will bring my lunch to work at least three times per week.

➤ I will choose an automobile that gets better gas mileage.

The not-so-funny thing about amassing wealth is that for most people it's a long-term affair. Only a tiny, tiny fraction of the population ever wins the lottery. (If you've ever thought you stand a better chance of getting struck by lightning, you're probably right.)

Chronos Says

Wealth, like happiness and fitness, is a habit. You get wealthy by developing habits of wealth. If you're on your way to wealth, it's probably those darn habits of yours.

You add to your net worth a little at a time. Gradually, inexorably, the wealth begins to build. *Fortune* and *Forbes* articles on wealthy Americans reveal that the majority got wealthy slowly. The book *The Millionaire Next Door* confirms that wealthy people developed a habit, early on, of living within their means—and one day found their nest egg had grown to a sizable sum. Wow, what a country! What a way to win back your time—by developing habits of wealth, breaking the cycle of deficit-spending, and amassing a sum that lets you to do what you want in life!

My Brilliant Career

Beyond what's already been discussed, the pursuit of career growth per se may be one of your priorities. If you've invested years in getting to be where you are, and if you like what you do, you may naturally look forward to rising within your industry or profession.

Independent of the monetary rewards, there's a high level of inner satisfaction among those who are highly learned and well-respected in their chosen fields. For goals you can choose in support of your career-growth priority, try these on for size:

➤ Read one new book a month by the top authors writing in your field.

➤ Subscribe to (or start reading in your company library) two important industry publications you don't currently receive.

➤ Form a monthly study group (with four to eight colleagues you respect) so that you each encourage each other in learning more about your chosen fields.

➤ Register to attend a conference this week (or submit a proposal to make a presentation of your own there).

➤ Return to school to get a graduate degree in your field.

➤ Undertake original research over the next six months, put your findings into article from, and pursue getting it published in a prominent industry journal.

➤ Complete the certification process in your industry by December 31, 200X.

➤ Volunteer for that special task force forming in April.

➤ Join your professional association, or (if you're already a member) run for office in it.

As society grows more complex (and, by now, you know it will), it will benefit you to become more of a specialist in your chosen field. Perhaps you could focus on biology—more specifically, marine biology, then marine biology restricted to a certain class of species, then marine biology in certain species restricted to the Hudson Bay. If you're among a handful of specialists in your niche, then wealth tends to follow.

One caveat: It only pays to specialize if you know your specialty is marketable and has long-term prospects (as some of my friends know from bitter academic experience).

If you're worried that becoming too specialized will restrict your intellectual diversity, fear not. What often happens is that once you decide on pursuing a highly narrow field and concentration, it actually expands. You begin to see things within your narrow focus that you couldn't have seen before making the choice.

I Think, Therefore I Am

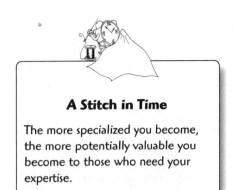

A Stitch in Time

The more specialized you become, the more potentially valuable you become to those who need your expertise.

When Supreme Court Justice Oliver Wendell Holmes was in his 80s (quite aged for his day), he was asked why he was reading the voluminous book, *Plutarch's Lives*. He responded, "To improve my mind." Rumor has it that the pursuit of intellectual growth—independent of career growth—is a worthy priority. Certainly education and intellectual development—for its own sake, and for that of your children—rank at the top of any list of priorities you may devise. In support of this priority, here's a smorgasbord of possible goals:

➤ Read one new book every two weeks that is not in your field and not connected to what you do for a living.

➤ Spend time with your children playing games such as Scrabble to help develop their vocabulary and love of words.

➤ Enroll in that local community college course you've been wanting to take.

➤ Send away for a books-on-tape catalog so you can listen to the classics rather than having to read them (because you already read way more than you want to).

➤ Take at least one international trip per year to a destination completely foreign to you so that you can learn firsthand about other cultures.

➤ Sign up for the lecture series sponsored by the local Chamber of Commerce so you can hear in person from visiting authorities on contemporary issues.

➤ Drop your subscription to, say, *People* magazine (sorry, *People!*) and replace it with, for example, a subscription to *Smithsonian* magazine.

➤ Watch at least one program per week on The Learning Channel or PBS.

➤ Rent a documentary rather than a feature film.

➤ Read a historical account instead of a mystery.

As more people go online and Internet technology marches forward, it will become progressively easier to enhance intellectual growth. (Wait a minute: People used to say that about television in the '40s, didn't they? Uh-oh....) It's worth a warning: Watch out. You can get hooked on the Internet far worse than you can get hooked on television. You can be sitting at your monitor at 7:00 p.m., look up, and notice it's 12:30 a.m.

Time Out

As with life priorities, you need some parameters before sitting down and simply freewheeling on the Net. Otherwise, rather than winning back your time, you'll watch it dissipate among an infinite number of seemingly intellectual pursuits.

Next time someone tells you to "get real," consider this reality you've already experienced: There are far more worthy and stimulating issues competing for your time and attention than you will ever be able to pursue. It takes strength to stay within the confines of a few pre-identified focus areas—while, of course, *occasionally* allowing yourself to freewheel all over creation. (You are, after all, only human, aren't you?)

The Spirit Within You

This is a vital subject that's ticklish to handle. I've known lots of folks who are sensitive about religion, sometimes taking offense where none was intended. I'm not assuming that your spiritual tradition is the same as mine, nor am I prescribing my own practices. Spirituality is a wellspring of the quality in life. The time that makes up an enjoyable and worthwhile life is well worth winning back.

Spiritual growth doesn't mean going to church every Sunday, although it certainly can involve that. Your spiritual growth can occur anywhere at any time. If you choose to seek active spiritual growth as a priority, goals like these can support your choice:

➤ Take at least one walk per week in a natural setting, and appreciate your surroundings.

➤ Decide to actually *read* the holy book for your religion during the next calendar year, or listen to it on cassette.

➤ Begin to live as if you recognize that every creature on earth is a divine creation. You can start this anytime, and the ending time is never.

➤ Practice the art of forgiveness by making three calls this week to people against whom you've held long-term grudges, and tell each of them that you forgive them. ("Do I *have* to do this?" Yes, if you're serious about your well-being.)

➤ Give thanks each morning or evening for all you have been given in life.

➤ Decide to regularly attend weekly religious services.

➤ Donate your time and energy once a month to a food service for the homeless, starting in May.

➤ Scour your home this week to find everything you can donate to the less fortunate.

➤ Listen to inspirational music.

➤ Pray for yourself and for others.

Okay, you already know many possible starting points.

That's seven possible priority areas we've looked at so far—and even they're not the be-all and end-all. You may have some that don't fit within these categories at all. That's fine, as long as you recognize what they are and choose goals that involve specific action steps and timelines in support of your priorities.

Spring into Action

To support the priorities you choose, here are some basic action steps:

➤ Write down everything that's important to you or that you want to accomplish in your life. A long list is okay.

➤ Several days later, re-examine the list. Cross out anything that no longer strikes your fancy. Feel free to add a few things if they come up.

➤ In another day or so, review your list and see whether any items can be grouped together. Then reword or relabel those choices. At all times, feel free to drop an item if you think it's iffy.

➤ Put your list away for yet another day. (I know, this is going to take a week or more!) Then review it again.

➤ Once more, combine, regroup, or delete things on the list as appears appropriate to you.

➤ Prepare the final draft of your list, recognizing that in time it may change. For now, these are what you've identified as your priorities.

Shrink Your List to Wallet Size

Maybe what this country *really* needs is a good portable priority list. At any rate, *you* can have one. If you have several fonts in your printer, print out your list in a reduced point size (or simply hand-print it in miniature) so that it's small enough to carry in your wallet or purse. Then review your list of priorities at least once a day. With so many other things competing for your time and attention, it's easy to lose sight of your priorities by 10:00 in the morning. It's not excessive to read your priority list several times a day.

Chronos Says

Some of the most accomplished people, who routinely appear to be in great control of their time, review their priority lists all the time.

The Least You Need to Know

➤ Deciding what's important to you is a key to efficiently winning back your time. Once you've identified your priorities, you're far more likely to make incremental progress toward them.

➤ Too many priorities, by definition, can't all be priorities.

➤ Traditionally, the top priorities for many people have been family, society, health and well-being, wealth, career growth, intellectual growth, and spiritual growth.

➤ To establish your priorities, write down everything that's important to you, re-examine the list, cross out anything that no longer strikes your fancy, add a few things if they come up, group similar items, reword or relabel any of your choices, and prepare the final list.

➤ Print your list in a reduced point size so it's small enough to carry in your wallet or purse; review it often.

Chapter 6

Supporting Your Priorities for Fun and Profit

In This Chapter

➤ Supporting your priorities with goals you'll follow through on

➤ The telltale signs that you're heading off course

➤ What commuting does to your time, and whether telecommuting is a viable option for you

➤ A neat way to manage your to-do list and balance short-term and long-term tasks

Suppose you identify your priorities and establish some goals in support of them. What will it actually take to ensure that you stay on your chosen path? It's easy to stray—you know it and I know it. If you had a nickel for every time you heard somebody decide to do something and then you watched them over time do little or nothing in support of the decision, well, by jove, you would probably be rich! You don't want to join *that* club. In this chapter, you'll learn how to reinforce your commitment to your newly established priorities, discover ways to recognize when you've derailed your progress toward achieving them, and learn one particularly useful way to make sure that your work priorities don't undermine the ones you've set for your personal life.

Reinforcement's the Key

Staying on track with your priorities means staying focused, of course. You can make it easier for yourself to keep that focus if you build some positive reinforcements into your day-to-day life. Here are some reinforcement techniques you can put to use in support of the priorities you've chosen:

1. Join others who have priorities and goals similar to yours—and who are supporting them. Perhaps there is a professional, civic, or social organization in your town that fits the bill.

2. Surround yourself with reinforcing statements, reminders, and self-stick notes so you don't lose sight of what you have already deemed important.

3. Create a cassette tape of your priorities and supporting goals in the form of affirmations: "I choose to visit the health club four times per week for a minimum workout of 30 minutes."

4. Prepare a budget to help determine exactly what it will cost to honor your priorities and the goals you've chosen to support them.

5. Develop rituals that support your quest. For example, if your goal is to lose 6 pounds by the end of June, begin taking the stairs instead of the elevator whenever you're heading down for lunch or to your car at the end of the day.

6. Keep your action steps bite-size. There's no value in choosing goals that are so difficult to achieve that you're not honoring the associated priority at all.

7. Report to someone. Have some significant other serving as a coach or watchdog to ensure that you do what you said you were going to do. (Don't be lulled into thinking that this ploy is only for the weak-willed. High achievers do this!)

8. Visualize the goal every day—while you're waiting in a bank line, when you're in the bathroom, when you're stuck in traffic. Olympic athletes aboard a plane, en route to their next meet, can actually improve their performance once they land if they visualize their event during the plane ride.

9. Set up a series of small rewards so that you're naturally reinforcing the behavior in which you've chosen to engage.

10. Contract with yourself. Author Dennis Hensley, Ph.D, based in Fort Wayne, Indiana, describes advancement by contract: "A contract takes precedence over everything else. For example, you make your monthly house payment rather than use the money for a vacation because you have to make that payment: The contract allows the bank to repossess your home if you do not fulfill your obligation."

    He suggests carefully selecting three to five major goals (in support of your priorities) and then signing a contract that aids you in reaching them. "Once under contract, you would have to succeed by a selected date or else face the consequences of defaulting on the contract." (It's worth remembering that in the business world, people who default can be sued or go unpaid for the work done to date.) Make three copies of your contract (this chapter includes an example). Keep the original. Give one copy each to your spouse, a trusted coworker, and a friend.

SELF-INITIATED CONTRACT

I, _____, agree to accomplish each of the following items
on or before _____ and hereby do formally contract myself to these
purposes.

These goals are challenging, but reasonable, and I accept them willingly.

A._____

B._____

C._____

Signature: _____   Date: _____

Review your contract when you find yourself becoming distracted by small details
or if you think you are not moving in the right direction.

11. Plot your campaign on the calendar. Start from the ending date (the deadline for
completing your goal) and work back to the present, plotting the subtasks and
activities you'll need to undertake.

Proceeding in reverse through the monthly calendar helps you establish realistic
interim dates that reflect not only your available resources, but also vacations,
holidays, weekends, other off-duty hours, and reasonable output levels. A sample
Calendar Block appears below.

CALENDAR BLOCK BACK

MONTH ____MARCH_____ YEAR _____

SUNDAY	MONDAY	TUESDAY	WEDNESDAY	THURSDAY	FRIDAY	SATURDAY
	1 Submitted Feb. 24	2 Deliver draft workshop planning report	3	4	5	6
7	8	9 Submitted to typing	10	11	12	13
14	15 Assessment of conf. capabilities Deliver profile revisions	16	17	18	19 Assessment of target audience, 52 pages Deliver	20
21	22	23	24	25	26	27
28	29	30	31 Deliver final workshop planning report			

*Start with a major
deadline, then work
backward to set realistic
interim dates for
achieving what you
want.*

61

Chronos Says

Give yourself flexibility; build in some downtime, vacation time, and so forth. Devise a realistic plan to accomplish your goal by the time you said you would.

Whoa, Horse—Get Back on Course

If you're like most people, then on more than one occasion (I'm being kind here) you're bound to get off course. When you do, revisit the list just given and initiate a new strategy in place of—or, better yet, in addition to—the ones you're using. Here are some warning signs that you're not following the path you said you would:

Time Out!

The drive to and from work can take a big chunk out of your day. Commuting is one of the worst time thieves. If you're serious about winning back your time, you'll consider moving closer to work. If that's not an option, strongly consider telecommuting.

➤ *You've talked a good fight, and that's all.* You said this undertaking was important to you, but you haven't scheduled any time on your calendar, budgeted any funds, or even thought about it.

➤ *You're late.* You said that working out four times a week was important; by the third week, you're making excuses to yourself about why you're not.

➤ *You've let piles of paper stack up.* Although you've chosen only a handful of priorities, you find yourself still wading through stuff that's nice, interesting, and not that important.

➤ *Your goals missed the mark.* Despite the toil, time, and thought you put into establishing your goals, it's apparent they're not supporting your priorities.

Is the Commute Killing You?

As you consider what it will take to pursue the goals that support your priorities, sometimes creative solutions will begin to appear. For example, imagine reducing the aggravation and wasted time of the fundamental act of getting to work as discussed in Chapter 2, "Time Flies Whether You're Having Fun or Not." For many people, it's an arduous undertaking.

So let's talk about telecommuting.

Stay in Touch by Bits and Bytes

As metro areas keep expanding, and as daily commuting becomes more trying, telecommuting is gaining popularity. At least 20 million people are doing some telecommuting these days. Telecommuters complete much of their work back in the traditional office.

The benefits to you include reduced commuting time; reduced personal cost for travel, clothing, and food; flexible working hours; more time for dependents; and potentially greater autonomy.

You can rack up significant time savings by telecommuting, as detailed in Table 6.1.

Table 6.1　How Commuting Adds Up to Lost Time

Round-Trip Minutes/Day	Hours/Year	Equivalent Number of 40-Hour Weeks
40	160	4
60	240	6
80	320	8
100	400	10

Believe it or not, the federal government is on your side when it comes to telecommuting! In 1990, the Clean Air Act mandated that all businesses employing more than 100 people in a single location reduce their employees' commute time by 25 percent. Employers could encourage the use of public transportation, car-pooling, condensed work weeks, or telecommuting. The act has since been implemented, primarily in the states with the worst pollution.

Maybe you can sell your employers on this trend. The benefits to them include potentially higher productivity; reduced office or plant costs; the ability to accommodate physically challenged employees; and the ability to motivate new employees with an attractive stay-at-home-and-get-paid option.

Stockbrokers, consultants, writers, and even top-level executives are finding that telecommuting enables them to maintain—even increase—their overall productivity. Jobs such as computer programming, translating, software engineering, sales, and system analysis are well suited for telecommuting. Other professions, such as word processing, book publishing, telemarketing, research, and architecture, also lend themselves to effective telecommuting.

Watch Words

Telecommuting is working outside the office (that is, away from your employer's base of operations) and staying in touch with coworkers via electronics, such as a computer, a fax, a pager, and a phone. It can be done from your home, a hotel, a satellite office, or even your car.

Despite all the technological breakthroughs, telecommuting thus far has been employed only marginally. Some employees have been directed to telecommute; others have requested the option. Yet, in business and government, most employees don't telecommute, even periodically.

Even on a limited basis, telecommuting can provide you with many benefits beyond the time saved by not commuting. These include cost-savings, as well as the freedom to focus on projects, initiate conceptual thinking, and exercise more control over your environment. Check it out!

Your To-Do List: Managing the Long-Term Versus Short-Term

Whether you telecommute or work in a traditional office five days a week—whether you've identified your priorities (and some well-chosen goals to support them) or are still stuck in old habits—it's likely you face an age-old dilemma: staying on top of all the things you need or want to get done.

People are always asking me about to-do lists. Do they need to maintain them? How can they go about fixing them? Everyone I know in the workaday world uses *some* kind of list as a tool for getting things done. I'm neither for nor opposed to any particular system you might use to stay efficient; judge by your results. (Chapter 12, "Neat and Uncomplicated Tools to Manage Your Time," explores some time-management tools and technologies.) If you maintain some type of to-do list, you can use it to support your priorities—by lengthening it for strategic reasons, without overloading yourself. Read on.

> **A Stitch In Time**
>
> If you haven't yet considered using the superlong to-do strategy, give it a try. Your first superlong list will probably fill two to five pages—it should be easy to move items up to the front as needed. You'll have a clear idea of what you face all on one big roster, and you'll keep your priorities sharp for years to come.

Long Can Be Good

The primary dilemma you're most likely to face is balancing short-term against long-term tasks and activities. Believe it or not, I maintain a 8- to 10-page to-do list! I have hundreds of things on my to-do list, arranged by major life priorities. How do I keep from going crazy? Most of what's on the list are medium- to long-range activities.

The first page of my list represents only the short-term activities—those I've chosen to do now or this week. I draw continually from the 10-page list, moving items to the top as it becomes desirable (or necessary) to tackle them.

In essence, I maintain a dynamic to-do list; it contains everything on this earth I want to get done, but always with only one page I need to look at: the top page. Yes, I am forever updating the list and printing out new versions, but there are so many advantages that I wouldn't think of doing it any other way.

My list is long, and it will stay long. I don't worry about all the things on the list because I know I can get only so much done in a day, a week, and so forth. I also know I'll review the entire list periodically, always moving items from, say, page 7 up to the front page. Thus any anxiety stays at a rather low level.

Sometimes it's One Thing, Sometimes Another

I keep the list on my computer—this is handy because virtually all word-processing programs contain word-search capabilities. If I'm working on something during the day and it appears there will be a breakthrough in my ability to tackle something *else* that's buried on page 8 or 9 of my list, I have only to search for a word or phrase, and I quickly come to the item. There is no need to dig through the hundreds of items on the list.

Maintaining a long to-do list helps me become more proficient in managing long-term or repeated tasks. If I'm working on a long-term project, I can continually draw from it those portions that can be handled in the short-term; I move them up to the front page. Likewise, if a task is a repeat or cyclical project—something I have to do every month or every year—I can choose a portion to get done and move into the short-term (up to the front page).

Making an End Run Around Your To-Do List

On occasion, you can short-circuit the to-do list and get stuff done without even entering it on your list. Here's how it works. Most people who encounter information worth retaining make a note or add it to a list; it may stay there for days or months. To deal with it faster, remember that useful information usually involves calling or writing to someone else. Rather than adding it to your to-do list try a fast-action option:

➤ Pick up a pocket dictator and fire off a letter, or do the same with voice-recognition software.

➤ Dictate or type a message on your computer for immediate transmission by fax, e-mail, or Internet message.

I was talking to someone who enjoyed the *Readers' Digest* section in which one editor reviews vocabulary words from books he's read. Many years ago, I would have made a note about this (and dealt with it in about six months, with any luck). Instead, I grabbed my pocket dictator and dictated a letter to the editor on the spot, indicating some words I thought his readers might enjoy. In cases like this, my transcriber types the letter and sends it to me on a disk; I copy it onto my hard disk and then send it. When I switch to voice-recognition software, (see Chapter 12) I won't need a typist. Either way, I bypass the to-do list.

Good Old Paper and Pencil

If you already suffer from too much technology, there's a simple system that will keep you on top of the goals that support your priorities. It works surprisingly well: Simply go to your nearest office-supply store and buy one of those washable wall charts or an oversized set of monthly calendars in cardboard stock or paper. Mount your calendars on the wall and use magic markers, washable felt-tip pens, sticky-note pads, gold stars, red seals, or what have you to represent what you want to accomplish by when. This isn't news to you if you work in an office where any number of people, vehicles, or goods need to be scheduled for optimum efficiency. On a personal basis, such calendar plotting works well; you're the boss of the calendar. Moving self-stick notes around is a one-second maneuver. High-tech or low-tech, do what works.

The Least You Need to Know

➤ Everyone needs reinforcement. Join others who have similar priorities and goals. Develop supportive rituals; report to someone; visualize your success; set up a series of small rewards.

➤ Telecommuting may be the biggest time-saver of your career.

➤ Create a superlong to-do list, and split it into short- and long-term tasks.

➤ A low-tech approach to managing your time has its charms. Calendar wall charts are easy to use and re-use.

Part 2
Appointing Yourself in Charge

Armed with all the great stuff you learned in Part 1, undoubtedly you're now ready to kick some derriere and stand up for yourself—first by lying down longer and more often, as in sleep. You're not sleeping enough, bucko.

When you're well-rested, you can better handle everything that everyone is asking you to do. Not just your boss, but also your family, friends, and neighbors may tend to ask more of you simply because you can do it. So you need some carefully considered excuses.

If you can reduce requests for your time, you'll finally be able to tackle your office and desk. (A desk, you may recall, is not a filing cabinet; window sills and the corners of your room are not permanent storage locations.) Then you can learn to manage piles and trials with smiles, and investigate some low-cost technology that won't drain your brain to use. When you make it to that point, you'll learn clever ways to handle all the messages that have been bombarding you.

Let's begin with an eye-opening look at why you're hardly able to stay awake days and (too often) find yourself up all night.

Chapter 7

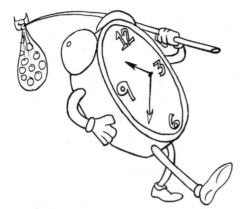

Money Comes and Goes—Time Just Goes

> ### In This Chapter
>
> ➤ Doing too many things yourself is not such a good idea
>
> ➤ You can always make more money; you can't make more time
>
> ➤ Trade your money for more time
>
> ➤ Getting helpers who can handle almost anything you need to get done

Too many people in Western societies practice rugged individualism, typified by John Wayne's movie roles. Not so curiously, 17 years after his death John Wayne was voted America's favorite actor. *He* took care of everything himself. Unfortunately, life is not a movie.

In the workaday world, you frequently see middle managers who attempt to leapfrog several positions in the company by taking on more projects, even though they're already working beyond optimal capacity. Among entrepreneurs, you may encounter someone trying to crack a new market—even while juggling several other balls, short-changing his or her health to keep that circus going.

It's Gotta Be Me

What are some danger signs indicating that you believe you have to do it all yourself? Consider these symptoms: You think you'll be able to overcome obstacles by working longer; you tell yourself (or worse, your boss) that you "appreciate the challenge." If the people around you think it can't be accomplished, all the better; you'll wow 'em by doing the impossible, right? You might become a little overbearing, but hey, you're in pursuit of an important goal, and *that's* what counts. Besides, you're the "only one who can do the job."

Certainly, working hard in itself is not a problem unless you maintain preposterous ambitions or let force of habit push you beyond the point of diminishing returns. If you're willing to stay late, work on weekends, and minimize your vacation time, you well may be your organization's star performer—hey, what a great deal for them!—but too many career-achievers fall into an endless cycle. These people feel their accomplishments are too small or too few; they experience disappointment, frustration, and health-threatening stress. To relieve these feelings, they work even harder in the hope they'll accomplish more and a golden rainbow will appear.

Attempting to "Do It All" Will Cost You

The notion that you and you alone must take care of everything is, in a word, erroneous. If working too hard is you way to gain the respect of others—or self-respect—it's time to rethink your whole approach.

Chronos Says

Admit to yourself that you can't do everything; acknowledge that trying harder in some instances may not be worth it. Contemplate the possibility of using help for selected segments of your life.

Some do-it-all people may have the ill-advised notion that the only way to exhibit competence is by constantly proving it to everyone else. Worse, if they never quite prove it to themselves, they live in dread of being found out as imperfect.

➤ Rather than focus on your weaknesses, accentuate the positive! Develop your strengths. Also give yourself realistic time frames for ambitious goals.

➤ Divide and conquer. Take smaller steps when setting larger goals so that you don't burst a spleen along the way. When progress is slow, try an alternative route, a new door, or a different mindset—anything but plod along the same as you've always done.

Misers Are Often Penny-Wise, Pound-Foolish

Especially when it comes to domestic tasks, do you get stuck in a miserly mode? Do you think that if you spend a few minutes here and there taking care of this and that you can handle all you seek to keep up with—and avoid shelling out the money to have others do it? Many people do.

Each time you avoid getting a service professional, helper, or part-timer—when such parties could aid you considerably—you're ensuring that you won't win back your time. If you don't enjoy mowing the lawn, for example, every time you do that chore you add to the cumulative total of undesirable tasks in your life (as discussed in Chapter 2, "Time Flies Whether You're Having Fun or Not"). Besides, you're incurring all that unnecessary tissue-and-decongestant expense during hay fever season.

Time Out!

Watch out if you start believing that you alone are the only one who can handle things. Many organizations tend to seek out people with such urges and expect them to over-perform forever. Only superheroes need apply.

You Can't Make More Time: You Can Make More Money

When I make presentations to groups around the country and explain the value of shelling out a few dollars to preserve your time, invariably someone asks, "What do I do if money is tight?" I don't presume for a second that you have loads of cash stashed away in a trunk somewhere. (Remember, most people spend more than they have.) And the thought of parting with some of your money to hire people to do what you've traditionally done yourself may seem like heresy at first.

But let's look at hiring others from the vantage point of your life's big picture. You have things to accomplish that can perhaps make you much more money than the $15 you pay somebody to mow the lawn or trim the hedges.

If you're an entrepreneur or self-employed, it pays to rely on outside services so you can focus on what you do best and make the overall business

A Stitch In Time

It makes perfect sense to pay a high-school kid $15 to mow the lawn if you can't stand mowing the lawn. In the long run, you won't miss the money and you'll be glad you're no longer stuck with a task you dislike.

prosper. If you work for an organization, there are still countless opportunities for relief; you *can* rely on others (at work and away from work) to alleviate the piddling tasks you don't enjoy doing. Thus you can be at your best, get noticed by superiors, and stand a better chance of getting those raises and promotions.

Overcoming the Urge to Do It All: Making a Little Money Go a Long Way

It's surprising how common the do-it-all urge is. Nanci Hellmich, a reporter for *USA Today*, uncovered some of it when she interviewed me for two articles. The first was a brief, two-column article; in it Nanci invited readers to write to *USA Today* and discuss their time-pressure problems. Several lucky readers would benefit from my counsel (aw, shucks). The second article would include the results of my counseling.

Over several weeks, Nanci received hundreds of letters; she selected respondents for me to call. I lived in Falls Church, Virginia, at the time, so I made the calls from the *USA Today* offices in Arlington, Virginia. I had lengthy talks with a female attorney and a graduate student, among others.

The attorney was perpetually racing the clock, getting her daughters to school in the morning, seeing her husband off on his (frequently long) business trips, plying her trade as a partner in a successful law firm, picking up the children, driving them to various after-school activities, making dinner for them, reading to them, and putting them to bed.

Chronos Says

You need to be rested and alert when you head into work. Having others take care of domestic tasks helps you in your professional career.

After listening to her story, I asked her why she didn't give herself the liberty of ordering dinner a couple of times a week rather than making it all the time. She said she'd never thought about it—and, on first hearing, it seemed a little extravagant. I asked her how much she earned. It was considerable. I asked her how much her husband earned. It was more than considerable.

"Okay," I replied, "between the two of you, you're clearing nearly a quarter million per year. Suppose you had Chinese food or pizza or chicken delivered to your home now and then—and you didn't cook at all on those nights. How much would it cost you, once a week, to have dinner delivered?" She thought about it and said, "Maybe an average of $16 a week, so that's $800 a year."

I said, "Would it be worth $800 a year if, once a week—particularly during hectic work weeks—you had dinner delivered instead of making it yourself? Would that free up some of your time? Would you enjoy it? Are you worth it?" She agreed on all counts. It's food for thought.

Booking It

The graduate student I spoke with also had a hectic schedule. Besides taking several courses, she worked in the afternoons and was a volunteer for a service organization two nights a week. Frequently she found herself arising in the morning barely in time to catch the bus. This kind of pressure was no way to start her day, yet it had become routine.

I listened carefully to her story and asked, "How much is the bus ride to school?" She said it was $1.75. I said, "How much would a taxi ride cost?" She was aghast. "I couldn't take a taxi!" I said, "Wait a second. How much would a taxi ride be?" She didn't know, so we paused our conversation. She called the closest taxi company and asked about the charges from her apartment to her class in the morning. The cost was approximately $4.50.

When she called me back, I asked her the million-dollar question: "How upsetting would it be to your budget if, occasionally, when you were running late, you permitted yourself to hail a taxi and pay $4.50 instead of paying $1.75 for the bus?" She thought about it and said, "Well, I suppose occasionally it wouldn't hurt."

I said, "You're right. You could hail a taxi as often as once a week, and in the course of a 15-week semester, you're only paying an extra $67.50 for the luxury of not being enslaved to the bus schedule. You could easily blow $67.50 on stuff all the time. Why not be gentle with yourself? Acknowledge that you're handling a lot in life right now, and occasionally you deserve to take a taxi ride to school." She relented.

Make Mine Manhattan

If you're a big-city career-type, the same principle applies. If you're up on East 78th Street in Manhattan and have to get down to 43rd in a hurry, once every week or so, it won't put a significant dent in your pocketbook to take a taxi rather than the subway or bus. Suppose it costs you $8 more per week. In the course of a year you're only paying $400. How many times have you blown $400 in ways that were far less beneficial to your overall health and well-being?

Time Out!

Don't get caught in the trap of false economies. How many times do you get stuck in a miserly mode, pinching pennies here and there, while blowing triple or quadruple digits on items of marginal value? If you don't watch out, you'll find you're sacrificing your time *and* wasting money.

A Flying Leap

What time/money trade-offs might make good sense in *your* situation? Consider a few:

➤ *Grocery delivery:* Many supermarkets and grocery stores will deliver for free or for a nominal fee of $5–$7. Some offer catalogs from which you can order by phone, by fax, by e-mail, or by Internet. For items you buy frequently, you can establish a standing order: Every week the market delivers eggs, milk, whatever. You can still shop for new or specialty food items now and then, lugging all those bags home so you remember what it's like. It will reinforce your inclination to use grocery delivery services.

➤ *Office supplies by phone and fax:* Those giant superstores splashed across the terrain—such as OfficeMax, Staples, and Office Depot—have delivery services and publish large supply catalogs (with 800- numbers so you can reach semi-knowledgeable attendants). The catalogs also contain 800-fax numbers; you can fax your order without even talking to anybody. Ordering via e-mail or the Internet is becoming a standard option. Most vendors deliver at no extra charge if your order is above $50. The orders usually are delivered the next day, right to your door. It's fast, accurate, and relatively painless.

➤ *Gift wrap it, please:* If you're buying presents and the store offers a wrapping service, pay the extra dollar and have them wrap it. Do you particularly want to fiddle with wrapping paper, tape, scissors, string, bows, and all that stuff? If you do, fine, that's your option. For another dollar (or whatever it takes), however, isn't it worth it to have that chore completed?

➤ *Online services:* Rather than doing it yourself, consider the online service vendors who maintain bibliographies, citations, dossiers, and indices for a fee. Sure, software can help you navigate the Net. Extracting what you need, however, takes time—*your* time—your *valuable* time.

A Stitch In Time

Every time you successfully use one of your many helpers, you're winning back your time!

➤ *Pick-up and delivery services:* Use vendors and suppliers who come right to your door. I use one firm that recharges my laser printer's cartridge for about half the price of buying a new cartridge every time. Virtually all the major express package delivery services will both pick up and deliver for home as well as office locations. You can start your own account even if it's from your home and you send only a few packages monthly.

➤ *Shopping services:* There are people who can go shopping for you to buy gifts for others, new shoes, or nearly anything. If you dislike shopping (or aren't too good at it) and someone you trust *is* good at it, this could make sense. The professional shopper can actually save you money. He or she knows where to get the best buys. Often the overall cost of the item-plus-the-hourly-fee is less than you would have paid (especially if you often hunt for items in five or six stores and end up paying full retail price).

Clean and Green

In my book *Marketing for the Home-Based Business* (Adams Media), one recommendation I make to entrepreneurs is to look for local service providers. The Maid Brigade, for example, was the service I used when I wanted to have my house cleaned quickly. Rather than hiring a service that sent over a cleaning person or two and required three or four hours to get the job done, the Maid Brigade would send six or eight people at once and finish the job within 45 minutes.

Here are other types of services that probably exist in your community (they'll be called something else in your city, of course).

➤ The Butler Did It (a catering service)

➤ Everything But Windows (housecleaning)

➤ Rent a Dad (house repair when there's nobody around who can drive a nail straight)

➤ The Tree Doctor (tree and hedge trimming)

➤ Jumpin' Jack Flash (pick-up and delivery)

➤ Walkin' the Dog (takes care of Pooch when you're gone—or when you're not)

➤ Gutters-R-Us (clears your gutters, saves you from roof duty)

➤ Shake a Leg (airport shuttle service)

There are plenty of part-time workers as well; some may be more suitable to your needs than others. These include part-time regular employees, retirees, temporaries, and students (high school, college, intern, foreign-exchange, grad school, and so on).

You probably can find a bright, motivated student to help you. Schools are full of intelligent, perceptive young men and women—many of whom are seeking an opportunity to gain some real-world experience or extra money. Their part-time status doesn't mean they're less intelligent or effective. Many can take a divisible unit of work and do a bang-up job on it.

Chronos Says

Most communities have high-school juniors and seniors who'd be thrilled to work for $.50 an hour above minimum wage while gaining more experience than flipping hamburgers. This might not seem like a lot of money to you, but it may to them.

What could helpers do for you? Fair question. Take a look:

➤ Route/sort the mail

➤ Answer requests for information

➤ Send out mailings of any sort

➤ Serve routine customer needs

➤ Make deliveries and pick-ups

➤ Survey customers and their needs

➤ Keep track of necessary data and news sources

➤ Type mailing lists

➤ Type anything, for that matter

➤ Keep things tidy, clean, and in good repair

➤ Study competitors, their literature, and their products

➤ Make first-round or lead calls to prospective customers

➤ Hunt for a product or service you need

➤ Catalog new information or products

➤ Proofread or double-check anything written

➤ Track inventory or arrange displays

➤ Do anything that a less-essential part-time employee could do without excessive guidance

Identify all those non-essential-but-bothersome tasks you've been putting off and that a part-timer can handle.

Seed work functions best when it's a distinct *unit* of work that's easily assigned to someone else. For example, suppose you want information on the eight other local companies in your field. A high-school student can easily open the phone book or a local trade publication, visit the sites, write for the brochures (using his/her home address), and summarize the information gathered. A more experienced employee could spot trends or innovations from this data, all with a minimum of your time spent on instruction.

Watch Words

Seed work is the sort of task you can easily assign to another because the downside risk if he or she botches the task is negligible.

Putting Your Service System in Place: Ten Steps

Whether you live in a community of 35,000 or 1,035,000, many service providers can help you with domestic as well as business tasks to free you for whatever makes the most money for you.

By now, you're probably mildly enthusiastic to downright excited about the prospects of bringing such providers into your life. Good. If you start using such helpers in a systematic way, you'll be far along the road to winning back your time.

Here are 10 suggestions for putting your service system in place:

1. Identify all the tasks you don't like to do. Make this list as long as possible. Be honest with yourself. Separate the list into domestic and career-related tasks.

2. On two separate pages (one for domestic and one for career-related tasks) create a matrix listing these tasks down the left side of each page. (There's an example Task Matrix lurking nearby in this chapter.) Across the top of each page, leave room for four columns; label them Option 1 through Option 4.

Task Matrix

	Option 1	Option 2	Option 3	Option 4
Task A	_____	_____	_____	_____
Task B	_____	_____	_____	_____
Task C	_____	_____	_____	_____
Task D	_____	_____	_____	_____
Task E	_____	_____	_____	_____
Task F	_____	_____	_____	_____
Task G	_____	_____	_____	_____

3. If you list seven tasks down the left side of the page for your domestic sheet, with four option boxes across the top of the page, potentially you have 28 cells to fill. Fill even half of them, and you'll be in great shape.

A Stitch In Time

Create an up-to-date file of key literature and information you encounter when seeking service providers; constantly add to it. Align your life with people who can free up your time. You're worth it.

4. Within the blank cells, write down every alternative you can imagine for not doing tasks you don't enjoy doing. You may find yourself writing down such options as delegating the tasks to your kids, your neighbors' kids, or someone you found in a shopper's guide or the *Yellow Pages*.

5. Take stock of your grid. If you don't have good options for some of the tasks, it's time for some fieldwork. Go to your local library, supermarket, or community center and read the bulletin boards. Often you'll find business cards or small ads posted by local entrepreneurial talents. Start collecting these leads.

6. Talk to your local librarian. Talk to the job-placement officer at your local high school, community college, or university. Ask around. You're likely to get many names of people who can help you.

7. Consider running your own advertisement. A small classified ad in a suburban shoppers' newspaper will probably cost you less than $10. Go ahead, splurge!

8. Start calling potential helpers (or better yet, get your seventh-grader to make exploratory calls for about $3.00 an hour; you won't miss the money).

9. Interview, interview, interview. Over the phone is fine, in person is better. Map out what you want done; break in your helpers gently but systematically.

10. Start a file of the literature or information you've collected on all the different types of helpers you've been seeking and talking to.

Once you have a file of helpers, keep adding to it, keep it current, and use it.

The Least You Need to Know

➤ You drop buckets of money on stuff that provides little benefit compared to the time savings you can readily enjoy once you forsake your miserly mode.

➤ Among the best time/money trade-offs are occasional taxi rides; delivery of dinner, groceries, and office supplies; and any other vendors who pick up and deliver.

➤ A wide variety of service providers can help you. They advertise in suburban shopper newspapers, on library bulletin boards, on electronic bulletin boards, and at odd places around town.

➤ Students can help you enormously, part-time. Many are ready, willing, and able; with some, the only drawback is that they're young—and if they learn fast, that's no big deal.

➤ Create a grid of all the domestic tasks—and then all the career-related tasks—you'd rather not be handling. Then identify as many as four options for each task.

Chapter 8

To Sleep, Perchance to Not Wake Up Exhausted

In This Chapter

➤ You're probably not getting enough sleep

➤ Can you really catch up on your sleep?

➤ How too little sleep hampers your effectiveness

➤ How to get more rest throughout the day

You're not getting enough sleep. If my guru-powers were fully perfected, I'd gesture hypnotically and give you eight full hours of sleep before you read this chapter. How do I know you're not getting enough sleep? It's not a lucky guess; study after study shows that most American adults have been depriving themselves of the proper amount of sleep they need.

The director of Stanford University's Sleep Center says that "most Americans no longer know what it feels like to be fully alert." A *Prevention* magazine survey showed that 40 percent of U.S. adults—tens of millions of individuals—"suffer from stress every day of their lives and find that they can sleep no more than six hours a night."

How important is sleep to you in your quest to win back your time? How important is it to your overall health and effectiveness? (Hint: highly, extremely, incredibly, all of the above. Choose one.)

Short-changing your sleep on any given night (provided it's only one) won't cause you much harm. Most experts agree that getting only three to four hours of sleep once a week is not likely to result in long-term problems. You might feel crummy the next day, but you can compensate by taking a nap or going to bed early the next evening.

No Sleep: A Disaster Waiting to Happen

In *The 24-Hour Society*, sleep-researcher Dr. Martin Moore-Ede found that repeatedly getting less sleep than you need day after day can lead to disaster. Moore-Ede contends that George Bush's collapse during his visit to Japan, Captain Joseph Hazelwood's ineffectiveness in piloting the *Exxon Valdez*, and a rash of plane, train, and other transportation mishaps can all be traced back to insufficient sleep on the part of those in question.

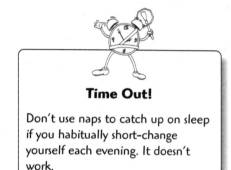

Time Out!

Don't use naps to catch up on sleep if you habitually short-change yourself each evening. It doesn't work.

How much do *you* need to sleep each day? It all depends—for some people, seven hours a night is great; for others, it's eight; for others, nine. Most adults need about eight hours. College students may need an average of nine to nine-and-a-half hours (whether or not they stayed up until three in the morning, they'd still *need* more sleep than a 35-year-old). As people age, some need more than eight hours a night; some need less.

Dr. Jack Edinger at Duke University's Sleep Center says, "The older one gets, the less smooth one's sleep pattern. It is normal for someone between 40 and 70 to be awake some part of the night." As you age, you may need *more* than eight hours of sleep nightly if it's punctuated by wakeful periods (not uncommon).

You've long known that you need to get enough sleep to function effectively. Yet you probably haven't been getting it. Who, or what, is the culprit? Here's a lineup of the usual suspects.

What Habits Have You Developed?

If you've gone to bed at 11:00 for the past several months, chances are you'll go to bed around 11:00 this evening. If you feel compelled to turn in after Jay Leno does his monologue, you've developed a habit of retiring late.

Alternatively, if you have magazines, newspapers, CDs, and all manner of things to read and hear surrounding you, it's tempting to stay up yet another 20 or 30 minutes—which can balloon into 40 to 60 minutes.

If you're among the lucky ones who doze off as soon as you begin reading, be thankful. Many people remain awake longer when surrounded by information stimulants.

Draining You of Energy

If you use drugs (especially alcohol), your sleep patterns will be disrupted and you're likely to get too little sleep. Alcohol might knock you out faster, but it can cause sleep difficulty and frequent wake-ups.

Microsleep, Scary Stuff

Your eyes may be open, but don't let that fool you. Moore-Ede found that many people engage in *microsleep* (the body's attempt to compensate for under-sleeping) throughout the day. For example, microsleep can occur when:

➤ bus drivers have full passenger loads.

➤ truck drivers are racing down hills hauling nuclear weapons.

➤ mothers are transporting their babies.

Watch Words

Microsleep is a 5-to-10-second episode when your brain is effectively asleep while you are otherwise up and about. Microsleep can occur while you are working at a PC or (omigosh) driving your car.

Drowsiness comes in waves. You can be alert one moment, drowsy the next, and not know the difference. Having too little sleep the night before (and certainly on an extended basis) increases the probability you'll engage in microsleep.

You Need Rapid Eye Movements

You've probably heard of REM—*rapid eye movements* that are a crucial part of your overall sleep cycle.

If you sleep too little or are awakened at inopportune moments, your REM pattern can be disrupted; hence, even eight hours in the sack may not yield the benefits of a solid eight hours of sleep. To win back your waking time, protect your sleep time. May I suggest the following:

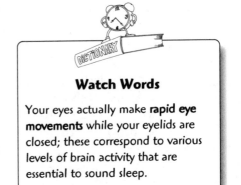

Watch Words

Your eyes actually make **rapid eye movements** while your eyelids are closed; these correspond to various levels of brain activity that are essential to sound sleep.

➤ Don't sleep with your head by a telephone that can ring aloud. Remove the phone from your bedroom, or install an answering machine and switch off the ringer. Too many people sleep with their heads by the phone because, say, they have aged loved ones far away; they worry about that one call in 15 years that might haul them out of bed at 3:00 a.m. Stop doing this; there's not much anyone can do at that hour. You'd be far better off getting 15 years of sound sleep.

➤ Once a week, get to bed by 9:00 p.m. Your body will thank you. Let yourself go to dreamland for 9, 10, 11 hours—whatever it takes. Remember, you're probably going to live longer than you think you will; to get to old age with grace and ease, allow yourself at least one weeknight in which getting sleep is your only objective.

➤ One Friday night each month, crash right after work and don't get up until the next morning. Have dinner or skip it, as suits you. If you want to experience a fabulous weekend, this is the way to start.

➤ Avoid caffeine for the six hours before retiring. This means if you're thinking about going to bed around 10:00, 4:00 in the afternoon (or before) is the last time to imbibe any caffeine. But hey, why drink this drug-in-a-cup anyway?

Time Out!

Dr. Martin Moore-Ede notes that if you stay up too late one evening, you are literally borrowing from the next day.

➤ Avoid alcohol in the evening. Sure, it'll put you to sleep quickly, but it tends to dry you out and wake you up too early. Then you have trouble getting back to sleep, your overall sleep time is reduced, and the quality of your sleep is poor.

➤ If you fall asleep when you read in bed, then do so to induce drowsiness. Don't overdo this. Dr. Edinger says it's important to make your bed and bedroom for sleeping (and, of course, sex) only. Don't set up your bed as a command station with your CD player, TV, or other appliances that reinforce the notion of your bedroom a place for anything but sleep.

➤ Go to bed when you're tired. Let your body talk. It'll tell you when it's tired. The problem you've had in the past is that you have ignored the message.

➤ Don't fret if you don't fall asleep right away. You may need a couple minutes or more. After 30 consecutive minutes of restlessness, do something else until you're tired again.

➤ If you're kept awake by your spouse's snoring—or if you're the one snoring—you need help. I recommend a snore-control device. Whenever your snoring is above a certain decibel level, you receive a gentle vibration that breaks the pattern and helps you return to quiet sleep.

➤ Moderate exercise several hours before sleep aids in getting sound sleep.

➤ Moderate intake of proteins, such as a glass of milk, also aids in sound sleep.

Is Catching Up on Sleep Possible?

The answer is an absolute yes—*and* no. No, from the standpoint that if you've been depriving yourself of sleep for the last three years, you can't literally add back all the hours you missed. That kind of "catch-up" sleep won't support the continuing need you face each day.

Chronos Says

Even if you've deprived yourself of sleep for a prolonged period, if you devote the next month to giving yourself all the sleep you can get, you'll be in reasonably fine shape.

Nevertheless, your body is extremely forgiving. Ex-cigarette smokers know this. Even lungs abused by years of smoking begin to cleanse themselves once the smoking stops for good. The effects of 10 years of abuse can greatly diminish in as little as one year. So it is with chronic undersleeping.

Developing Good Sleep Habits

Getting enough sleep, as with engaging in other healthy practices, is a habit. Albert Gray, a successful businessman of yesteryear, said, "Every single qualification of success is acquired through habit. Men (and women) form habits, and habits form futures. If you do not deliberately form good habits, then unconsciously you will form bad ones."

You can rationalize about it until doomsday, but depriving yourself of sleep *is* a bad habit. Yes, I know all the excuses. Of course you have a lot to do. No one will debate that. You'll get it all done more effectively and more efficiently with sufficient sleep, not with less sleep.

Here are several suggestions to develop (or perhaps redevelop) the habit of getting sufficient sleep:

➤ Let others know about your newfound quest—this means family members who might otherwise impede your progress.

➤ One weekend day (or more) per month, linger longer in the morning before getting up—you know, sleep in!

➤ Any time you're traveling for work, try this trick as a reminder: Give the TV channel-changer to the front desk at the hotel. You can't afford to be still clicking away at midnight. Get sleep when you're on the road (more on this shortly).

➤ Schedule extra sleep any time you're on vacation as well. An extra 30–45 minutes can make all the difference in the quality of your vacation.

➤ Recognize that at first you may have to force yourself to get into bed, even if it's 9:00 or 9:30 on a weekday evening and you'd rather be up and around. The way I see it, the opportunity to get precious sleep is too good to miss!

You may have to break the flow of your normal evening activities to get that sleep. Next time they start to make claims on your time, consider them as if they were traffic. I remember, at the end of a workday years ago in Washington, D.C., heading west on M Street to get to Arlington, Virginia, when there was absolutely no break in the traffic. There I was in my car, trying to take a left; literally eight minutes went by without an opening. I concluded that no opening would be provided, no matter how patient, respectful, or needful I was. So I stepped on the gas, careened across the intersection, and made my break. You have to take the opportunity to get the rest you need. You're in the driver's seat.

Your Body Rebels Against Too Little Sleep

In *The Organic Clock*, Kenneth Rose says that each part and function of your body is timed. Each has its own rhythm—heartbeat, breathing, speaking, even hiccuping. If you sleep too little for too long, you disrupt well-developed cycles that took millions of years to evolve.

Rose also found that every bodily function has internal controls for its basic rhythm. Each body function is reset every 24 hours to parallel the natural light cycle of the day. You are subject to this *circadian rhythm*. Trying to alter that rhythm for a prolonged period can be contrary to your own physiology. Your body won't like it.

If you find you can't sleep more even when you try, or if you seem to need almost endless amounts of sleep, it may be an indicator of depression or another clinical problem. See a physician, in this case.

For proper functioning, you need to get the right amount of sleep most days. When you are sleep-deprived, you incur changes in brain waves and literally cannot be as effective. Your immune system and mental skills decline. In *The 24-Hour Society*, Martin Moore-Ede finds that certain times of the day are especially important to sleep through. Human physiology is at its lowest level of alertness between 2:00 a.m. and 5:00 a.m. Highest alertness is between 9:00 a.m. and noon, and also 4:00 to 8:00 p.m. Your alertness will vary according to hours of consecutive work, hours of work in the preceding week, your regular hours, the monotony you face on the job, the timing and duration of naps you take, lighting, sound, aroma, temperature, and cumulative sleep deprivation, among other factors.

The Sleep You Get and Don't Get

I'd guess that your sleep deficiency ranges between 45 and 90 minutes daily. If you're deficient by more than 10 hours a week, as a benchmark it'll take you about a month to "recover." Again, this doesn't mean you can replace all the hours you've lost. It means that you *can* get to the point where you're fully functional and minimize (maybe eradicate) the effects of past deprivation. To get there, start at square one: Make a list of indicators that you're probably not getting enough sleep. Some of these may be familiar; some may be news to you:

➤ You bump into things more frequently than is normal for you.

➤ You slur your words.

➤ You have trouble digesting food.

➤ You're short with people when normally you wouldn't be.

➤ Your eyes are tired.

➤ Your *joie de vivre* is missing.

➤ You don't enjoy sex as much as you used to.

➤ You need to wake up by alarm clock (many people wake up when they want to, on their own).

➤ You don't want to face the day.

➤ Even small tasks seem to loom larger.

➤ Your life has achieved a level of fine monotony.

➤ You find it easier to engage in tasks that don't involve talking to others.

➤ As much as you hate going to the dentist, you find leaning back in the dentist's chair rather relaxing.

➤ You find yourself nodding off in what are otherwise interesting and/or important meetings.

➤ You zone out for unknown periods of time while working.

Do You Need More Sleep or Not?

Only you can determine how much sleep you need. I know I've had all the sleep I need when I'm ready to bolt out of bed in the morning, ready to face the day. I recognize it as a signal that I'm well-rested. To determine your optimal sleep time, consider the following:

➤ Experiment with the number of hours you sleep each night for a week. Start with eight hours, say 10:30 p.m.–6:30 a.m.

➤ If eight hours feels good, stay right there; no need to move on. If not, increase the amount by 15-minute increments.

➤ If you're waking up before you've slept eight hours (and you're not napping excessively during the day), perhaps you need less than eight hours. (More on naps in a moment.)

➤ To make your test valid, give up your alarm clock! Yes, give it up (any time you can afford to—not, of course, when you have a plane to catch). Any time it wakes you up, you don't truly know how long you would have slept.

If you have the opportunity, taking naps throughout the day (even on a weekday) can enhance your overall effectiveness and put you in the driver's seat of winning back your time.

Nap-taking 101

Some people nap without problems; others can't nap at all. One study found that if you nap for 30 minutes each afternoon, you actually have a 30 percent lower incidence of heart disease than people who don't nap at all—such a deal. Napping increases your alertness for the rest of the day. Although many people feel a little groggy for a few minutes after a nap, it gradually subsides and they feel more alert (and in a better mood—try it).

Chronos Says

The extra edge napping provides can last for 8–10 hours. So if you can steal one, you could be good for hours! However, naps are not designed to be substitutes for missed nocturnal sleep.

Short naps are actually more productive than long naps. A short nap will leave you refreshed, whereas a long nap may interfere with your sleep that evening. The experts say that the best nap time is between 2:00 p.m. and 3:00 p.m. Any later, and your nap may be too deep, interfering with your nightly sleep. If you can, nap in a bed or a cot, but not a chair. Your quality of sleep will be much higher and the immediate benefits more apparent. The only caveat: Naps are not a substitute for the proper amount of sleep.

Watch Words

When you're **hydrated**, your body's tissues are sufficiently filled with water. To be **dehydrated** is to be parched.

Are You Sleepy or Are You Dehydrated?

Hydration and dehydration play an important role in how much sleep you need.

About half the time I feel tired during the day is because I haven't taken in enough water. Nutritionist David Meinz of Norfolk, Virginia, says every chemical reaction that occurs in your body requires water. In fact, your brain is 75 percent water.

Meinz says that your thirst mechanisms lag behind your true need for water on a continual basis. Even a 2 percent reduction in your amount of body water will render you less productive than normal. A 5 percent reduction can seriously decrease mental functioning. Here are Meinz's suggestions for ensuring you're sufficiently hydrated:

➤ Eight cups of water a day is the standard, but don't wait until your thirst reminds you that you need water. Drink before you're thirsty.

➤ If you work out a lot, your body requires a full 24 hours to regain the water supply that you need. Hence, you have to have much more water than you think when you work out.

➤ Try drinking 8 ounces of water before starting your workout. During your workout, drink as often as you can.

➤ Sign on with the best water-delivery service in your area, or buy bottled water. The best choices for bottled water are distilled water or spring water.

➤ If you use tap water, let it run about 30 seconds so any sediments can clear out.

Meinz also says to take a multivitamin every day to reduce feelings of lethargy and ensure that you're getting most of the basic nutrients. Along with sufficient water intake, this will help you feel more vibrant more often during your day.

More Ways to Be More Rested

In addition to previous recommendations, here are other ways you can get more rest throughout the day without putting a dent in your overall output:

1. Find a quiet place in your office, such as an empty conference room or a coworker's office, where you can simply sit in a chair for a few minutes and be still without fear of interruption. Even two or three minutes in a semi-reflective state can help recharge your batteries.

2. Go outside to a bench, your car, or some other safe haven where you can do the same.

3. Don't bolt right away from the table after eating your lunch. Linger for an extra minute or two; give your food a better chance to be properly digested.

4. Rest while you walk. This sounds like a contradiction, but you can walk hurriedly or restfully. On your way back from the restroom, a coworker's office, or lunch, stroll mindfully down the hall in a rhythmic fashion, fast enough that no one will accuse you of being a zombie, but sufficiently slow that you're hardly exerting yourself. This can work wonders.

5. Practice the same restful habits outlined here on Saturday and Sunday as well as during the week. Who says you have to go all out during the weekend? Obviously, the opportunities for outright naps are much greater on Saturday and Sunday, so take them.

What about when you're feeling drowsy but you have to be awake and alert? In that case, think light and cool. With bright lights, your sense of alertness is enhanced and your brain is switched on. In essence, brightness equals wakefulness.

If your office or workspace is somewhat on the chilly side (say, 68 degrees or less), you're also likely to stay more attentive and alert. As a rule of thumb for making presentations, it's better to have an audience cool and awake than warm and sleepy.

Sacking Out on the Road

You know the scenario. You're bedding down for the night in a hotel and need a good night's sleep so you can summon enough energy to hold your own at the meeting the next day. Unluckily, the guest from hell is in the next room and apparently is trying to break the decibel barrier at 2:30 a.m. Normally you're a sound sleeper, but this time you find yourself tossing and turning for four hours before you finally doze off. What can you do after checking into your hotel room to make sure you get a good night's sleep every night, regardless of the quality of your sleeping accommodations?

Paging the Hotel Manager

Noise is invading the room you've rented. If it's easy enough to determine the direction of the sound, and if the intrusion is from the room to the left or right, you could try tapping (gently but firmly) on the wall. This alone sometimes works. In many hotels, the phone system allows you to readily dial adjacent rooms. If the noise is from across the hall or above or below you, you could call and ask the night manager to handle the situation.

Watch Words

A **sound screen** creates a sound "barrier" that breaks up, masks, or mutes the effects of louder sound from beyond the barrier by using **white noise** (a sound much like that of rushing water).

Sleep-Enhancing Technology

To maintain greater control of potential sound disturbances, there are some essential items you can use before checking into any hotel room: a "sound screen," earplugs, and a timer.

1. The Sound Screen® is a portable white-noise device developed by the Marpac Corporation. The Sound Screen emits different frequencies and amplitudes of a droning, non-disruptive blanket of sound. You can use this device to minimize the effects of startling or disruptive sounds outside your room. By placing the screen about 10 feet from your head in the direction of any disruptive noise, you are able to minimize the intrusive effects immediately. If you're interested in this product, contact the Marpac Corporation at P.O. Box 3098, Wilmington, NC, 28406-0098. You can fax them at 800-999-6962.

2. Create your own white noise. If you're awakened and the offending noise isn't too outrageous, use an empty channel on your TV set or radio as a white-noise machine. If you're using a TV this way, turn the brightness down to nothing, or cover the screen set with a blanket or towel to minimize light from the screen. If the TV isn't bolted down, put it between you and the noise. Experiment with your room's thermostat. Perhaps you can turn on the fan (or the heating or cooling system, depending on the season). Use the ventilation system as a white-noise device; adjust the number of blankets and sheets you need accordingly.

   Space-age earplugs called Noise Filters® are available from the Cabot Safety Corporation. They cost little and weigh even less. Airline gate and runway crews (employees who guide planes to and from their gates) use these industrial-strength plugs to shut out heavy-duty noise; they can provide you with a near-silent world. The plugs expand in your outer ear canal, blocking out sound in ways traditional earplugs cannot. You can get these godsends in Walgreen's and CVS pharmacies.

3. The third essential device is your own alarm clock or timer. You can wake up on cue and be free from having to keep your room phone plugged in. When you remove the plug from the phone, be sure to position the cord so the end is exposed to you; it will remind you to plug it back in when you get up.

How to Know You're Well Rested

If you're committed to getting back to the level of sleep and rest you need—and if you're looking forward to being more awake, alert, and refreshed during the workday—you're already well on the way to making this happen. While you'll *feel* the difference, nevertheless here's a checklist of indicators that let you *know* you're getting the amount of sleep you need.

➤ You look forward to facing the day.

➤ You no longer need an alarm clock to get up.

➤ You awaken with energy, feeling great.

➤ Your eyes look clear, not red and bloodshot.

➤ You put in a full workday and have a deep-down satisfaction about what you've accomplished.

➤ You have sufficient energy for activities after work as well.

➤ You look forward to sex.

➤ Your *joie de vivre* is back.

Time Out!

You might have been able to get away with sleep starvation in your 20s. You might even have managed to get to work and do a decent job. However, the chance of successfully continuing this behavior diminishes every day.

The Least You Need to Know

➤ Within a month, you can largely recover from a prolonged pattern of insufficient sleep. Start tonight.

➤ Insufficient sleep has a heavy impact on your effectiveness. Don't pretend otherwise.

➤ Safeguard your sleeping area by removing the phone and converting your bedroom back to a bedroom (not a den or living room).

➤ You may need to take a nap during the workday. Get some type of brief rest. You definitely need to drink more water.

➤ You know you're getting enough sleep when you bolt out of bed in the morning without having to use an alarm clock.

Chapter 9

Volunteering a Little Less—and Liking It

In This Chapter

➤ What to do when your boss wants you to be a workaholic

➤ Defend your calendar, because it's your life

➤ Learning to say no with grace and ease

➤ How to get off—and stay off—mailing lists

The ever-growing array of widely available office technology provides you the opportunity to do far more in a day than your predecessors of yesteryear. Concurrently, it also gives your boss and organization the opportunity to get and expect more *from* you. You used to be able to generate a handful of letters each day, if you were lucky. Now, with a few keystrokes, you can crank out 1,000 letters and still have time to work yourself to exhaustion before the end of the day.

The great paradox of today's work environment is that the more you can do, the more is expected of you. Unfortunately, expectations about what you can accomplish rise immediately with the introduction of tools that facilitate greater accomplishment. This explains why you frequently feel squashed in the gears of your work life like a present-day version of Charlie Chaplin in *Modern Times*. Instead of working on a real assembly line with which you can't keep pace, your "assembly line" is digital, byte-sized, and cyber-driven at nearly the speed of light.

You know you're a good worker. You're only too happy to help your organization in meaningful ways. Unfortunately, not all organizations make meaningful or reasonable demands.

Let's explore how to further take charge of your turf and win back your time—starting with the vital challenge of managing your boss.

Managing to Manage Your Boss

Whole books have been written on this subject! Fortunately for you, I'm going to encapsulate them into the following single sentence:

> Ultimately, you'll be treated by your boss in the way you teach your boss to treat you.

There, I've said it. A gross oversimplification? Look around your organization. Who gets stepped on the most? Who is handled with kid gloves?

Time Out!

You don't want to be an office wimp, a routinely unsung hero who's asked (or is that commanded?) to perform great feats of productivity simply because you can, with no regard to your personal well-being and personal balance.

Generally, the office wimps get used as doormats, and those who are a bit more particular as to how their workday unfolds are treated with a tad more respect. The key to not having your boss consume the time in your life beyond the normal workday involves re-examining the issues discussed in Chapter 1, "I Know I Can Finish Most of This (If I Stay Late)," and learning some specific phrases that you can offer as needed. Read on.

Wanted: Workaholics We Can Deluge with Work

You've got this great position in this great organization; there's only one itty-bitty little problem: Your boss is a workaholic and expects you to be the same. This situation requires great tact and professionalism because you're not likely to change your boss's nature. You are likely to be confronted with his or her workaholism and its effect on you. Here are key phrases that might help unstick you. (They work even better if your boss is *not* a workaholic!) Commit these to memory; in many cases it's essential that your retort be automatic.

➤ "I'm overcommitted right now, and if I take that on I can't do it justice."

➤ "I appreciate your confidence in me. I wouldn't want to take this on knowing my other tasks and responsibilities right now would prohibit me from doing an excellent job."

➤ "I'd be happy to handle this assignment for you, but realistically I can't do it without foregoing some other things I'm working on. Of tasks *a* and *b,* which would you like me to do? Which can I put aside?"

➤ "I can do that for you. Will it be okay if I get back to you in the middle of next week? I currently have *a, b,* and *c* in the queue."

➤ "The number of tasks and complexity of assignments I'm handling is mounting. Perhaps we could look at a two- or four-week scenario of what's most important to you, such as when the assignments need to be completed and what I can realistically handle over that time period."

Even workaholic bosses are appreciative of your efforts on occasion. When the boss knows that you naturally work hard, he or she is not as likely to impose on you so often. A great time to make a sterling effort is when the boss is away. Most people follow the old adage, "When the cat's away, the mice will play."

Therefore, it behooves *you* to be the one who's able to go into the boss's office after he or she returns and say, "Here's that big report you wanted. It's all done."

A Stitch in Time

If you're the one who works hard when the boss is away, you help to convey a message that he or she doesn't need to constantly keep heaping on assignments.

When the boss is outside the office, perhaps on travel or simply downtown on appointments, that's when he or she is most likely to monitor who's doing what back at the office. That's when the boss calls in more frequently, inspects things a little more closely upon returning, and is more on-edge, knowing that most employees tend to slack off. Hence, this is your chance to shine, to teach this workaholic that you don't need to be over-monitored—and to make great strides toward controlling your time.

Your Calendar and Your life

It's a strange phenomenon: When you look at your calendar months in advance and there's nothing scheduled, that's when you fall into time-traps. Suppose Jim comes in and asks you to volunteer with him three months hence for a charitable cause he supports. You open your appointment book or look on your scheduling software and see there's nothing going on that day. So you say, "Sure, why not?" You mark it dutifully on your calendar. You even intend to honor your commitment.

Two months pass. As you approach the date on which you promised Jim you'd volunteer, you notice that you now have responsibilities in and around it. A day or two before the time you're supposed to help Jim, your schedule is jam-packed. Suddenly, Jim's long-standing request looks like an intrusion. How dare he! Yet, when he asked and you agreed, it all seemed so harmless. All of which leads to *Jeff's Law of Defending Your Calendar*, which states (among other things):

An empty calendar is not such a bad thing.

Why are you inclined to schedule tasks, responsibilities, and events for which you volunteer, but you aren't inclined to schedule leisure-time activities, particularly those on a weekday after work? Hopefully, you have no trouble scheduling a vacation. What about scheduling calendar-pockets of fun, leisure, and relaxation throughout your week? You need to defend your calendar on a continual basis.

Now hold on, Bud. I'm not saying that volunteering to help someone isn't worthwhile. On the heels of 5,000 other things you have to do, however, it may not be appropriate—or even feasible—for you to take on another task at this time.

Your life, as discussed in Chapter 1—as well as your career, year, month, workweek, and day—are finite. If you are similar to other professionals, your calendar essentially is your life—therefore, you need to defend it.

As an exercise, I suggest you go review old calendars and examine the appointments, activities, and tasks that you scheduled back then. You'll gain perspective on how many things you scheduled that you could've done without. In reviewing my own prior calendars (before I got all this wisdom), I observed that 40–50 percent of my activities were nonessential. Some could've been cut given my knowledge of their results. Most, however, could be cut simply because they weren't in accordance with my priorities and goals. I either yielded to the whim of the moment, or I hadn't developed the ability to say no.

Ducking Out on Future Commitments

Here's a quick list of techniques to help you determine whether you can safely avoid adding some future commitment to your calendar:

Time Out!

If you don't defend your calendar, it will surely be filled in with all manner of "worthwhile activities."

➤ Is it in alignment with your priorities and goals?

➤ Are you likely to be as prone to say yes to such a request tomorrow or next week?

➤ What else could you do at that time that would be more rewarding?

➤ What other pressing tasks and responsibilities are you likely to face around that time?

➤ Does the other party have other options besides you? Will he or she be crushed?

➤ Do you like him or her?

➤ If none of the above work, make your decision in three days hence, particularly when you can respond by phone, mail, or fax. It's much easier to decline when you don't have to do so in person.

Say No, but with Grace and Ease

The bigger your organization, the more requests you receive to attend or support various functions. If you're an entrepreneur, a student, or a retiree, you still are likely to face a number of requests, the brunt of which are best handled with a polite "no." With Joe's retirement party, Megan's baby shower, Kevin's summer bash, Aunt Millie's 64th birthday party, the Little League parade, and who knows what else, it would be easy for you to fill up your calendar and never get your job done—let alone do the things you *want* to do in life.

You don't need to bone up on the teaching of Amy Vanderbilt, Letitia Baldrige, or Miss Manners to be able to say no with grace and ease. If you simply employ any of the following responses as they apply, you'll be in great shape:

➤ The easiest technique you can use to decline a request is to say that your child's birthday/recital/graduation/sex-change operation will be occurring at that time, and you couldn't possibly miss it. This is not a lie; undoubtedly, your child will be doing something that merits your presence.

➤ Closely related is anything your family has planned. For example, "Oh, that's the day our family is taking our annual fall foliage trip. We've been planning it for months, and the hotel reservations have already been made. I do appreciate your asking, however."

➤ You may be able to work up enough guts to say, "You know, I'd like to, but I'm so overcommitted right now I couldn't work it in and do it justice, or be fully attentive, or offer the level of support that I know you'd appreciate."

➤ "I wish you had asked me a couple of days ago. I already committed that time to helping XYZ accomplish ABC."

➤ "Could I take a rain-check on that one? I've been working myself dizzy lately, and I've scheduled that time to be with my...therapist...masseuse...mistress...bookie."

If you have no legitimate prevailing circumstances, here are other possible responses:

➤ "Let me get back to you by tomorrow on that." Tomorrow, use the aforementioned phone, mail, or fax to politely decline.

➤ Offer a gently worded "Thanks, but I'll have to pass on that."

Unglutting Yourself

You face so much that competes for your time and attention—perhaps a workaholic boss, an overfilled calendar, or scads of future commitments. You need to think about controlling the number of demands coming at you. Don't volunteer to have others hit you with even more tasks that will compete for your attention. Do you open your intellectual kimono willy-nilly and permit newspaper, magazine, and newsletter publishers to sign you up?

The effect of all this is having too much to respond to, feeling overwhelmed, and having no sense of control over your time. The next time somebody calls with a highly worthwhile publication you can subscribe to, use what you've learned in this chapter to politely decline. In addition, the following techniques for handling magazine subscriptions may be of use to you:

➤ As each of your magazines subscriptions expire, don't immediately renew. Wait two to three months to see if you actually miss having the magazine. If you don't, then you've saved some money and a whole lot of time. You can always view several issues at a local library. Most importantly, recognize that in a society where information flows abundantly, no particular magazine (unless it's highly specialized) is that crucial anymore.

➤ If, however, you do miss it, then resubscribe. The publication will take you back, I promise—in many cases, you'll even get a better rate.

➤ For the magazines you do receive, immediately strip them down; tear out or photocopy only those articles or passages that appear to be of interest to you. Then recycle the rest of the publication. (More on this in Chapters 11, "Filing: Your Simple Salvation," and 12, "Neat and Uncomplicated Tools to Manage Your Time.")

➤ One of the great benefits of having an online service is that you have the ability to quickly skim articles from dozens of publications; if they seem worthwhile, download and save them on hard disk. Then you can read them at will, without ever having to handle paper at all. After reading them, you can wipe them off your disk or keep them. Either way, you avoid glutting your physical systems—filing cabinets, desk drawers, and file folders.

A Stitch in Time

Without thinking, do you add your name to mailing lists, thereby openly surrendering yourself to more data and more offers? If you make yourself aware of which organizations or businesses sell their client or membership lists, you can avoid the mailing-list blues.

➤ For existing subscriptions, experiment with giving away every second or third issue. Even chemists, engineers, and highly technical types agree they could skip every third issue of their technical publications and not be less informed; most periodicals have an inherent redundancy.

➤ Each year, many magazines publish a roster of all the articles that they featured in their final issue of the year. Such indices can be invaluable; you can highlight exactly which articles you would like to see.

➤ Some publications maintain a readers' service, whereby you can order only the articles you desire.

Getting Off—and Staying Off—Mailing Lists

By extending the principles of reducing your magazine glut to your mail, you ultimately can save even more time. To get off—and stay off—mailing lists, write to the addresses listed here and ask to be removed from the list. Those organizations represent some of the most formidable mailing lists in the United States.

Advo Inc.	Director of Lists 239 West Service Road Hartford, CT 06120-1280
National Demographics & Lifestyle	List Order Services 1621 18th Street #300 Denver, CO 80202-1294
Donnelley Marketing	1235 North Ave. Nevada, IA 50201-1419
Mail Preference Service	Direct Marketing P.O. Box 9008 Farmingdale, NY 11735-9008
Metro Mail Corporation	901 West Bond St. Lincoln, NE 68521-3694
R.L. Polk and Company	List Services Division 6400 Monroe Boulevard Taylor, MI 48180-1884

Some strategies follow; you can use them to ensure that your name is removed from the mailing list(s). Some of them may seem like a lot to do, but once you get rolling, the peace of mind and time savings you reap from having less junk mail cross your path will be well worth the effort!

➤ When you write to these organizations, include all variations of your name, such as Jeff Davidson, Jeffrey P. Davidson, Jeffrey Davidson, J. Davidson, J. P. Davidson, and so on; do this for all others in your household for maximum effectiveness.

➤ Thereafter, write to the organizations at least once every four months with a follow-up reminder; any purchase you make by credit card or check is likely to get your name back on the direct-mail rolls.

➤ Create a printed label that says:

"I don't want my name placed on any mailing lists whatsoever, and I forbid the use, sale, rental, or transfer of my name."

➤ The Direct Marketing Association, in Washington, D.C., has published a pamphlet entitled Direct Marketing Association Guidelines for Ethical Business Practice. It offers a comprehensive review of your rights regarding unsolicited third-class mail. For example, consider Article 32 on "List Rental Practices."

Under the heading "Use of Mailing Lists," the DMA states, "Consumers that provide data that may be rented, sold or exchanged for direct marketing purposes periodically should be informed of the potential for the rental, sale, or exchange of such data." It further states, "List compilers should suppress names from lists when requested from the individual." To reach the ethics department of the Direct Marketing Association write to this address:

Ethics Department
Direct Marketing Association, Inc.
1126 6th Avenue
New York, NY 10036
(212) 768-7277
Fax (212) 768-4546

➤ When you are besieged by third-class mail from repeat or gross offenders, and when such offenders have included a self-addressed bulk-mail reply envelope, feel free to use the envelope to request that your name be removed from their lists. Also, review their literature to see if there is a (toll-free) 800-, 888-, or 877-number by which you can make such a request, at no cost to you.

➤ For those who do not heed your request, lodge a complaint with the Direct Marketing Association or the U.S. Postal Service.

➤ Sometimes the fastest way to deal with repeat offenders is to simply write the words "Speed Reply" right on the communication from them that you've received, and underneath those two words write this message: "Please remove me from your mailing list now and forever." Sign your name, date it, and send back the items or communication that you received. Be sure to address it to the mailing list manager of the offending organization.

➤ At all times and in all places, inform the parties with whom you do business that you do not appreciate having your name added to a mailing list and being inundated by catalogs, announcements, brochures, and fliers. This is particularly necessary if you place an order by fax, make a purchase by credit card, fill out a magazine subscription form, or procure any other type of good or service other than by cash.

As an extreme measure, I once carefully wrapped up a brick, and on the outside of the wrapper included this note to a gross offender: "I respectfully request that you remove my name from your mailing list. This is my eighth [or whatever the number] request, and if unheeded, I shall send 10 bricks next time." After wrapping up the wrapped-brick-and-message, I affixed the bulk-mail-postal-reply face of the envelope sent to me in the latest mailing. I taped it securely to the package and dropped it in a mailbox. Technically, of course, the post office didn't have to deliver it (I'd defaced the reply envelope), but the delivery went through. It seems I made a dramatic, costly impact on the original mailer, who then chose to heed my request and eliminate my name from their rolls. (They called me and surrendered.)

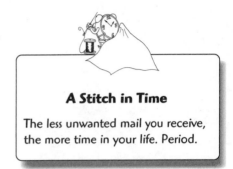

A Stitch in Time

The less unwanted mail you receive, the more time in your life. Period.

By now, you may be thinking, "This guy's got a vendetta against junk mail." Actually, I don't. I am not fond of waste—especially the waste of time in relation to the delivery of mail I never wanted to receive in the first place.

The Least You Need to Know

➤ If you have too much scheduled, too many commitments, or too much to read, remember who invited all that hassle into your life: You.

➤ If you have a workaholic boss, memorize key statements that you can spring at appropriate moments.

➤ Defending your calendar is synonymous with controlling or winning back your time. Beware of future commitments: They get vexing as their time draws near.

➤ Practice saying no with grace and ease, in front of the mirror or with family members. Use legitimate reasons (such as your kids, family, or prior commitments) to respectfully decline offers and requests from others.

➤ Manage your magazine subscriptions. Keep your name off mailing lists.

Chapter 10

Making Your Office Work for You

In This Chapter

➤ Managing your desk and guarding the flat surfaces of your life

➤ Handling paper more quickly and easily

➤ Self-stick labels and long-life stampers yield maximum advantage

➤ What to chuck and what to retain

On the road toward taking charge of your turf, you've learned two major principles thus far. In Chapter 8, "To Sleep, Perchance to Not Wake Up Exhausted," you read about the dramatic impact sleep can have on the quality of your life and your effectiveness, both on and off the job. In Chapter 9, "Volunteering a Little Less—and Liking It," you saw some ways you volunteer (perhaps unwittingly) to have more assignments, commitments, and information thrown your way—and that it's possible to keep much of this at bay.

Now it's time to tackle the vital notion of whipping your office into shape. You can rule an empire (okay, a little empire) from a desk if you know how to do it correctly. Too many people neglect their offices and their desks.

Take Charge of Your Desk, or It Will Take Charge of You

Have you seen the mid-1980s movie *Top Gun*? Tom Cruise plays a Navy fighter pilot. Among his many responsibilities in flying some of the nation's most expensive aircraft is landing Navy jets safely on aircraft carrier decks.

A few months after seeing the movie, I read an article in *Smithsonian* magazine about how aircraft carrier decks have to be completely clean and clear before a plane can land. "All hands on deck" on an aircraft carrier deck traditionally meant that everyone—even senior officers—picked up a push broom and swept the deck completely clear when a plane was due to land. Now they have giant blowers and vacuums to do the job. The goal is the same: to leave nothing on the surface of the deck, not even a paper clip. This ensures the highest probability of a successful landing. What happens if there is debris on the deck as a plane approaches? Or—oh boy—if an earlier plane has not left the landing strip? The approaching plane is likely to crash and burn.

Chronos Says

Your desktop, gentle reader, is like the deck of an aircraft carrier. If you take the next pile of stuff you get and simply park it in the corner of your desk with some vague notion that an organizing fairy will come by and do something with it, good luck when the next thing lands!

Nobody is coming to help you manage your desk; each new item you pile on will (figuratively) crash and burn into smoldering ruins as your work accumulates, unless you take charge of the situation.

All other things being equal, if you have but one project, one piece of paper—whatever you're working on—in front of you and the rest of your desk is clear, you're bound to have more energy, focus, and direction. Conversely, if all manner of distractions compete for your attention—piles of reports, memos, and faxes—how can you have the same focus, energy, and direction on the task at hand? I think you know the answer.

The Top of Your Desk Is Not a Filing Cabinet

What to keep on top of your desk is uniquely individual. As a general rule, anything you use on a daily basis (such as a stapler, roll of tape, or pen), gets to stay on top of your desk. Remove anything you can safely eliminate from your desktop. Where does it go? You might have a credenza behind you. In case you're thinking, "Well, you asked me merely to shift my stuff from one surface to another," you're right. And it works!

Inside your desk, retain items you use at least weekly, if not daily—but don't start storing supplies there. Those belong further away from you, in file cabinets or supply lockers. Your goal is to maintain the optimal number of items on and in your desk—enough so you work efficiently every day, but not enough to clutter up the works.

A Stitch in Time

The fewer things you have in these vital places, the greater the sense of control you have over your immediate environment. So clear out the unnecessaries and start enjoying a new, more efficient work life.

After you've cleared your desk of what's unnecessary, apply the same principle to the top of your filing cabinet, closet shelves, and other areas. What about your dining room table, a work bench, or the trunk or glove compartment of your car?

Your goal is to have in front of you what you need and not much more. Oddly enough, once these flat surfaces are under control, you also gain a heightened sense of control over your time. Such a deal!

Getting a Workout in Front of the Computer

Time out for a quick aside to computer users. Because you sit at your desk so often, for so much of your work day, in many instances facing the monolithic computer monitor, here are a few tips (assembled from various office equipment manufacturers) for overcoming the sedentary inclinations that facing a PC tends to propagate:

➤ Breathe in slowly through your nose, hold it for two seconds, and then exhale through your mouth. Repeat this several times, and you'll likely experience an energy boost.

➤ Roll your shoulders forward five or six times using a wide circular motion; do the same thing, this time rolling in the opposite direction.

➤ Turn your head slowly from side to side and look over each shoulder. Count to three. Repeat the exercise 5–10 times.

➤ While in your chair, slowly bend your upper body between your knees. Stay this way for a few seconds, then sit up and relax. Repeat this once or twice to stretch your back.

105

➤ Hold your arms straight out in front of you. Raise and lower your hands, bending them at your wrists. Repeat this several times; it stretches the muscles in your forearms and gives your wrists relief.

➤ Fold your arms in front of you, raise your elbows to shoulder level, and then push them straight back. Hold this for a couple of seconds. This gives your upper back and shoulder blades some relief. Repeat 5–10 times.

A Stitch in Time

Hereafter, manage your desktop as if it's one of the most important elements to winning back your time—because it *is*.

Also, take a break now and then. By working more effectively with this piece of office equipment, ultimately you'll get more done. And if you do even a few of these exercises, you'll feel better about your time during the workday and afterward.

Master Your Shelves, or, Yup, They'll Master You

Ah, shelves! What an invention. Do you ever consider what goes on a shelf versus what goes in a filing cabinet? Because filing is the subject of Chapter 11, "Filing: Your Simple Salvation," let's focus on the first part of the question here; what goes on your shelves. In a nutshell, your shelves are the home of the following items:

➤ Items you're bound to use within the next two weeks

➤ Items too large for a filing cabinet (or collections of such items)

➤ Projects in progress

➤ Supplies that can go in supply cabinets

Let's examine each of these individually.

Items You're Likely to Use Within the Next Two Weeks

These include reference books, directories, phone books, manuals, instruction guides, books, and magazines (especially large ones, annual directories, and theme issues).

Items That Are Too Large for a Filing Cabinet

Because it's difficult to file some thick items such as books (and some magazines) in a filing cabinet, any such item is better housed on a shelf. Any oversized item that simply won't fit in a file cabinet (and any item that is part of a continuing series) is probably best housed on your shelves.

If you receive a key industry publication and it makes sense for you to hang on to back issues, these also belong on your shelves. In this case, you could acquire magazine holders—essentially precut or preassembled boxes (corrugated cardboard or plastic) that hold about 24 issues of a monthly magazine. The box itself enables you to stay in control. It's visual; you can stick a face-up label on it. It's easy to grab one issue from among the many you're retaining; it's easy to replace the issue.

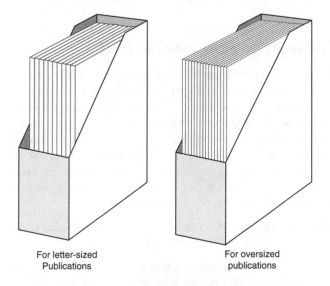

Cardboard magazine holders help you stay in control of incoming items.

For letter-sized
Publications

For oversized
publications

Calling All Projects in Progress

Similarly, if you're working on a project that requires a variety of items, the magazine boxes work well. If you keep your shelves behind your seat at your desk, keep one shelf compartment clear so you can lay incoming file folders flat on it. You'll have a place for new stuff while keeping your desk relatively clear. The prevailing principle is that it's better to have these materials *behind* you than right in your immediate work area. Undoubtedly you face many demands during the day; you may have to draw upon several folders for different projects or tasks. It makes sense to have a single flat surface (even among your shelving units) readily available to accommodate active files.

Supply Cabinets and House Supplies

Most professionals today have little difficulty filling up their shelves. Supply catalogs, a Chamber of Commerce directory, guidebooks, or new software manuals all are capable of consuming a few inches of precious horizontal space.

Your inclination might be to get more shelves, but it's best to avoid that. Your goal is to keep your office in shape within reasonable parameters—using the desk, filing cabinet, shelves, and supply cabinet you already have. If any of these is always overfilled, okay, I'll concede: perhaps you need to go get another. More often, lack of space is an excuse for not being able to manage an office.

Keep supplies in a supply cabinet (isn't logic beautiful?) because there you can store them in bulk. Stack them horizontally, vertically, or one type of item on top of another. Treat your shelves as somewhat sacred; align them so you can pull out key items at will. If it takes you longer than 30 seconds to find something on your shelves, refine your system.

Now a Word About Filing for Fun and Profit

While "filing for fun and profit" will be covered in detail in Chapter 11, it's important to look at the relationship between your files and your office in general. Filing is a dynamic process. Items you place in your file folder today may find their way onto your shelves, re-emerge in some other form, or be chucked. What's on your shelves may (in some mutant form) find its way into your files. If you have a big reference book on a shelf, you may have to extract a few pages from it, discard or recycle the larger volume, and retain only a few essential pages in a folder in your filing cabinet. The relationship among all your storage areas is dynamic; your prevailing quest is to boil down what's crucial for you to retain—keep only the essence.

Information is power; if you can't find what you've retained, it's of no value to you. Worse, the time you took to read and file the items would then be wasted.

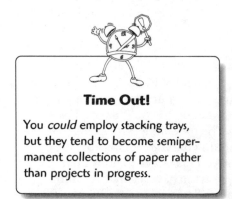

Time Out!

You *could* employ stacking trays, but they tend to become semipermanent collections of paper rather than projects in progress.

Are you fearful about tossing something because you just know you're going to need it tomorrow? Chapter 19, "It Pays to Travel Light," will help you here. Suffice it to say for now that if there are no discernible negative consequences to tossing something, toss it. Most of what you're retaining is readily replaceable anyway. Office efficiency experts claim that 80 percent of what executives file, they never use again. Even if that's only partially true, it still means a significant chunk of what you're retaining is deadwood.

Clearing this deadwood out of your desk, files, and office keeps your office in shape. That enhances your capacity to properly handle new demands (and you read Chapter 3, "With Decades to Go, You Can't Keep Playing Beat the Clock"; you *know* more is coming). It also raises the probability that you'll be able to get your mitts on (find) those items you actually need.

Consider the cumulative time savings you could potentially chalk up if you cut your search time in half—let's say you'll save 12 minutes per day, at minimum. That adds up to an hour per week and 50 hours per year. That's like creating an extra week for yourself. As a kicker, others in your office get a clear message that you're someone who is able to remain in control, find things quickly, and stay on top of situations. Hence, you get a multiple payoff for keeping your files (and your office, in general) in shape.

Chronos Says

The great paradox of keeping house is that getting things in shape takes time. But don't give up. The small time investment you make in developing your newfound efficiency will pay off over and over again down the road.

Paper, Paper Everywhere

Even with the advent of the PC, the fax/modem, e-mail, and the Internet, paper is still the dominant means of communication and the scourge of your career. The most repetitious task you face, day in and day out, is handling paper. To win back your time is to win the battle with paper.

When you receive a catalog, magazine, or other thick publication, strip it down to its essence. What few articles, pages, or items of interest do you want to retain? Once you identify those, recycle the rest and reduce the potential for office glut.

Immediately reduce books, manuals, and long reports to their essence; manually scan the entire document (using your eyes, not a hand-held scanner). Copy the few pages you wish to retain, along with title page, table of contents, and any critical addresses, phone, or fax information. Your goal: Retain the few pages that seem important, and recycle the larger document.

Your Copier Can Help You, if You Let it

When new items arrive in your office, consider the creative ways you can strip them down to their essence, particularly using the copier. Can you create a single sheet, perhaps front and back, that captures the essence of the larger document? Can you create a single sheet that captures the essence of several small scraps or tidbits you wish to retain?

When I speak at conventions, sometimes I ask the audience members to hold up their wallets. This gets a chuckle, but the exercise is well worth undertaking; if their wallets are thicker than half an inch, they're carrying too much in them.

Mr. Lakein's Junk Drawer

Alan Lakein, a management specialist of yesteryear, had a nifty idea about what to do with the mounting piles of stuff you can't deal with just now but want to review when

Time Out!

When confronted with too many scraps and information tidbits, it's easy to fall into the habit of parking them in your wallet, on your desk, or in your drawers.

you have a chance. He suggested putting everything in what he calls a "C" drawer, meaning it's not an "A" or "B" item. You can't chuck it at the moment, but you certainly can't deal with it at the moment, either.

In this drawer, you temporarily house what you want out of sight and out of mind. Go back to your "C" drawer when you have the time and strength, take out the items and see what needs to go into your file system (probably not much), what you can immediately chuck or recycle, and what goes back into the "C" drawer. I maintain a "C" drawer and find it helpful, particularly when I'm working toward a deadline and I encounter something that I don't have time to review immediately. I pop it into the "C" drawer and get back to what I was doing.

What About the Paper That Keeps Coming Your Way?

When you're confronted by yet another report, document, or who knows what, ask yourself these questions:

➤ *What is the issue behind this document?* What does the paper represent? Is it an information crutch (data that you already know)? If so, chuck it. Does it represent something you think might be important in the future? If so, put it in the "C" drawer. (See Chapter 11 for a variety of other files you can create to house such documents.)

Often the issue behind the paper flood is, in retrospect, too minor to merit your attention. Sure, it looms large at times, but what doesn't seem important when it arrives in screaming headlines? For years, newspapers have been able to sell their wares simply with clever use of language and font size. The issues addressed often have precious little to do with the typical reader.

➤ *Did I need to receive this at all?* This can be an insightful question to ask yourself. In many cases, the answer is no; that means you don't have to spend another second on the item. Now and then, something you didn't need to receive comes your way and is of interest. (Rare, but possible.) You can chuck most of these items immediately.

➤ *How else can this be handled?* Can you delegate what needs to be done regarding this new piece of paper? Referring back to Chapter 7, "Money Comes and Goes—Time Just Goes," on using helpers, is there someone else in your cosmos who can handle this for you and free up your time for more important things?

If no one else but you will do, how else can you handle it so as to have (in good old computer biz-speak) "quick and easy throughput"? Can you fax instead of mail? Can you e-mail instead of fax? Can you pay by check instead of in person? Can you pay by credit card by fax instead of by check? Can you highlight the five items in the important company memo that merit discussion at the next meeting instead of trying to get a handle on all 22 pages?

➤ *Will it matter if I don't handle it at all?* This is a critical question. Much of what confronts you requires no action on your part. For example: announcements regarding upcoming publications, ads that tout prices or services, and anything addressed to "current resident." If you don't pay your rent or your mortgage, you'll be contacted by someone interested in collecting the money. If, however, you don't participate in the office pool, don't attend the local charity ball, don't make an extra copy of that recipe, or don't learn about that software game, *your life will not change.*

Discarding the Discardable

Without equivocation, go through your office on a search-and-destroy mission. Trash anything that fits these categories:

➤ Outdated manuals.

➤ Back issues of publications you haven't touched in more than two years.

➤ Drafts, earlier versions, and outdated versions of letters, correspondence, memos, reports, and documents that have already been produced as final (unless you're in the legal department of your organization; then it's your job to hang on to such—ahem—*material*).

➤ Carcasses of once-useful stuff: dead bottles of white-out, dry pens, pencil nubs, or business cards whose vital information is already logged in your database.

➤ All scraps and tidbits of information, used Post-It notes, and the like that have accumulated around your desk, in your wallet, and elsewhere. Get them on a single sheet or log them into a file on your computer.

➤ Excess vendor supply catalogs.

➤ Manuals you will absolutely never open again.

➤ Outdated catalogs, flyers, annual reports, brochures, and promotional materials.

➤ The hoard of thumbtacks, pushpins, pennies, and paper clips that gathers in the corners of your desk drawers.

➤ Take-out/delivery menus from restaurants you never visit (or visit so frequently that you've memorized the bill of fare).

➤ Lingering stacks of irrelevant documents, extra copies of relevant documents. Keep what you need. Discard the rest.

Items to Acquire

Nothing is mandatory for you to acquire. The following items, however, may help you keep your office in shape:

➤ Color-coded file folders, tabs, labels, and long-life stampers (more on these in Chapter 11 and Chapter 13, "Are You a Slave to Your Beeper?").

➤ Magazine holders for your shelves.

Long-life stampers can cut down on the time you spend handwriting or organizing material.

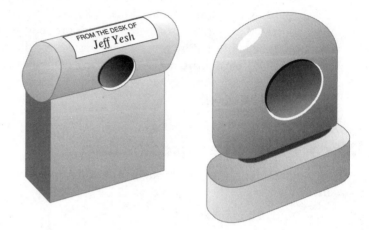

➤ A few three-ring notebooks for storing and maintaining similar items.

➤ A mechanical arm that hoists your monitor over your desk. You can use it to bring your monitor closer or move it aside, depending on how much room you need for your work (if your computer's disk drives are in a tower case, you've just freed up another square foot or so of desk space).

➤ A larger wastebasket.

Near your desk—but not *on* it—go the loving and familiar items, such as pictures, plants, and motivators. Also install any supporting accouterments (from VitaLites to ocean-wave music, if they support your productivity, efficiency, and creativity) near—but not on—your desk.

The Least You Need to Know

➤ Your desk is among the most important areas of your life. Take charge of your desk, and you help take charge of your time.

➤ Refine your office setup so you can find whatever you're looking for easily. (That's right, *easily*.)

➤ Everyone faces a continuing barrage of scraps and information tidbits. Corral these and copy them all onto a single page or into an appropriate computer file. Do not let them accumulate.

➤ Continually discard what does not support you, and acquire what does. Get ruthless about this.

➤ As often as possible, clear your desk of everything but the one task at hand.

Chapter 11

Filing: Your Simple Salvation

> **In This Chapter**
>
> ➤ As the world grows more complex, filing becomes more important
>
> ➤ The essential tools for mastering the high art of filing
>
> ➤ It's both what you file and how you file it
>
> ➤ Design your filing system to uniquely serve the way you work

Do you look upon filing as drudgery? If so, you're not alone! You don't see people shooting movies, writing Broadway plays, or producing hard rock albums on the topic. It's rather mundane, pedestrian, and (shall I say it?) even a tad boring. Yet it's an unheralded key to winning back your time.

As discussed in Chapter 10, "Making Your Office Work for You," when you're in control of your desk, office, files, and the resources you've assembled, you are a more focused, efficient, effective professional. In this chapter, I focus exclusively on filing. Don't give me that look; it's going to be engrossing, and it'll give you a career edge.

Filing: The Big Picture

First, it's important to ask the big question: Why file? Here are two big answers:

1. Files have value—ideally, you file items because you believe that they will come in handy. (Most items don't have value, which is why you may regard filing as unproductive.)

2. There are consequences for *not* filing. You save receipts from business expenses so you can be reimbursed by your organization and comply with IRS regulations. Filing tax receipts makes sense: It keeps you out of jail.

If you're in sales, you file information that will enable you to make greater sales in the future. This includes notes on customers and perhaps their catalogs, brochures, and reports.

Consider everything you have ever filed! Each item presumably had (or has) potential future value, if only enabling you to cover your derriere. Why do people avoid the mere thought of filing? Beats the heck out of me. Maybe they don't see the connection between filing and its future impact on their careers and lives.

Actually starting the process is very time-consuming, but it is one of those necessary tasks that save time later. Rather than spend hours searching for an item, you'll be able to find it—pronto. So it's well worth a day or two during downtime to create a system that supports you.

Time Out!

Most of what confronts you will have little impact on your career or your life—exceedingly little. Therefore, most of what crosses your desk is a clog that dares not find its way into your files.

Simple Tools to Make it All Work

Filing requires only a few simple tools and the proper mind set. The tools are listed here:

➤ *A chair*. You can file while standing if you have a four-drawer filing cabinet and you're dealing with the top drawer. Usually, your filing activity is easier if you're in a chair—particularly a swivel chair. If you're way behind in your filing, you won't want to be on your feet.

➤ *A desk or flat surface*. This comes in handy when you staple or unstaple, paper-clip or un-paper-clip. Often you'll have to mark the folders you insert in your file cabinet, making notes on what you're filing, folding, ripping, or taping together. A flat surface means never having to work in mid-air.

➤ *File folders*. File folders are essential. Rather than the two-cut or three-cut manila folders that have been around since Moses crossed the Red Sea, you can get folders in blue, green, brown, red, pink, or black—any color you want. They can be letter-size, legal-size, or have a protruding label area.

➤ *File folder labels*. These can be color-coded as well. You don't have to order the same old white labels. You can easily have subsections within your green file folders by using labels of different colors.

➤ *Filing cabinets with ample space.* The next time you visit your doctor or dentist, ask to see how the patient files are stored. Healthcare providers often use a modular stacking shelf system (see the illustration in this chapter) that gives them immediate access to the record needed.

➤ *Color-coded dots.* These help you find files quickly, even if you're already using color-coded files and labels. You could put a small red dot on files you anticipate using in the next week or two. The real value of the dots, however, is that you can leave the files in the file drawer instead of on your shelf or desk.

A shelf system like this one provides the room you need to set up any kind of filing system.

➤ *Staplers, paper clips, and other fasteners.* Keep these on hand; you never know when you'll need to fasten or unfasten items before you file them.

Chronos Says

Unlike the Ten Commandments, what you file is not etched in stone. You can move things around, chuck them, add or delete files...go wild. Your goal for now is to get things into their best apparent home.

Staying Sane by Filing Soundly

I've touched on these principles in previous chapters (particularly Chapter 10), but now I'll get to the particulars. Suppose you face a mass of items (or is that a *mess* of items?) on your desk. How would you tackle it? How would you whip that stuff into shape?

Toss it Without Passion

Wade through everything rapidly, and determine what can be tossed, as well as any duplicate or outdated items you don't need. Some items won't fit in your file folders anyway; it's best to copy the handful of pages you need from them, file those pages, and recycle the rest.

"When in doubt, throw it out." These immortal words, uttered two decades ago by efficiency expert Edwin Bliss are still true. If you're not sure about keeping something, in most cases you've already answered the question: NO. If you're like most professionals, you have a tendency to overfile, which gluts your system and helps hide anything you need to find. If you ever file too much stuff, use the "C" drawer discussed in Chapter 10 as a pit stop for potential file items.

If you question whether to file an item, put it aside for a day or two and look at it again. Often the answer will present itself. Ask yourself, "What will happen if I pitch this?" If there's no significant downside, chuck it gleefully.

Birds of a Feather

In that great mass (mess?) of stuff before you, if eight items refer to delegation, that's a clue to start a file folder labeled "Delegation." Do the same with other groups of like items.

Plow through the entire pile; toss what you can and group like items until everything is tossed or grouped. Yes, some items will stand alone. Not to worry.

When approaching each of your mini-piles, ask yourself these questions:

➤ Can I consolidate each pile by using the backsides of documents, single-page copies, and shorter notes?

➤ Can I consolidate scraps and tidbits by using the copier to create a dossier page or stapling them into a packet?

➤ For piles that have only one or two items each, is there a way to group them? (An article on office chairs might join your notes on using room dividers in a pile called "Office furniture.")

A Stitch in Time

If you haven't ordered file folders before, you're in for a revelation. Open up any office supply catalog and let your creative juices flow. Colored file folders enable you to stay organized with less work. How so? You can use green file folders for anything that relates to money, red for government, blue for (true blue) customers, and so on.

Managing the Mini-Piles

Go through the materials you've put in mini-piles; see if any of them should go into all-encompassing files, such as "Copiers" or "Insurance." Always, *always* seek to have a few large files of like items, not a gaggle of small files. It'll be easier to find what you want in the course of your day, week, year, or career.

Use date-stamping, if it suits you. Some efficiency experts suggest putting a date stamp on every item you file. If you've been holding on to an item for months on end and haven't used it, maybe it's time to chuck it.

It's not mandatory to use date-stamping; an item's future relevance isn't always linked to how long you've had it. Generally, the longer you've held on to an item without using it, the smaller the chance is that it will be of future importance—but it ain't always so.

Customized File Headings

This is the part where filing gets to be fun. (You're laughing. See? I told you.) By using customized file headings, you can devise compartments that enable you to give the materials that cross your desk a good home, while you remain anxiety-free, guilt-free, and fat-free. For example, if you often don't know where to file items, you can create a file called, "Where to file this?" (I use one called "Check in one month.")

Other handy file names you could use include these:

➤ Read or chuck

➤ Read when I can

➤ Review for possible linkage with ABC project

One profound question you face when you consider filing any item is, "Where does this go?" Your quest then is to find an appropriate file where you can park the item and find it again easily. Often that means relabeling files. That's fine; you're further refining your system and putting your smarts into developing a personal information-retrieval system.

Watch Words

Tickler files automatically remind you of when you need to deal with a particular task. When the request for the task hits your desk, you can place it in the tickler file for the appropriate future date. Every day of the month, check your tickler file for that day to identify tasks to take on for the day.

Tickler Files: By the Day and By the Month

You can benefit greatly by creating file folders for each month. Then, when something crosses your desk in December but you don't have to act on it until February, into the February file it goes.

You can have a 31-day tickler file as well. If you receive something on the second day of the month but don't have to deal with it until the 14th, put it in the file marked the 14th—or give yourself some extra time and put it in the file marked the 13th. (Think about it.)

You can use this system to pay bills on time. Write the checks in advance, sign them, seal them, stamp them, and put the envelope in the appropriate folder of your 31-day rotating tickler file. Review that file at the start of each week, and perhaps once or twice during the week; you'll know automatically when it's time to pay a bill or address a date-filed item. (More on this in Chapter 13, "Are You a Slave to Your Beeper?")

The monthly files and 31-day tickler files will help you reduce clutter while offering you peace of mind. Simple? Yes. It's also remarkably efficient.

When you view something several days, weeks, or months after first filing it, you often have greater objectivity and a new chance to act on it, delegate it, or toss it. If a lot of stuff gets tossed, fine; at least you had those things out of your way for all that time.

Creating Files Before You Need To

Suppose you're planning to go to graduate school for a master's degree. One way to accommodate the growing body of literature you'll be assembling is to create a file folder in advance of having anything to file. When stuff comes in that appears worth saving, it'll have a home.

You might think that this is merely a way to collect more stuff. Please reconsider! Creating folders in advance of the need can be a potent reminder and affirmation of your future goals.

Suppose you come across a brilliant article on how to finance your degree in a way that considerably reduces your burden. Where are you going to put that article? Park it on top of something else, where it will sit for weeks or months? You still won't know what to do with it, but you'll want to hang on to it—right?

A Stitch in Time

You can start a new file folder, label it, and park it in your file drawer without anything in it! Yup. Are you insane to do so? Nope.

What are some files you can create in advance of having anything to put in them—merely because it makes sense, based on where you're heading in life? Here are some suggestions:

➤ Your child's higher education fund

➤ Your retirement home

➤ Your vacation next year to New Zealand

➤ Assistance for your aging parents

➤ Evolving technology that interests you

➤ A new medical operation that might affect you

Chronos Says

Actor, writer, and film producer Woody Allen once said that 85 percent of life is just showing up. At least 50 percent of dealing with all the piles of paper you confront is simply making room for them!

Creating a file in advance of having anything to put in it works on a computer hard disk as well. If a new project is about to start, or if you'll be scanning information on a new topic, why not create a directory for it on your hard disk? I do this when I bring on a new part-time helper.

Suppose Bob is going to start in a few days. The first thing I do is create a directory named "Bob." As the days pass, I move files into Bob's directory so I already have assignments for him. As he takes them on, others develop; I move them to his directory.

I have a directory called "Inprog" that I go to at the start of each day; from there I might move an item to "Bob" or (once it's finished) elsewhere on my hard disk. You get the picture.

Giving Your Files a Home

I'd like to spend the next 150 pages on the value of housing your files, but there are limits on our time and space, so I'll simply do it in two. Your goal is to keep closest to you the items you use frequently; keep rarely used items farthest from you. Much of what you file *won't* be used frequently.

Of course, certain factors—the nature of your work, tax laws, or other regulations—may require you to hang onto more than you'd like. Whatever you have to hang on to—plus what you *want* to hang on to—can be stored away from your immediate workspace. I'm going to take the leap and assume your organization already has systems and procedures for storing files. What about you? Are you hanging onto all kinds of stuff you cannot bear to pitch? Here's a plan of attack:

1. Group like items, put them in a box or storage container, and mark the box with something descriptive, such as "Check again next April," or "Review after the merger."

2. Before storing a container, quickly plow through it once more to see what can be removed. This will simplify your task, and you'll thank yourself later.

3. Once the box is out of sight, build a safeguard into your system. Put a note in your "April" file that says to review the contents of the box located at XYZ.

Sometimes, instead of storing vast volumes of material, you can simply scan it and keep it on disk.

Can anyone else in your organization or family harbor such items so you don't have to? If the box holds reminders of some dear, departed one, perhaps the best solution is to rotate it among the siblings—four months a year at your sister Sally's, four months at your brother Tom's, and four months with you. People do this all the time, especially with stuff they know they'll never go through again but can't bear to chuck.

It's easier emotionally to sell your child's baby clothes if somebody wants them. When you sell items and they meet a need, you feel good. Afterward, when you have to pack up what wasn't sold and give the items to charity, you might not feel as good, even though it's a commendable gesture. Perhaps there's some kind of emotional relief in getting money for the goods—and emotional blockage when you end up giving them away. Perhaps there is the lingering notion, "I should hang on to these items for posterity. Maybe my child, as an adult, might open the box and appreciate them." You'll need to decide the exact disposition of your goods before you hold a yard sale.

Storing Stuff for Money

If the stuff you've boxed is valuable and compact, maybe it makes sense to put it in a safety-deposit box in a bank. If it's voluminous, maybe consider putting it in a commercial self-storage unit (available in most metro areas).

Paying to store materials brings up the issue of what you're retaining. Is it worth it to pay a bank or a company to retain the stuff? If it is, then you'll feel all right about forking over the dough. If it doesn't seem worth the cash, you've just found a good indicator that you don't need to hang on to the stuff.

Watch Words

When you rent a **self-storage unit**, you get a garage–like space you can cram full of any items you don't need on a daily basis. For example, you may want to store old files in a smaller self-storage unit. See "Storage" in the *Yellow Pages* to learn what storage options are available in your area.

Recycle and Win

An effective way to pare down the mountain of pages confronting you down to a molehill is to watch constantly for what can be recycled. Can you give a report, memo, or article to a key associate or junior staff person whom it will benefit? If so, it's far easier to let go of what you're retaining.

Can you use the clean back sides of sheets for rough drafts, scratch paper, internal memos, notepads, and hard-copy fax responses? If so, it will be far easier for you to recycle materials that come across your desk. In this case, you're supporting the environment by getting double use out of your materials. All the folders you use are potentially reusable. Label them over again and give them new life. Recycling also gives you a quick and socially acceptable means of dealing with much of the paper and clutter that arrives during the day.

If you don't take control, you're setting yourself up for glutted files, glutted systems, and glutted thinking. Rather than winning back your time, you'll be giving it away. You're at your best when you're a lean, mean, working machine.

The Least You Need to Know

➤ Filing is a necessary response to working in an environment of continual over-load.

➤ When you're in control of your desk, office, files, and the resources you've assembled, you're a more focused, efficient, and effective professional—and you're certainly more in charge of your time.

➤ Effective filing is an opportunity for you to devise a personal information-retrieval system that supports the way you work and live.

➤ The tools for effective filing are simple. Colored file folders, labels, and dots help you organize what you're retaining. Purchase them with reckless abandon.

➤ Remove anything from your immediate environment that you don't need to encounter for weeks or months.

➤ Recycle whatever you can of the stuff that comes across your desk. This will automatically help you win back your time, keeping your files lean and mean.

Part 3
Communicating at All Speeds

Now that you're in charge of your turf—or a least know what it takes to get there—it's time to get into a higher and more efficient gear when it comes to staying in touch with the rest of the known universe. The four chapters in this section examine the ridiculous to the sublime in terms of options available for staying in touch.

The key to making the most of these is to recognize that the Revenge Effect is alive and well and waiting to wreak havoc on your day, depending on what tools of technology you're prepared to abuse. In other words, you can both save or waste oodles of time using electronic pagers (jeepers creepers, I'll call them beepers), e-mail, the Internet, and snail mail. Since you'd rather save oodles of time, we'll focus on that.

So, comrade, appropriately use or apply all the tools and methods of communication discussed here. Otherwise, you will quickly find yourself behind the no-time 8-ball faster than you can say "The dog ate my homework."

We'll begin with an alarming, insightful, and totally thoughtful look at a tiny little gadget that threatens to decimate your life (but only if you let it) and turn civilization into a smoldering heap of ashes.

Chapter 12

Neat and Uncomplicated Tools to Manage Your Time

In This Chapter

➤ No need for guilt and anxiety

➤ Technology time traps

➤ Speakerphones, headsets, and two-way recording

➤ Simple technologies, affordable prices

A lot has been written about new technology, making the most of your online time, and how to not get left in the dust by all the techno-twits out there. The only time you have to adopt a new tool or technological device is when: (1) your organization or boss requires it, (2) your clients already use the technology, or (3) you'll gain a strategic competitive advantage.

Don't Race Ahead of Yourself

In the mid-1990s, mass advertising suggested that tapping onto the Internet was the be-all and end-all. While there's no denying the awesome power of online information, it's important to keep things in perspective. "Driven by our obsession to compete, we've embraced the electronic god with a frenzy," says Bill Henderson, leader of the Lead Pencil Club. "Soon, blessed with the fax, voice and e-mail computer hook-ups and TVs with hundreds of channels, we won't have to leave our lonely rooms—not to write a check, work, visit, shop, exercise, or make love. We will have raced at incredible speeds to reach our final destination——nothing."

Look around your office and your home. Have you been caught in the trap of gathering information or acquiring an item far in advance of your ability to use it? Have you bought any technological items in the last two years that you simply don't use? I'm talking about hardware and software, instruction manuals, scanners, additional printers, adapters, cassettes, videos, CD-ROMS, phone systems, fax machines, and who knows what else.

Ten Times the Advantage

Peter Drucker, the noted sage of management, made the observation that for new technology to replace old, it has to have at least 10 times the benefit of its predecessor. I don't know how he arrived at that figure, but who am I to doubt Dr. Drucker?

All technology holds the potential to either help you be more efficient or further slide you into the morass of the overwhelmed. In his book *Technopoly*, Dr. Neil Postman says that the introduction of any new technology into your life brings both benefits and detriments. The manufacturers, advertisers, and dealers are adept at helping you focus on the benefits—especially in the rare case that you happen to become one of the world's expert users of the system they're offering. How often, however, do you actually read about the downside of acquiring new tools and technology in your life?

Upside and Downside

Consider the car phone: If you're the parent of three children, it can give you great comfort to call them on the car phone after school. Car phones, indeed, can be wonderful tools. The newest models offer voice commands that enable you to "Call Joe Smith," "Call home," "Answer the phone," or "Hang up the phone."

Some car phones have built-in fax and data communications that allow for transmissions from your car. Some connect to your horn, providing a security feature. Others allow for emergency dialing. Nearly all have some type of anti-theft alarm. A growing number offer wider display screens, brightly lit for easy use at night, speed dialing, speed re-dialing, and one-touch dialing.

But there's a downside, too. By adding a car phone to your automobile, what else have you added to your life that perhaps you didn't want? (Note that more than half of these developments have an impact on your time.)

➤ The ability of anybody to reach you at any time

➤ Disturbance of one of the last sanctuaries that you had

➤ The need to change your brochures and business cards to reflect your car phone's number

➤ The potential for driving less safely

➤ Added expense as you engage in unnecessary conversations

➤ The new-found annoying habit of making one extra call before reaching destinations—to make sure that plans haven't changed

➤ ...Thereby leading to heightened insecurity and anxiety

➤ Another invoice to examine at the end of the month, and another check to write

➤ Involuntarily opening up your percepters to notice other ads about other cellular phone systems

➤ The annoying feeling that your system is insufficient and that you need more range, more power, and less cost per call

It seems paradoxical that a device created to make you more efficient or save you time holds nearly equal potential for doing the opposite.

The Revenge Effect

"The Revenge Effect is the curious way the world has of getting even, defeating our best efforts to speed it up and otherwise improve it," says Professor Edward Tenner of Princeton. The failure of technology to solve problems, Tenner says, can often be traced to the interaction between machine and man. Freeways, intended to speed travel, lead to suburbs—urban sprawl *out* instead of *up*, so commuting times climb. Computers make it easy to copy and print files, so you end up copying and printing many more files, and your paperless office fills up with paper.

You Set the Rules

When you view each new technological tool as both beneficial and detrimental, you're in a far better position to stay in control of your time. With a cellular phone, you could make the purchase with predetermined rules of use, such as only making calls to loved ones and for crucial appointments, limiting calls to under three minutes, and not listing your car phone number on business cards or brochures. Or, you might employ other ground rules.

The crucial element is that *you* define your personal set of rules for using the tool.

A Stitch in Time

Consider both the benefits and the detriments of the time-saving technological tools you operate. If you never become a master at using everything that tool provides, you'll gain still greater benefits if you're able to eliminate some of the detriments that may arise.

Many types of "neat tools" follow. Some represent sophisticated technology, and some are rather simple. Each represents great potential for you to win back your time. With your own rules of use, you'll feel better about how and when you use the tool, and you'll avoid potential time traps.

Talk Your Way to High Productivity

To be more productive in your office and make maximum use of your travel time, use a pocket dictator or voice-recognition technology. I've used dictators to capture notes, offer immediate thank-you's to people I meet, and produce whole books—yes, even this one.

If you are already proficient in using your own personal computer, lap-top, or note-book computer for word processing, there still are many advantages to becoming skilled in using portable dictation equipment—particularly if you have other staff members who can transcribe your golden words. By using portable dictation equipment or voice-recognition technology, you can approach your productivity potential. Few things in life will have this type of dramatic impact on your ability to manage your time.

Have Dictator, Will Travel

Portable dictation equipment allows for mobility. You can dictate almost anywhere. Microcassette recorders accommodate up to an hour of taping on each side. If you compose directly on a word processor, you may be able to type between 40 and 80 words a minute. With a little practice, you can dictate at 100–140 words a minute. When you type while you are thinking, your mind races ahead of your fingers. Many of the ideas and phrases you compose in your mind are lost.

Once you become familiar with the ease of operation and the pure joy of finishing written items in one-third of the previous time, there is no returning to old ways. With dictating, you can handle whatever you wanted to write but never found the time to actually do.

Your Master's Voice

Voice-recognition technology (let's call them VRTs, for short) available as of this writing enable you to speak into the system's headset and dictate at a slightly slower speed than you're used to talking. In 20–40 minutes—depending on the system and how adept you are at it—the software "learns" your voice pattern and from that discerns what words to throw on the screen as you speak.

With practice, you'll soon be able to speak at a normal speed and spend little time "training" the system—perhaps five minutes or less. In fact, systems will be available soon enough where no training is necessary and anyone's voice can be interpreted.

Chronos Says

In a few years, you won't have to talk to use VRTs. You can simply don a headband, issue thought commands, and have the computer diligently obey!

Gettin' Better All the Time

VRTs are convenient when it comes to dictating brief letters and e-mail responses, creating lists, and developing other documents that are not voluminous. As the mighty microchip continues to decrease in size and become more powerful, VRTs will be ready right out of the box and have awesome capabilities, such as discerning 300,000 or 400,000 words instead of 20,000 or 30,000, have automatic syntax and idiom checkers, and, in general, take the pain out of composing new text much like word processors took the pain out of making corrections to text. The instruction booklet—if there's one at all—could be four pages or less. Perhaps you'll just need a single card.

Don't See What You Get

Much as with dictating equipment, you're better off not looking at the screen while you're using a VRT system. Continual monitoring is only going to *hamper* your progress. You're better off composing your memo or letter, letting the system do its job, and then seeing what you have. If the wrong word was inserted here or there, or you want to make a correction, do it afterward. If you attempt to compose on the fly, your progress may be uneven.

Pause at Will

Dictating in 20- or 30-second blocks what may have previously required 2—5 minutes to write negates the need for visual review. If you are able to file and extract materials readily—and if your desk is well-organized, and if your shelves are neat (you followed all my advice!)—, chances are, you'll be good at dictating with portable equipment.

A Stitch in Time

If you avoid dictation because you can't write without being able to visually review what you've written, consider this: A good outline is a prerequisite to *any* effective writing. When dictating with a good outline, key words can readily be expanded to sentences and paragraphs. And the Pause feature allows you to easily start and stop, to gather thoughts, and to articulate complete sentences and paragraphs.

How to Overcome Mike Fright

Dictating expert Jefferson D. Bates recommends the following steps in overcoming the fear of speaking into a microphone:

➤ Pick a subject you know well.

➤ Jot down a few ideas on the subject in outline form.

➤ Study the words for a few moments while the ideas sink in.

➤ With the microphone in place, close your eyes and take several deep breaths. (This helps put you in a creative state of mind.)

➤ Imagine you're talking to a close friend or associate, anyone you feel comfortable with and trust. Picture that person in your mind.

➤ Start talking. If you still have hang-ups about getting started, take something you have written earlier and start reading it aloud into the mike. When the words are flowing smoothly and easily, close your eyes and keep talking.

Look Ma, No Hands!

Whether you use the telephone five times a day or all day long, simple, inexpensive technology is available to immediately double your phoning efficiency. If you need both hands free to take notes or maintain better organization during a phone call, the typical phone receiver is not practical. Speakerphones aren't much better, and the sound quality is dreadful. Cell phones free your feet, not your hands. A far better solution? The telephone headset.

Headsets are provided by a variety of communications and telephone equipment companies and generally entail a set of light-weight earphones with a long prong bending toward the mouth. This ear-and-mouthpiece set is attached by a cord to a desktop dialer. With many competitors in the market, you can shop and compare.

Brother, Can You Stand to Save Some Time?

A major benefit of using a telephone headset is mobility. When you wear a headset, your hands are free to take notes, shuffle papers, or open file drawers. Yet, the sound quality of your voice equals or exceeds that of a traditional handset phone.

While talking to someone on a headset phone, for example, you can use your computer more conveniently, address an envelope, or just relax with your arms free. Headsets have evolved from large, heavy "earmuff" equipment to extremely light-weight pieces contoured for a comfortable fit.

Five Ways to Feel Better by the End of Each Workday

➤ Don't put anything more on today's to-do list late in the day.

➤ Tackle the issues you face in descending order of importance.

➤ Work on one thing at a time.

➤ Pause periodically, if briefly, throughout the day.

➤ Acknowledge yourself for what you *did* accomplish.

Hold That Thought

➤ You are not your tasks; you are not your job; you are not your title.

➤ Some people are late bloomers; James Michener wrote his first book at age 42 and wrote books for over 40 more years.

➤ Most millionaires make their first million slowly, over many years.

➤ You'll never be younger than you are right now.

Time "Speeds Up" and You Seem to Have Less When. . .

➤ You take in more information than you can absorb.

➤ You work in front of a clock to meet an unrealistic time-frame.

➤ You jam-pack your calendar with activities and appointments.

Time "Slows Down" and You Seem to Have More When. . .

➤ You close your eyes for one full minute and imagine a pleasant scene.

➤ You delete three non-essential items from your to-do list *without* doing them.

➤ You clear your desk of everything except your primary task.

Try These to Catch Up with This Week

➤ Telecommute at least once a week.

➤ Get dressed each morning quietly, sans radio or TV.

➤ Do something fun once a week on the way home from work.

➤ Regard each piece of paper entering your "personal kingdom" as a likely traitor.

➤ Make a lunch date with a friend, not a coworker or client.

You Know You're Winning Back Your Time When. . .

➤ You leave home in the morning with grace and ease.

➤ You enjoy a leisurely lunch.

➤ You often depart from the workplace at normal closing hours—and feel fine about it.

➤ You stay in shape and at your desired weight.

➤ You have time to be with and enjoy friends and relatives.

The Top Ten Tips for Winning Back Your Time

1. Leave the office or your workplace on time at least several workdays per week, having accomplished what you sought to accomplish *within a normal workday*.

2. Watch less television; cruise the Internet less.

3. Pay others to do tasks you don't want to do so you're free to address more important stuff; break the cycle of spending for items that don't free up your time and then having to work harder to pay the bills.

4. Recognize that while nobody loves filing, hereafter it's essential to staying in control.

5. Buy any device *you can easily master* that you believe will make you more efficient.

6. Get into the habit of doing one thing at a time. Stop doubling up on activities such as reading the paper while on the treadmill.

7. Get a solid night's sleep (eight hours for most adults) at least five to seven times a week.

8. Enter the "wholesale throwout" business—throw out accumulating piles of newspapers, magazines, and reports that offer little to your career and life.

9. Earmark several hours each week during which you'll take in no new information and have nothing to read or do (especially Saturdays and Sundays).

10. Read this book; pick some changes to make. Incorporate each one slowly and thoroughly; let it sink in, then move on to the next.

Five of the Worst Mistakes People Make with Their Time

➤ Spending time on concerns that are not chosen priorities.

➤ Underestimating the time that tasks or activities will actually consume.

➤ Allowing too many interruptions.

➤ Saying "yes" too frequently for requests for their time.

➤ Not getting help.

Five Unbelievable-but-True Facts About Your Time

➤ You're likely to live longer than you think you will—perhaps ten or more years longer.

➤ Anything you do for an average of 30 minutes each day (equal to over 180 hours for 365 days) consumes *a full week's time for every year of your life.*

➤ You're likely to spend eight years of your life watching electronically how other people (supposedly) live.

➤ You're working about 360 hours more annually (equal to nine 40-hour work weeks) than people in Germany.

➤ You may be engaging in 10-to-15 second bouts of "microsleep" while driving your car!

alpha
books

tear here

Far Less Fatigue

An advantage often cited by headset users is less fatigue. If you make and receive many phone calls, a most efficient way to handle them is to reserve a specific block of time—say, two hours in the afternoon to return and generate calls. Repetitive phone use, however, is tiring. A telephone headset alleviates this strain. Ten to 15 calls used to be drudgery. Now, I mow them down with no fatigue! You can move around a bit, stretch your neck and back, and combat the tiring feeling of sitting in one spot.

A Stitch in Time

You can respond to questions much faster when your hands are free to look through the files for answers. And, when the task of making phone calls is more comfortable, you don't give in to the temptation to waste time between calls.

Finally, using a headset helps you to minimize distractions. While you're wearing earphones, you don't hear a lot of the background noise that is typical of regular phones. You're not likely to hear phones ring in the next office, and you're less tempted to divert your attention.

Not Created Equal

All headsets are not equal. The simplest models sell for as little as $49.95, while the most elaborate can climb to $300 or more. Some are versatile enough to be plugged into a hand phone, allowing fairly instant conversion when you need it. Some are specially designed for high-noise environments, with earphones that insulate you from outside noise particularly well. Headband and mouthpiece designs vary, as do warranties and service policies.

Here are some suppliers. I suggest first getting their catalogs.

➤ GN Netcom Incorporated, 10 Victor Square, Scotts Valley, CA 95066; phone 800-995-5500 (a full-line supplier)

➤ Plantronics, P.O. Box 635, Santa Cruz, CA 95061-0635; phone 800-544-4660 (a full-line supplier)

➤ Ziehl Associates Inc., 115 Meacham Avenue, Elmont, NY 11003-2631; phone 516-437-1300 (offers Cradle Mate and other telephone headset accessories)

Cord-Free, as Free as the Wind Blows

Some vendors offer headset models that are cord-free. One such model enables you to move up to 100 feet from your desk and still maintain a clear, solid connection with the other party. You're hands-free to write, open cabinets, flip through books, pick up materials, check equipment, or even straighten your tie—all while listening intently to the other party.

Look for models that offer noise-canceling microphones, which automatically filter out background noise so that your own voice transmits clearly.

Headset in the Air

Along the same lines of donning a headset, if you fly frequently, you might want to consider a new generation of active noise-cancellation headphones. The Sharper Image version is designed to generate "anti-noise" waves, which neutralize the irritating drone of an airplane engine and surrounding cabin sounds. With less distractions, you can get more work done, hence be more in control of your time.

Say No to Noise

If you fly from say New York to Los Angeles non-stop, at the end of your flight, you'll actually feel rested and relaxed. Noise does a number on each of us, often in ways we can't discern. Some models of noise-cancellation headphones allow you to use a two-prong adapter so that you can listen in to the in-flight music or programs offered while receiving the benefits of hearing less engine and cabin noise. In fact, you can hear every word of the programs being offered.

Lightweight Batteries to Save your Head

Many systems run on simply AAA alkaline batteries. The systems are lightweight and pack easily. They're also affordable, at under $100. If you fly at least 20–30 times a year, noise-cancellation headphones could be a godsend for you.

Keep in mind, however, that noise cancellation headphones do not diminish all noises around you such as other people talking to you, an announcement over the plane's public address system, or a radio or ringing telephone. This is because the anti-noise waves that they generate are geared toward plane engine and cabin sounds.

Speakerphones Come of Age

A variation on the theme of using a telephone headset is a high-fidelity speakerphone. Traditionally, speakerphones have been less than useful, particularly for executives.

Out with the Old

The obvious problems, if you've previously attempted to use a speakerphone for any quality conversation, are many-fold:

➤ When you speak, it sounds as if you are at the bottom of a well (hellooooo down there...).

➤ If the other party begins speaking before you finish, you lose a syllable or two of what you or they said.

➤ Because your tones are not crisp and clear, the other party is not sure of what you said, even if he actually heard all the words.

➤ The other party may feel other people are in the room listening to the conversation, or that you're preoccupied with some other matter and speaking to him as a secondary activity.

All the above combined to render use of the speakerphone as inappropriate and ill-advised. Are you getting the picture?

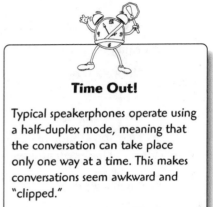

Time Out!

Typical speakerphones operate using a half-duplex mode, meaning that the conversation can take place only one way at a time. This makes conversations seem awkward and "clipped."

It's a New Generation

Full-duplex speakerphones have been available for several years, but with price tags exceeding $1,200. That's not exactly a sum you'd plunk down tomorrow, but read on!

The best of the duplex systems offer high-fidelity stereo speakers and noise-canceling microphones. So you can speak hands-free and have it sound as if you were on your good old phone with your good old handheld receiver. Now that prices for some units have dropped under $400—and undoubtedly will drop someday to under $100—speakerphones are a neat tool of efficiency whose time is about to come.

Chronos Says

Full-duplex systems capture every word that you say with the vibrancy and amplitude with which you offer them. If the other party interjects while you're speaking, you'll still both hear everything—and it won't sound like you're at the bottom of a well. Indeed, the other party has no clue that you're on a speakerphone at all.

135

As with most electronic gadgetry, a variety of options are available. With some speakerphones, you can rest your telephone headset on a platform and then speak and listen as you normally would; no special hookups or lines are necessary. Most models have a mute option and a hold option, some have caller ID, and some have re-dial capability.

Advantages? Let Me Count the Ways

The beauty of speakerphones over that of cordless headsets are fairly obvious:

➤ No weight on top of your head.

➤ No fatigue.

➤ No looking like you're a Martian when others pass your office.

➤ Free and complete range of motion. You can scratch your head, you can take your glasses off and on, you can keep the pencil behind your ear.

The drawbacks are few:

➤ You have to stay within a recommended distance.

➤ If you move around while speaking, the other party may get the notion that you *are* on a speakerphone.

➤ Background noise in your office may also be transmitted.

Still, when your hands are free and you can engage in conversation with somebody 12 blocks or 12,000 miles away, you're going to be much more efficient.

Time Out!

Detectives, snoops, and spies have long recorded conversations for purposes of collecting evidence or for entrapment. Clearly, there's a negative connotation to the notion of two-way telephone conversation recording among the under-informed.

Two-Way Phone Recording Equipment

Some people have used two-way phone conversation recording for years as a means of keeping a log of conversations to help document highly complex transactions.

I'm all for reversing any perception among anyone that using two-way recording is anything other than a marvelous timesaver. As a speaker and author, I find it convenient to be able to record conversations, both ways, with the touch of a button. When a meeting planner is giving me essential information over the phone, my ability to capture those words on tape can mean all the difference when it comes to delivering a dynamic program. There's no way I can take notes as fast as I can capture the meeting planner's words via taping.

Let the Sparks Fly

When I'm interviewing someone for a book, letting other people simply talk—at whatever speed they wish—facilitates effective conversation. The sparks fly. I ask a question, they answer. Later, when I review the tape at my own speed, I am able to glean the essence of what they said—not what my half-baked notes reveal or my even less effective memory recalls. Often when reporters call me and they're not armed with two-way recording equipment, I volunteer to tape the conversation for them and mail them the tape.

With two-way recording I can give a lot more information in a lot shorter time. It'll be higher quality information, and it will flow in the manner in which I intended.

How About You, Buddy?

Undoubtedly there are countless instances where you could tape-record a conversation, play it back, and be more effective at what you do. This could include conversations with coworkers, clients, suppliers, and so on.

The Ethics of Two-Way Recording

While legally you don't have to tell the other party you're recording the conversation, you may feel that *ethically* it's best to do so. I eliminate this potential dilemma by simply saying to the other party at the outset, "Let me capture this on tape," or "Do you mind if I capture this on tape?" Only a handful of times in hundreds of recordings has anyone said, "I'd prefer not," and I've respected that.

Otherwise, I've been able to capture conversations from mentors giving me advice, peers brainstorming with me on a problem, and the aforementioned meeting planners and journalists.

Any consumer electronics store carries a vast array of phone systems with two-way conversational recording capability from which to choose. Most models sell for less than $100, and so there's really nothing to stop you.

A Stitch in Time

A common misconception about two-way recording is that it's illegal. Not so. You may tape-record any conversation at any time in any of the 50 United States. What's illegal is when *neither* party knows that the tape recording is being made. That's called wiretapping or eavesdropping, and even law enforcement officials who engage in this first need to secure permission for doing so.

The Least You Need to Know

➤ Buy portable, expandable, flexible technology.

➤ Each tool designed to increase your efficiency carries the seeds of both great benefit and significant drawback.

➤ You learn most technologies when you need to—no need to feel anxious by advertising designed to make you feel inadequate.

➤ Adopt new technology when your organization requires it, your clients use it, or you see strategic, competitive advantages.

➤ Simple technologies such as dictation equipment, headphones, and two-way telephone recorders can also benefit you greatly.

Chapter 13

Are You a Slave to Your Beeper?

In This Chapter

➤ Voluntary versus involuntary beeper enslavement

➤ The Faustian bargain

➤ Keeping in touch, or fanning anxieties?

➤ A negotiable issue

In this world are two types of pager- (or, as I like to call it, beeper-) enslavement: voluntary and involuntary. It's voluntary when you buy a beeper of your own accord, and no one made you do it—this is the most insidious kind of enslavement, for a variety of reasons. We'll cover voluntary enslavement in the first half of this chapter.

Involuntary enslavement—wearing a beeper because your job requires it—poses a different set of challenges. We'll cover this in the second half of the chapter.

A World Unpopulated by Beepers

There was a time when the world was not populated by people with beepers—and, for that matter, cell phones. You could go to a movie or a play and not have somebody in the row behind you demonstrate the essence of crassness by allowing his or her pager to go off during the performance.

Two decades ago, wearing a beeper was actually a mark of distinction. It meant that you were a top executive who made major decisions that impacted thousands of people or millions of dollars. Perchance, you were in the healthcare field and every day made crucial decisions, some of which meant the difference between life and death for your patients. Or, it signified that you were in the military, perhaps in command of strategic operations and, thus, the fate of nations—or perhaps hundreds of thousands of lives—hung in the balance.

TV Commercials Designed to Get You to Wear a Beeper

➤ A man in a sport utility vehicle up in the mountains surrounded by majestic scenery but not breathing a sigh of relief until he gets a beeper message that the deal has been completed.

➤ An 11-year old pleading with his father to buy him a beeper so that they can stay in touch.

➤ A young postal worker explaining how his girlfriend can stay in touch with him at any point throughout the day because, after all, he always wears his beeper.

➤ A school nurse getting in touch with a parent immediately because little Johnny skinned his knee.

Some people wear a beeper in the name of freedom—the freedom to be in touch with others at any given moment. Being "locatable" by beeper, however, is not much different in concept than a pet who's kept within the bounds of a back yard via an invisible electrical fence.

Fools Rush in

Today, any darned fool can wear a beeper—and practically every one of them does. These electronic leashes are worn by

➤ real estate agents and brokers.

➤ pimps and prostitutes.

➤ surgeons and orderlies.

➤ drug dealers and carriers.

➤ journalists and copy editors.

➤ cabinet-level secretaries and interns.

➤ junior high school principals and junior high school students.

➤ carpenters and lumber yard laborers.

➤ practically everyone in between.

It's Like, So Cool, Dude

Between 1992 and 1997, the number of pagers (beepers) doubled in the United States. In 1995, one in 14 teenagers carried a beeper. By 1997, it had climbed to one in seven.

One high school on Long Island, which recently allowed students to wear beepers in class as long as they were on "vibrate" instead of "beep," reports that about three-quarters of the students are now wearing them! Yikes! Does anyone in civilized society believe that students need to be sitting in class with beepers on their belts? Does anyone believe that beepers don't interfere with education?

Beeper Message Codes	
Code	Message
423	Call me now.
143	I love you.
00100	I feel very alone.
121	I need to talk to you alone.
50-50	It's all the same to me.
007	I have a secret. (As in Agent 007).
1040	You owe me big-time.

A Valid Way to Keep in Touch?

I know, I know. The prevailing argument is, "If I am electronically connected to the great mass of humanity at all times, then I can be available when people need me,

Time Out

Is it any wonder why attention spans are dropping to all-time lows in modern civilization? Is an entire generation doomed to grow up believing that being chained to a beeper is the way it is? Will there be anybody left who can go for hours—let alone days—without getting all bent out of shape because they're not "in touch?"

Watch Words

Shady deals have been called **Faustian bargains** because the lead character in *Dr. Faustus* by Christopher Marlowe—named Faust, of course—sold his eternal soul to the Devil for a better time on earth.

respond to emergencies, and, in turn be in touch with others when the need arises." It's a Faustian bargain, however, because the price for this sense of security is the elimination of the following luxuries:

➤ Being alone

➤ Dwelling on one's own thoughts without fear of interruption

➤ Working in harmony with one's own internal rhythms, with no break in the action

➤ Becoming comfortable, happy, and even content with the entity known as yourself

A True Connection?

The typical, yet odd reasoning behind wearing a beeper all day long is to stay connected to others. Yet, is this being connected to others in a meaningful way? Or is it a disguise for individual and mass anxiety?

A generation of people are experiencing no sense of being spiritually in touch with one another, for they are *electronically* in touch around the clock. Consider that the people you love and like and are most in touch with in this world have, if you've let it develop, a spiritual connection with you. Sure, an occasional message via a beeper—similar to an occasional e-mail or an occasional phone call to someone who wasn't expecting it—can help brighten their day.

The need, however, to constantly keep in touch about everything ranging from the magnificent to the utterly mundane, from that of utmost importance to that which is absurdly trivial, spells a much deeper and insidious problem. Overcommunication is not necessarily effective communication.

Chronos Says

In May 1998, 30 million beepers—about half of them installed in America—stopped working. Galaxy 4, a communications satellite, went bonkers, and all of a sudden gazillions of messages from one earthling to another never went through. High school students had to briefly return to old-fashioned note passing because they couldn't send coded beeper messages in class to one another. Spouses couldn't get in touch with each other, people missed rides, and drug dealers missed major connections. The Associated Press remarked that the failure of the "beeper satellite" was "one of the worst communication breakdowns of the information age."

Braddock Senior School in Miami, Florida, has 5,000 students. Based on estimates from the assistant principal, 40 percent (2,000 students) carry beepers. While they're officially banned—along with other classrooms nuisances such as cellular phones and automatic weapons—enforcement of the "no beeper rule" is difficult because beepers are easy to conceal.

A Giant Technological Step Backward

Bob Morse, writing in the *Arizona Republic,* muses on the effects on society if some contemporary technologies were not available:

Time Out

"Let me put it this way," said a 17-year-old whose day was apparently shattered when the communications satellite Galaxy 4 beeped out, "every other minute you're getting beeped, and then all of a sudden, you not getting beeps at all; it's like silence."

➤ "If some popular online services went away forever, Americans might have their anonymous interactions face-to-face, the old-fashioned way."

➤ "If computers were taken out of the classroom, children might actually learn the fundamentals of reading, writing, and 'rithmetic."

➤ "If cell phone systems disappeared, people could actually drive their cars instead of proceeding along in projectile phone booths."

Morse reports that he attended the Republican Convention in 1996 with a beeper in his pocket. "Instead of giving full attention to the panoply of the rich…I would sit there dreading a certain buzzing feeling on my thigh. This was not a good vibration." Morse reports that there are ways to escape this kind of "electronic house arrest." It's not that he's anti-technology; he's anti-*certain* technologies, one of them being "devices that put a beeping electronic leash on your belt."

The Family That Beeps Together Keeps Together?

There are people who profess that families who beep together keep together. Some families maintain codes that indicate everything from "Come home in time for dinner" to "Pick up a loaf of bread." This is a seemingly positive development. After all, bread is a staple of the American diet.

Still, you can't help wondering if the beeper isn't overused by a factor of, say, 15, when you think about a traditional form of communication, such as talking to one another. Some people talk all day long because they have some things to say, and some people talk all day long because they want to hear the sound of their own voice. Is this the case with beeping, too?

Time Out

Dr. Peter Crabb, a professor of physiology at Pennsylvania State University, has been studying technology's impact on behavior. He says that the instant gratification brought on by beepers can end up enslaving the user. Those who voluntarily—or, for that matter, involuntarily—wear a beeper essentially are giving the message to all others that it's okay to interrupt whatever is going on with them.

I'll Concede, There a *Few* Valid Uses

To be sure, there are valid uses of beepers by people who need to have information on demand. Volunteer firefighters use beepers for a quick response to a fire—and, if your house is burning, you're darned glad of it.

The newest generation of beepers can, of course, beep or vibrate and can display phone numbers and text messages of up to two lines. Some models offer ski and weather conditions, hourly stock market reports, and even your email. These sound like pretty useful benefits—and depending on how you're employed and who you serve, they may well be.

What about the ability, however, to retrieve your e-mail any moment of the day? That's analogous to the telephone gently ringing in your ear wherever you are all day long. It's like having the postal carrier personally deliver each letter addressed to you as it arrives at the post office. Yikes!

Bit by Bit to Death

When the big book of human civilization is written, someone will look back and say that the beeper was among the most dubious developments in the course of humanity. We don't need drips and drops, tiny bits of information coming to us all day long. It's not the best way to function—and indeed it may be deleterious to effective functioning.

Involuntary Beeper Attacks

As you've learned throughout this book, the most effective way to manage your time is to stay in control of it, to protect yourself from unwanted intrusions. Receiving mail, e-mail, phone messages, or beeps around the clock all disrupt your potential for highly productive, clear, cool thinking. You need peace and quiet when you're pondering how to best make a new product or service offering, reflecting on what you've accomplished, or fathoming where you or your organization is heading.

A Stitch in Time

In *The Artist's Way*, Julia Cameron recommends that when someone who is trying to be creative feels blocked, there is a simple cure. Rather than bombardment by the thoughts and words of others, for one week give up reading (except, of course, this book) watching television, and listening to the radio. This exercise helps the person searching for his or her own ideas and creativity to encourage them to emerge.

Fenced in Like a Junkyard Dog

The following letter, which I received from a man after a speech I gave, is perhaps one of the saddest commentaries on humanity and working in contemporary society that I have ever encountered:

> *While you were lecturing, my cell phone, pager, voice mail (mental and physical torture device) vibrated no less than three times. Usually I leave the room to listen to the voice mail and return the calls. During your presentation I just let it vibrate. However, I can't turn it off. I carry the phone as a requirement of my job. I must carry it whenever I am officially on the job. Yet, I know peers who are on-call 24 hours to their organizations. They are interrupted by pages and cell-phone calls at dinners, church, the theater, everywhere.*

> *I also have peers who are expected to work with their PC until the battery dies. As mobile computing increases through the availability of high bandwidth, facilitating wireless satellite communications to the Internet, technology issues will become more complex and frustrating. I can foresee employers expecting employees to retrieve e-mail while traveling, at weekend outings to the beach, and everywhere in between!*

If the above scenario even mildly describes your situation, it's time to take control in major ways. This is your day, your career, and your life. If you don't take control, who else on the planet will do it for you? Emancipating yourself from your beeper is a task that you and you alone must face.

Chronos Says

The *Christian Science Monitor* reports that some theaters in London now request attendees to turn off beepers and cell phones before the performance begins. In the United States, many business establishments, such as highbrow restaurants, are adopting strict policies regarding the use of beepers and cell phones, with some places regarding them with the same disdain as cigarettes, pipes, and cigars.

Electronic Communications Etiquette

Dr. Jaclyn Kostner, author of *Virtual Leadership*, advises displaying proper etiquette when you wear a beeper or take a cell phone with you:

➤ Turn off your device when attending face-to-face meetings, such as with customers, the team, and so on.

➤ Turn off your device during lunch, dinner, or other professional occasions you are attending face-to-face.

➤ Turn off your gadget in nonbusiness public places, such as restaurants, movies, and performances.

➤ Turn off your beeper or cell phone to be with your family and friends.

It Says Right Here in My Contract...

If your employment is based on a contract—and, increasingly, this is true of top managers and executives—then you have some options for not being enslaved to your beeper. When it's time to renegotiate your contract, insert a clause allowing for specific times throughout the day or week when you expressly are not responsible for being on call.

If performance reviews and/or appraisals don't happen frequently enough for you where you work, or if one is not slated until the distant future, arrange a meeting specifically to address this issue. After all, depending on how long you've been wearing the beeper, how many beeps you receive per day, the nature of your work, and how disruptive the overall effects have been, you don't want to let too many more days or weeks pass before elucidating your views to those who would otherwise have you wear a beeper around the clock and never have another word on the topic.

You Are Not the Energizer Bunny

As tactfully and professionally as possible, inform the powers that be that maintaining ever-ready responsiveness with a beeper diminishes your capacity for creativity in those tasks and responsibilities where it's needed.

Surely there are stretches throughout the day and week where even your supervisor will agree that it's not mandatory for you to be wearing the beeper. Indeed, if he or she sees the wisdom of enabling you to do some of your best creative and conceptual thinking, and if this mandates that you be beeper-free, who will insist that you keep the thing on around the clock?

Create a Message Hierarchy

If most of your beeper messages originate from a central source, such as an executive assistant, instruct that person as to when it's okay for you to be contacted and when it's best to keep the messages for later transmission. For example, you could use a system such as the one laid out in the table below:

A Stitch in Time

Whether your employment is based on a contract or not, negotiate to achieve the same results. Whenever it's time for a performance review and appraisal—be it yearly, semi-annually, quarterly, or monthly—take the opportunity to discuss with your immediate supervisor the potential disruption to your psyche and physiology of being constantly on-call.

Time Out

Knowing that any nonwork activity can be disrupted is deleterious to your breathing space. When you can't eat, sleep, make love, or go to the bathroom free of beeper or cell phone-related anxiety, you're not free to live.

Table 13.3   Redirecting Beeper Messages

Level 1	Contact me now.
Level 2	Contact within X hours.
Level 3	Contact me sometime today.
Level 4	No need to contact me at all.

To make this system work, you decide in advance precisely what represents Level 1, so that Level 1 summoning of you is indeed rare. These would be absolute and dire emergencies where your input is absolutely essential. Everything else does not require beeping you every bleeping minute!

Nonemergencies and Lower-Level Stuff

Level 2–4 issues can wait. Level 2 represents important bits of information but those that are not necessarily urgent. Level 3 represents messages that you could receive at any time during the day because they're not time-related in any way. Most of the messages you receive in a day undoubtedly will fall in this category. Once your assistant becomes adept at recognizing that most messages are Level 3, you'll find you have more stretches of uninterrupted time during the day.

Level 4 represents those messages that your executive assistant might have sent previously, but now based on a clearer understanding of what needs to be transmitted and what doesn't, fall into the "no need to contact me at all" category. These represent questions that are already addressed by existing printed materials, such as these:

➤ Policies and procedures manuals

➤ Memos

➤ Faxes

➤ Other items the assistant can retrieve on his or her own

Extinguish Unnecessary Beeping

You want to admonish the assistant anytime he or she sends a Level 4 message because, indeed, you didn't need to be contacted. You can curtail your assistant's behavior in this category by pointing out, "That was a Level 4 message" whenever you receive one.

Using this system, you'll find that in a matter of weeks—and, more often, in a matter of only days—your assistant will begin to understand with relative accuracy what level to assign to information that potentially could be beeped your way.

Engage All Options

Another measure on the road to managing your time and staying as beep-free as possible is to use all relay and forwarding options available. Leave instructive messages on your voice-mail or telephone-answering devices that let callers know when and where you can best be reached.

Also leave instructive messages that enable callers to have a higher probability of being served by you without necessarily having to contact you immediately. This can be done by employing the various voice mail boxes available on many systems: "Press number one if you have a question about XYZ," Press number two if you have a question about DEF," and so on.

Deflect and Win

Get in the habit of specifically announcing that such-and-such person can take care of ABC, that you'll be reachable Tuesday from 2 p.m. until 4 p.m., or that the best way to handle GHI problems is to send an e-mail to accounting. In this manner, you may be able to deflect half or more of the messages that would otherwise disturb you.

Out of Beeper Range

At certain times on some days, don't wear your beeper or carry a cell phone at all, and inform others that you will not be so equipped. Once the umbilical cord is disconnected, certainly your staff—and many others who've gotten into the habit of sending you a message at the drop of single byte—will begin to learn new ways to proceed on matters without instinctively and incessantly beeping you.

When You're the One Sending Messages

How about the situation where you're supervising others, and you're the one continually sending messages to them so that they're beeped all day long? You've gotten through this chapter thus far, so perhaps you have a newfound appreciation for what you're putting your staff through.

Can you find it in your heart, and does your newfound awareness lead you to the conclusion that you could be sending fewer messages per day? Chances are highly likely that you could. In most professions, effective managing does not encompass micro-managing around the clock.

If you've selected the right people, have trained them accordingly, have given them the opportunity to develop on-the-job skills, have given them appropriate feedback, are available for coaching, and give them adequate tools with which to perform their assigned tasks, why the heck do you need to be beeping at them all day long? Walk a mile in their wingtips or penny loafers, and you'll quickly see that just as you feel psychologically battered and abused, besieged and overcome by messages you're receiving each day, so does your staff.

The Least You Need to Know

➤ The need to constantly make contact with others is not effective communication; it is anxiety.

➤ If you lack a spiritual connection with someone, beeping and other e-communication is unlikely to create one.

➤ Tell your immediate supervisor about the disruption to your psyche and physiology. Bargain for time off the beeper.

➤ If primarily one person beeps you, indicate when it's okay for you to be contacted and when it's not.

➤ Sometimes don't take your beeper with you, and inform others that you will not be so equipped.

Welcome. You have **A TON** of mail.

Chapter 14

All About E-Mail

In This Chapter

➤ Coming at you at high speed

➤ Not making e-mail the most urgent thing in the morning

➤ The value of brevity and clarity

➤ Delegating e-mail messages

Perhaps you're not among those who are chained to a beeper or obsessed with a cell phone. The odds are much better, however, that you do send and receive e-mails every work day—and sometimes in between. And the number of e-mails you receive is probably growing at a frightening pace.

Speeding Your Way Every Second of the Day

Nearly 110 million people now use e-mail, collectively receiving 7 trillion messages annually, according to the Electronic Messaging Association. Depending on which study you read, the typical executive today receives 150–190 e-mails a day. Even after accounting for spam, you're still looking at 80–120 e-mails per executive per day. Any way you cut it, that's an awful lot of communication coming at you at high speed.

More than 35 percent of 400 managers polled by the American Management Association and Ernst & Young say they use e-mail the most of any communication tool. That beats the 26 percent who use the phone most frequently and the 15 percent who rely on face-to-face meetings.

Table 14.1 Preferred Ways of Communicating in the Workplace

Communication Tool	% of Respondents
E-mail	35 percent
Fax	26 percent
Mail	15 percent

If you're new to the world of e-mail, or if you're a veteran user, the advantages are abundantly clear. E-mail is fast; it's transmitted nearly instantaneously after you push the send button.

Chronos Says

Only the Internet Service Providers (ISPs) on your end and on the recipient's end have any real say as to when the e-mail actually shows up in the other person's mailbox, but in most cases it's under a couple minutes.

Table 14.2 50 Million Users in Record Time

Radio gains 50 million users	40 years
Television gains 50 million users	13 years
World Wide Web gains 50 million users	4 years

Source: Time Magazine

Where else on this earth can you get a message from somebody, type in a few words of reply, click one button, and have it sent back to them? No paper, no toner cartridge, no stamps, no envelopes. No trip to the mailbox, no second-guessing as to whether you had the right postage, no nothing. It just goes—which is why, as you've already undoubtedly concluded, you receive so many of the darned things every day. It's too easy to send to anybody about anything! So, in the context of managing your time, keeping your job, and having a life, how do you handle e-mail? Let us count the ways....

Next Subject: The Subject Line

Don't get caught up about the subject line. Some people, for reasons I'll never fathom, go bonkers when it comes to composing the subject line for their e-mail. They stare and they stare and still don't know what to type in. Why bother? Your e-mail will go through whether you include a subject or not.

If you can't live without listing a subject, wait until you have first composed your message. Then look at what you've said, and extract two or three words (usually together), making a phrase that you can throw into the subject line. Voilà! You've got it. That's one small step for you, one microscopic step for humankind.

Subject Lines When Writing to Friends

If your e-mail is non-work-related, then you've got it made in the shade. All you have to do in the subject line is put something like *hi, greetings, it's me again, hey, good day, long time*, or something equally harmless. A friend is a friend and is probably glad to hear from you. What does he or she care if you say *hi* in your subject line? It probably suits your message well, anyway.

Watch Out for Banned Words

If you use the same type of words in your subject heading that spammers use, chances are your e-mail might get discarded before it's even read. Hence, you've lost the time you spent composing the e-mail—and you'll waste yet more time trying to get a reply from a party who never read your message to begin with. What are the banished words? You already know most of these:

➤ Sex

➤ Free

➤ Naked

Time Out!

It's easy to receive many more e-mails that you can possibly respond to. It's also easy for you to send e-mails to others when no message is needed or wanted. Are you unknowingly glutting the mail In-boxes of others? The more you send, the more you get in return. As a guiding principle, send as few as possible to do the job and still have a life.

A Stitch in Time

If you don't send a subject, on many systems, the recipient receives an e-mail from you that says in the subject line, "No subject." That alone will make your e-mail stand out, unlike most of the rest that the recipient receives that day. Consider listing no subject messages when you possibly can, and relax.

- ➤ Money
- ➤ Exclusive
- ➤ Incredible
- ➤ First time
- ➤ Adults only
- ➤ Make money now
- ➤ A one-time offer
- ➤ Limited time only

…and anything with stars, plus signs, equal signs, or other attempts at using typographical figures as art work. The most efficient use of your time, when compiling e-mail messages that you intend to be read, is to offer a vibrant subject line—or, short of that, at least a passable one so that the other party will indeed open up your mail.

Words and Phrases to Avoid in Your E-Mail Subject Line

Don't use any of these words or phrases in the subject line of your e-mail, if you intend for any non-*Enquirer* subscribers to read your e-mail:

Free Guide	Grand Cayman Tax Shelters
Cyber Sex	Fly for Free
You Were Carefully Chosen	Limited Edition
Hot Nymphs	Stop Psoriasis Now
Consolidate Your Loans Now	An Urgent Message
Make $50,000 in Just Three Days	Make Money at Home
How to Stop Belching	ANNOUNCING...
More Web Hits Instantly	Your Dream Vacation is Waiting
You Can't Ignore This	Get into the College of Your
Pay Zero Taxes...Legally	Choice
A Friend Gave Us Your Name	Don't Ignore This
Make More Money Than You Know	Retire Now
What to Do With	Secrets Now Revealed
With Over Ten Million E-mail Addresses	Instant Web Site
You Can't Ignore This Offer	We Believe You Would be
Amazing Pet Training System	Interested...
	Lowest Air Fares Ever

Check Once, Check Twice, and Be Gone

Unless you're waiting for some critical response via e-mail, it's best to check your mail about twice a day, and perhaps a third time, if you're feeling particularly ahead of the game.

It may surprise you to know that I do not advocate checking your e-mail first thing in the morning unless your job requirements specifically call for such a procedure. Among many reasons, the most compelling is that you need to do many other things in and around your desk—and in the non-cyber world in general—before logging on.

Time Out!

Some people get obsessed with checking their e-mail at every spare moment. These are people who are usually not doing a great job anyway, sending off epistles to loved ones, trying to pick up new acquaintances in chat rooms, and sending and receiving the latest jokes to and from the usual gang.

Offline Preparation Yields Online Efficiency

The "administrivia" that you tend to first thing in the morning often enhances your productivity in both sending and receiving e-mail.

➤ Perhaps you need to prepare files on your hard drive.

➤ Perhaps you have addresses to correct.

➤ Perhaps you've received phone and fax messages that will fuel your e-mail responses.

Chronos Says

E-mail is relatively inexpensive. In most locales, you pay one flat monthly fee to have e-mail service. Of course, within your organization, e-mail is included as a communication tool at your disposal, much like the telephone on your desk is. Besides being fast and cheap, e-mail is also extremely convenient when you get totally objective about it!

I normally start my day at 7 a.m. Egad—I know it sounds like slave hours, but you have to consider that my boss is a pretty driven guy (I work alone!). Kidding aside, I start the day early, and I end earlier than most.

From the time I check in at 7 a.m., it's usually between 60 and 90 minutes before I log onto e-mail. Once I do, I allow anywhere from 30 to 45 minutes to handle the 15–25 messages I'll have waiting for me. Overall, if I'm free and clear of the morning administrivia and e-mailing before, say, 9:00 or 9:30, I consider that to be a great start; if it's before 10:00, that's normal.

Okay, Check at Lunch if You Must

I confess to checking in a little after lunch to see if anybody sent me anything, but then I log off rather quickly. I certainly check in at around 4:30 each day, to catch the closing e-mails that might be arriving from East Coast correspondence and from those on the West Coast who know to get their messages in before 2:45 Pacific Coast Time.

Use Only as Directed

In my work as a speaker, I've had the good fortune to make presentations to many groups across the nation. One time, I was privileged to be involved with a series of America Online meetings. At one such meeting, the group played a video of America Online executive Robert Pitman, who told the troops point-blank that e-mail is for sending data and getting answers. It's not a substitute for conversation.

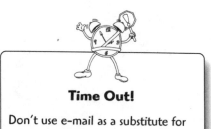

Time Out!

Don't use e-mail as a substitute for conversation because you will tie up endless amounts of time. Robert Pitman of America Online says it could easily take a dozen rounds of e-mail for two people to achieve the same level of communication and understanding that's possible with two minutes of conversation.

Make That Call

If you feel that a conversation is warranted, you're probably right. Go ahead and make the call. If you need a yes or no answer, or to easily transmit the data that someone has requested or is waiting for, then go ahead and use e-mail.

Here's a brief roster of appropriate use of e-mail:

➤ One-word or short answers

➤ Approval or disapproval

➤ Forwarding vital information to appropriate parties

➤ Articles, reports, outlines, and guidelines that have been specifically requested by the recipient

➤ Updated information such as price quotes, progress reports, and summaries of activities, again when the other party is expecting or requesting such

A One-Way Wonder

Dr. Jaclyn Kostner, based in Denver, Colorado, offers the following list of inappropriate messages for one-way media, such as e-mail and voice mail:

➤ The complex

➤ New ideas

➤ Issues requiring clarification

➤ Solicitation for agreement

➤ The emotionally charged

➤ Material that has a strong personal impact on the recipient

Once you've determined that your message is suitable for one-way media, Kostner observes you have one more choice: Should you relay your message by e-mail, or is voice mail preferable? Here are her guidelines:

Choose e-mail (not voice mail) in these situations:

➤ When a written record is needed.

➤ When language is a barrier. In multi-language teams, written words are frequently easier to understand than spoken ones, especially when accents are heavy or language skills are less than fluent.

➤ When the team's normal business day hours in each location do not match.

➤ When you've been unable to reach the person interactively but know the person needs the details right away.

On the other hand, as the economists say, leave a voice mail or answering machine message for these situations:

➤ When the sound of your voice is key to understanding your message.

➤ When the recipient is mobile. Voice mail is easier to access than e-mail, in most cases.

➤ When your message is urgent.

And be forewarned: Treat any e-mail you ever send at work or at home as having the potential to revisit you. Even if you bleep it from your system, it still may reside on your Internet service provider's system. If you write in disparaging terms about someone else and send it to a third party, expect it to come back to haunt you. The London edition of *The Financial Times* reports that few e-mail users recognize that "deleting a controversial e-mail message from a desktop PC does not always get rid of it. In most cases, the message is also stored more permanently on an Internet server or network server computer. If the lawyers come knocking on the door with subpoena, this is the first place they will look."

Brevity Is the Soul of E-Mail Wit

A good e-mail message often requires no more than a few choice paragraphs. Just because you're a fast typist doesn't mean you need to ramble on forever and ever. Guy Kawasaki, author of *How to Drive the Competition Crazy*, says that most people send e-mail messages that are too long. Most of the action is in the first and last paragraphs. If it's longer than four paragraphs, watch out—you're not using the medium for which it was intended, and you're tying up your time.

A Stitch in Time

When composing an e-mail message to someone who's not expecting it but whom, nevertheless, you wish to influence, aim for one screenful or less. Pretend the other person has a 14-inch monitor, and that the area in which he or she receives e-mails represents roughly one-quarter of the screen. Given this narrow parameter, craft your message to fit neatly into the allotted space.

Rambling On, and On, and On...

Think about the e-mail messages that you receive that go on and on for far longer than the first screenful. Especially among those that are unsolicited, do you ever stop and read them all? If you do, how many of them do you actually save? Chances are, the longer ones tend to get discarded more quickly.

Undoubtedly you can shorten many of your messages—and maybe you already do. If you don't, it's time to start practicing. Prune your prose. Say it once, and be done.

Prune but Don't Over Prune

Occasionally you'll get an e-mail from someone who uses such cryptic language, chops key words from sentences, and uses so many abbreviations, that the meaning of the message is all but lost. For example:

Time Out!

If Net abbreviations were universally known, used, and understood, they'd represent a tremendous savings in terms of composing and reading e-mail messages. The problem is that they are *not* universally known, used, or under-stood. When you use such abbreviations, you'll likely confuse the other party—and that's not a time-saver for anyone.

looking fw'rd 2 c'ing u this eve. is 7 gd, or do u thk earlier is btr? Also, R U getting tix or me? I'll B in to 5. later, TGB

Don't be among those who prune beyond reason—and beyond the recipient's ability to extract your meaning. And forget all those semi-neat Net abbreviations you see in other books, such as "BTW," which means by the way. You're more likely to confuse the other party than effectively communicate with them.

People actually e-mail back and forth regarding what the abbreviations meant! Now *that's* a waste of time.

Needless Drivel

When you want to get ruthless about the splendid use of your native tongue, why would you want to include something that began with "by the way" anyway? It tells the other party that what you're about to announce either is not important or that you didn't know how to effectively juxtapose the item with what you've already written. If you instinctively include some beginning remark such as "by the way," type away and then at the last moment chop the "by the way" part. Your message ought to read cleaner and neater.

A "Net" Savings

Once you begin pruning your prose effectively, you'll find that e-mail can be a valuable tool. After all, even if you're inundated with the number of messages you receive daily, there is a Net savings in the form of less mail, fewer faxes, and fewer telephone calls (hopefully) from these same parties.

If you're able to productively handle your e-mail, you effectively reduce your time and tasks associated with other forms of correspondence.

A Stitch in Time

Companies that implement Internet-based e-mail services will be able to slash telephone call-related labor costs by 43 percent, according to Forrester Research, based in Canada.

Keep Your "CC's" to a Minimum

Some Netiquette experts suggest that no more than three parties receive any message that you're sending. So, you'd send to one principal recipient, with circulated copies to two others. If you're the manager of a small group of say six, eight, or ten people, perhaps it's necessary for you to send to all six, eight, or ten. If you're the president of an organization of thousands and you want to send out an all-purpose e-mail to all of them, let 'er rip.

Watch Words

Netiquette is etiquette for those on the Internet, hence the combination of Net and etiquette, forming the new word.

In general, when you CC more than three or four parties in your e-mail for a rather pointed message, you're giving a signal to most recipients that they can safely ignore your message. As with failure to prune your prose, you're doing more work than is necessary, such as rounding up more addresses in the CC line and potentially glutting other peoples' e-mail In-boxes. You don't really want to do that, do you?

Showing Your Responsiveness

With a multitude of e-mail messages piling up in your In-box, even a brief time away from your PC means you'll have scads of e-mails to respond to upon returning. A mere two days out of the office will result in your coming back to at least two to three times the normal number of e-mail messages you encounter.

So, you have two basic strategies. You can let it make you crazy, or you can practice triage.

Watch Words

Triage is the practice of quickly poring over a variety of items and allocating them based on what needs to be handled immediately, what can be handled later, and what can be ignored altogether.

Triage or Die

Practice triage for all e-mail messages. First, you want to quickly eliminate the inane. These include all forms of spam. In general, any time you receive mail that has lots of Xs, all capitals (which is regarded as shouting), or otherwise makes excessive claims, don't waste a nano-second on it. Bleep it into where ever it goes into cyberspace. One writer commented, "You can safely bleep anything that has lots of exclamation marks, assorted promises, and come-ons, or if it looks like it was written by someone who pants for a living."

After eliminating the obvious, the next question is which e-mails can you park—that is, place in a holding folder, bin, file, or whatever your system calls them. Some are entirely worth saving but simply are not urgent. Some are from friends and loved ones, and you want to pore over what they've written. Some have told you in the letter that the reply time need not be immediate.

A Stitch in Time

Even if a message isn't urgent, if you're able to respond to it effortlessly and instantaneously, why park it? If the message is staring you in the face, all you have to do is type a few words and hit the reply button, then send it off and get on to the next e-mail!

The last category are those e-mail messages you receive that require quick-to-immediate action. *Quick* means sometime during the day. *Immediate,* as I use it here, means reply right now, while you're online. Hopefully the number of messages you get that fall into the quick or immediate categories is small.

For those e-mails that mandate your present, earnest, and rather speedy attention, do your gut-level best to handle them so that they're out of the way and you're mentally—as well as physically—clear of them.

Stock Your Messages

If you've returned from several days away from your PC, or the number of e-mail messages in your In-box is ganging up on you, here's a viable temporary solution to this dilemma: Have stock messages ready—such as that you have just returned from traveling and will respond by mid-week, or anything else that conveys your sense of responsiveness.

When I receive an acknowledgment message from someone (even an automated acknowledgment), I regard that person highly. At least he took the time, or set up his system as such, to let me know that he received my message and intends to do something about it. That's a far cry from those you don't hear from for days, much of the time suspecting that you'll *never* hear from them.

Any of the customized e-mail programs on the market enable you to save stock messages and easily retrieve them as needed. Also, many feature filters, which enable you to sort e-mail as it arrives. The filters find and delete e-mail that contains specific key words, such as those that spammers frequently use, or which were sent from specific addresses. Some of the leading e-mail programs in this area include Eudora, Claris E-mailer, CyberDog, and Microsoft In-box and Exchange.

Danger! Overusing E-Mail

If you rely on e-mail too much—such as sending e-mail when a face-to-face conversation was more appropriate—you may be seen as somewhat aloof. Managers looking for a way to avoid face-to-face conflict will often use e-mail, says Linda Talley, author of *Business Finesse: Dealing with Sticky Situations in the Work Place for Managers.* "It's an easy way out," she says.

Sometimes an e-mail message can make you seem as if you're curt or abrasive. It's not that you intended to ruffle any feathers; it's just that e-mail, unless worded carefully, can sometimes come off as impersonal, cold, and uncaring.

Chronos Says

According to Derek Scruggs, president of Distributed Bits (a firm specializing in e-mail usage), "E-mail is the second most widely used application on the Internet after research." Yet studies show that only 20 percent of customer-to-business e-mail is answered within one day—and 60 percent is never answered at all. "Imagine," says Scruggs, "if customer telephone calls were treated the same way."

Management 101

The best suggestion on timesaving tactics for using e-mail has been saved for last. If you're a manager and have any type of administrative or supportive staff to manage well, you need to delegate and forward many of your e-mail messages each day to your staff. If you're not, just as prior to the advent of e-mail, you're not managing well. You're holding onto too much!

Not delegating has cost many an executive a vital promotion—and worse, has led some to the unemployment line.

All it takes using virtually any e-mail software program to forward a message you've received to one of your staff is to simply hit the forward button, insert your staff person's e-mail address in the address column, and hit the end button.

If you want to be highly efficient when forwarding email, use aliases. This essentially means that you make some modifications to your e-mail address book; thereafter, all you have to do is type another person's initials, and his e-mail address appears. Keep a copy of what you send in the online "file folder" you maintain for messages related to that person. Thus, you're instantaneously able to forward tasks and catalog them. If you need to write anything in the body of the message at all, it could be as simple as, "Please handle this." Hey, what could be simpler?

The Least You Need to Know

➤ The more e-mail you send, the more you get in return. Send as few as possible to do the job and also have a life.

➤ Avoid using the same type of words that spammers use; chances are your e-mail might get discarded.

➤ Check your e-mail twice, maybe three times daily—but that's it.

➤ Don't fall into the trap of using e-mail as a substitute for conversation.

➤ Delegate e-mail as often as you possibly can.

Chapter 15

On and Off the Internet

In this Chapter

➤ Getting onto the Web: who uses it—and why?

➤ The rise of misinformation

➤ Search engines worth your while

➤ Living with the Internet

The Internet—and, more specifically, the World Wide Web—is putting more information at your fingertips than you ever previously imagined existed. By now, you're probably acutely aware of an ever-increasing number of topics and areas in which you cannot keep up. You can surf the Web for hours, but you pay a price. Is what you do on the Internet worth the time you spend? If you're finding key information quickly, then yes. Anything else, and the answer is suspect.

Fortunately, you don't have to become a victim of the overinformation age. The keys to maintaining control when you're on the Internet is to realize that 1) the sooner you quit trying to keep up, the better you'll feel, and 2) you need to continually and carefully choose where to give your time and attention. This chapter will help you achieve both those goals.

Who's On, and Why

By the late 1990s, Internet users had an average salary of $59,000, compared to the U.S. average of $20,690. According to one study, the average age was 33 years old. Based on findings in *What Makes People Click*, by NetSmart, 97 percent of users want to be better informed, 81 percent want to research product and service information (with many becoming buyers), and 57 percent go online just for fun.

What about the average bookmarks per user? A Georgia Institute of Technology survey of 17,000 users found that 18 percent bookmark 1–10 items, and 19 percent bookmark more than 100.

What Makes the Web Different?

Even if you don't surf the Internet much yourself, you probably have enjoyed its amazing capabilities of delivering previously obscure or hard-to-locate information. For all the news and information it provides, however, it's important to remember that the Web is first and foremost a marketing vehicle for those who host Web sites.

"Every other kind of marketing prior to the Web has been 'push,'" says Web guru David Arnold, Ph.D, the co-author with Gail Rutman of *Business on the Internet: The Concise Handbook* (http://www.daspeaks.com). "Direct mail, print and broadcast media advertising, telemarketing, billboards—they all involve pushing information at people. The message reaches an intended market and has an impact whether the communication is welcome or not." Web sites, however, must draw visitors to them. This means even the world's best site will have no visitors unless people are drawn to the site.

A Stitch in Time

Think of the World Wide Web as an information guidebook and advertising directory with 50 million entries that is updated or changed every pico-second.

Time Out!

Much of the Web is self-serving hype about the Web itself. Many people are trying to show off the "cool" graphics they can make, offering little else. That won't improve your life or end your work day any quicker. Don't waste your time on such sites.

Be Selective or Use Up Your Life

In the days of horse and buggy travel, drivers placed blinders on their horses to keep them from being startled by things they didn't need to see. Similarly, you can choose to travel the information superhighway wearing electronic blinders that enable you to view only the information that affects your microniche.

The Web Exacerbates Information Overload

Your house and garden plants need to be regularly shorn of dead leaves and stems to promote healthy growth. Likewise you need to trim yourself of deadweight thinking: believing that you need to endlessly strive to keep informed and up to date.

Why is overinformation a pervasive problem in society?

➤ The sheer volume of information that besieges the typical manager is staggering. There has been an exponential, not linear, growth in the amount of information you encounter every day.

➤ Few people are prepared as undergraduates, in business school, or even in doctoral business programs for handling the flood of information that one now routinely encounters daily.

Hundreds of e-mail messages glut the in-boxes of managers as soon as they log on in the morning. Voice-mail messages are retrieved around the clock. Faxes arrive all day long. And the Web? It beckons at all hours. You know it's there, like television—an information drug available in unlimited quantities and ready to rob you of your time at any moment.

Weed with a Vengeance

Before you even log on, eliminate what is not useful to you. Here's how: Create a default Download directory on your hard drive, and specify this directory in the Preferences sections of your Internet software. This way, you will always know where to find freshly downloaded files instead of having to search your computer system.

Then create permanent directories into which you'll transfer important files from your default Download directory—after you've confirmed their long-term usefulness.

Before you face the mounds of new information, delete outdated documents and unnecessary downloaded files from your computer. Download from the Internet only the information that will truly support you in your work. Instead of downloading files you'll use just occasionally, record their addresses and leave the information on the Internet.

Time Out!

More people than ever are competing for your time and attention—and the Internet only exacerbates this trend. Get selective—stay lean and mean.

Misinformation Rears its Ugly Head

In her book *Backlash*, Susan Faludi points out how market forecasters make a fortune reviewing popular media such as newspapers, television, and movies and then concluding what trends are looming in America. The problem with this method of forecasting, Faludi notes, is that it tends to promulgate what only a handful of editors, publishers, and directors believe. Hard data supports few of these forecasts. But they are spread as facts.

The Web Speeds the Spread of Misinformation

Along with the wealth of useful information you can tap into on the Web comes volumes of misinformation. Vast stores of what passes for data are the opinions of those who post the Web pages. Worse, too often the information is outright false—but it spreads at hyperspeed. The truth rarely has a chance to catch up.

Verify, Verify, Verify

In addition to false or misleading information, the Web is rife with what is called "spoof data"—information spread merely as a joke but presented as true. Why does this abound on the Net? Until the mid 1990s, the majority of Web users were college students, predominantly male. A few of them with an immature sense of humor can create a huge swath of ruin. Spoof data, however, can come from *anywhere*.

A clever junior-high student can generate spoof data that appears to emanate from the White House. It's not hard to create. The good news is that the Web—while massive and growing explosively—has the tools to help you become deft at securing the information you need.

Start Your Search Engines!

To find the information you need, or to specifically learn more about a product or service, most people head for one or more of the online search engines and request a key word search. "Some search engines scour the Web, locating and indexing new sites as they appear," says David Arnold, Ph.D. "Others, like Yahoo (www.Yahoo.com), list only those sites that are submitted to them." Does this mean you should use only those search engines like Yahoo that are more selective? No. Different engines convey different information. For a roster of search engines that lists their specific areas of focus, visit http://www.nueva.pvt.k12.ca.us./~debbie/library/research/adviceengine.html.

A Stitch in Time

PC trainer and Web expert Trish Santos suggests visiting http://searchenginewatch.internet.com to learn everything you want to know about mining for Internet informational gold. This site teaches you how to make the most of the search engines and also how to get your own site listed. It also lists and evaluates all the major and specialty search engines out there.

Giant Indexes Taking Over the Earth

Trish Santos, president of IMP Training (IMPtrng@aol.com), explains that search engines are basically indexes. You type in words, and the search engine finds the Web pages in its index with those words. To do this, they use what are called "robots" to index tens of millions of Web pages.

Santos suggests several strategies to help you use search engines like a hard-core geek. One is to use a variety of engines with the same search criteria until you settle on the few that give you the best results consistently. A few of the more popular ones right now include these:

➤ http://www.hotbot.com

➤ http://www.lycos.com

➤ http://www.infoseek.com

➤ http://www.nlsearch.com

Nlsearch.com also includes the full-text articles from more than 5,000 journals and magazines (with more being added all the time). You can get the abstract for free and the full text for a reasonable charge. If you use this search engine more than a few times, you may want to pay the nominal monthly fee.

Metasearch engines submit your search criteria to a number of different search engines for you. One such metasearch engine is http://www.metacrawler.com.

With all these engines available, you want to find the most efficient way to use them. That's where word-searching comes in.

Multiple Word Searches: Not as Difficult as You Think

When conducting a search, the first principle to learn is this: The more words you use, the more accurate your results. Virtually all search engines use quotation marks to identify phrases. For many, you can put the plus sign before any word you need to find included on the Web page, and the minus sign for those that should not be there.

For example, when searching for entries on professional speakers, you might want to make sure to exclude the words "stereo" and "car," or you'll get entries on sound systems. Each search engine is a bit different, however, so look for the buttons (labeled Options, Help, Hints, Tips, or Advanced) for online assistance on how to use the site.

Santos suggests that you turn to hotbot.com because that site uses drop-down lists and other simple tools to set up your multiple word searches. Look for other buttons that will expand your search for you as well. Usenet, for example, features thousands of newsgroups that you can tap into. (More on this later in the chapter.)

Web Sites Worth a Return Visit

When you find an information-rich site upon which you can rely, you're most likely to want to make a return visit. Everyone who's on the Web regularly has their own favorites. Make sure to bookmark such sites. Here are a few ideas on what makes a site worth bookmarking:

➤ Periodic updates: Something significant changes on the opening screen once a week, once a day, or more often.

➤ Up-to-the-minute information: Trends, breakthroughs, results, and so forth make it a place worth visiting daily for late-breaking news or public service messages.

➤ Quickly engaging: Encourages immediate participation; gives visitors choices, such as the opportunity to vote for something or send an opinion.

➤ On-line tutorial: Teaches visitors something and offers short, to-the-point instructions or guidance on something of interest.

➤ For members only: Offers exclusive features to its members. This is important if staying informed among such privileged users is important to you. You'll need a password to enter.

➤ Article series: Gives readers continuing information.

➤ Survey or polling results.

➤ Rating guide: categorizes products or services you might use.

➤ Review service: Provides reviews of movies, books, software, programs, courses, or the Web itself.

Who Can You Turn to?

To learn about key sites, find others who are willing to trade site suggestions with you. Peers can help enormously, and clients or customers may be helpful. In addition, Web specialists might know of sites you'd never find for yourself.

The Best Leave Clues

Good Web sites have certain features in common. If you find a site that offers most of the features listed below, it will help to optimize your time online:

➤ Keeps visitors from getting lost. A good Web site includes multiple links that take you back to the home page, to the previous page, or to another value-packed page of your choice. It ensures that you can quickly return to something familiar or move forward to something new.

➤ Goes easy on the graphics. Many Web sites truly are works of art by master graphic artists. Smaller graphics and text-only hyperlinks, however, help you navigate much faster.

➤ Includes multiple contact links. Good sites contain clear links that point you to contact information such as e-mail, fax, snail mail addresses, and phone numbers, if appropriate.

➤ Are visitor-focused. A good site focuses on your needs, ensuring you the most direct access to information that is most valuable to you.

Chronos Says

Much of what you find on Web sites is time-sensitive, or is updated on a daily or weekly basis. Other sites post information for the long run. My site, includes both dynamic and static information (see http://www.BreathingSpace.com). One feature is called "Book Digest," which summarizes nearly 100 books. Visitors may download book digest selections of their choice each month for free. I add to the digest periodically, but it is basically a static portion of the site.

Newsgroups Give Answers You Can't Find Elsewhere

What are newsgroups? How can they help you stay in control of your time? First, a little history. In *Business on the Internet: The Concise Handbook*, co-authors Arnold and Rutman explain that a network called Usenet started as an electronic bulletin board served by just two sites: the University of North Carolina and Duke University. Today, Usenet newsgroups have grown into a global collection of thousands of discussion groups where people post messages and replies on specific topics of interest.

People Who Need People

Usenet—short for users' network—is actually a connected network of people, not computers, say Arnold and Rutman. "Usenet newsgroups reside at specific, accessible computer sites, and in the early days operated independently of the Internet. Like a community bulletin board in a public hallway, people stopped by, read comments, added their own, and checked replies."

Similar to the Internet, no particular person or group owns or runs Usenet. It operates according to certain conventions, using a system of universally recognized categories.

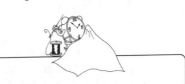

A Stitch in Time

Server sites around the world use the Internet today to share newsgroups and pass the postings from server to server throughout the computer network. Tap into this rich informational resource.

What if I'm New to Newsgroups?

If you're already browsing the World Wide Web, or if you intend to, you probably have what you need to access desired discussions. "The major Web browsers (Netscape Navigator and Microsoft Internet Explorer) come with built-in newsgroup readers that let you view, write, and reply to the postings of the groups you specify," says Arnold. He observes that, generally, the readers will ask you which server you're pulling the postings from, and that will probably be your ISP's computer. Software from online services like AOL include a preconfigured reader.

Pick Your Poison

Two basic categories comprise newsgroups, according to Arnold. The first, most highly controlled category, contains the following headings:

➤ comp: Computers and related topics (hardware, software, technical discussions)

➤ news: Usenet itself (announcements, software, and other information

➤ rec: Recreation and hobbies, entertainment, and the arts

➤ sci: Science (excluding computer science)

➤ soc: Social issues

➤ talk: Debates on controversial topics

➤ misc: Everything else, including "help wanted" postings

The second and less stringent set of categories includes these:

➤ alt: Alternative groups

➤ bionet: Biology

➤ bit: The most popular topics from Bitnet electronic mailing lists

➤ biz: Business, marketing, advertisements

The major group headings under each category are further broken down into subtopics, each separated by a dot in the address of the group. Arnold remarks that as the separators grow, the topic area shrinks. You may, for example, see a newsgroup identified as biz.books. Here you would expect to see information about all kinds of books on business. People participating in biz.books.technical, however, would be specifically interested in technical business books.

Using Newsgroups to Extreme Advantage

Deja News at http://www.dejanews.com is a useful site for uncovering discussion groups. The Deja News search engine is devoted entirely to newsgroups, and the site contains information and tools to help you find and use the groups that interest you.

After you've visited a few and gotten a feel for how they work, you may find the best to suit your needs.

Research

By following groups in a certain field, you can gauge trends regarding particular issues, products, or services. For example, take the example of SilverPlatter Information, Inc., publishers of CD-ROM information products. The top executive assigned staff members to peruse newsgroups related to the company's industry. Information gleaned from discussions on technological developments and areas of concern to buyers was passed on to management, who used it in strategic planning. It's that simple.

Visibility

You can join a group and get to know it, then let group participants know you exist. Offer information that they'll value. Arnold tells of Rohn Engh, owner of PhotoSource International and publisher of photomarketing subscription newsletters. When engaging in an online discussion, Engh offers to share information by sending a sample of one of his newsletters. This way he promotes his product while satisfying the information-exchange expectations of the group.

Consulting Help

When you become comfortable in the group, ask questions, solicit ideas, and request feedback. The owner of an executive recruiting firm needed fresh ideas to increase business, so he posted a message with a discussion group for advice. From the numerous replies he received, he found one that he put into practice. He figures that piece of advice brought in several thousand dollars of new business.

The E-Phones Are Coming, the E-Phones Are Coming

Just when you thought you'd heard it all, a new breed of telephone will enable you to browse the Web, visit newsgroups, or check your e-mail without going online. These e-mail telephones (e-phones, for short) offer a combination of phone receiver, keypad, and small screen that enable you to read and reply to e-mail directly from the phone.

Such e-phones range in cost from $250 to $600, but they'll soon drop to a price range everyone can afford. On top of the purchase price, you pay an Internet service provider between $15 and $25 per month for basic service.

E-Mail on the Fly

To check your e-mail from the phone, you select e-mail from a drop-down menu or click an icon that appears on your screen. Your e-phone then automatically dials your Internet service provider. ID information is instantly transferred, and the Internet service provider automatically transmits your messages to your screen.

Each message appears with the name of the sender, the subject line, and the date. You click on the listing to read the body of the message. You can reply, delete, or simply go on to the next listing. You can program the phone to check for e-mail periodically throughout the day, or you can dial up at will.

For now, e-phones lack the capability to send or receive attached files with e-mail. That means no graphics and no downloading of voluminous files. Stay tuned, however—that's bound to change in a hurry.

Time Out!

Real audio and video, and sites that feature tons of graphics do not currently load on an e-phone screen, and Web surfing is very slow. Stick with data-rich sites with lists and text-based articles.

Cruising the Net by E-Phone

Getting online to cruise the Web from your phone works much the same way as retrieving your e-mail. You either press a button or click an icon. The phone automatically dials your Internet service provider, and once you're online you'll see your familiar home page. Depending on the model of e-phone you buy, the size of the screen and quality of the graphics can be quite presentable.

A Phone by Any Other Name

The phone portion of this system has much the same features you get from any of the Baby Bells. But as these phones grow in popularity, more people are expected to use them for electronic shopping and banking.

As the technology unfolds, it's likely to save you and your family a ton of time. After all, you can plug in an e-phone anyplace with a phone jack. You don't need nearly the same amount of desk space as you do for a PC. Having the ability to simply pick up a phone, tap a few digits, and retrieve your e-mail from your kitchen or den without having to boot up your computer and go online may redefine the role and use of e-mail in society.

The Internet in Perspective

How many times do you take a minute before or after logging on and off the Internet to take a deep breath and get yourself focused? For the rest of your life, the volume of information available via the Internet and all other sources is going to accelerate.

Allow yourself to acknowledge that it will always be that way, and give yourself the opportunity to pause for a moment and relax.

The Least You Need to Know

➤ Much of the Web is self-serving hype about itself. Skip that part.

➤ Before you wade through scads of new information, delete old and unnecessary documents and files from your computer.

➤ Use top search engines (such as www.hotbot.com, www.lycos.com, www.infoseek.com, and www.nlsearch.com) to aid you in your searches.

➤ There will always be far more information available than you have time to keep pace with. Focus on what's vital and let the rest go.

Part 4
Springing Yourself From Time Traps

Consider what you've been up to in the first three parts of this book: leaving the office on time, choosing priorities, getting help, and recognizing that we are all in the same boat. Then you went in quest of getting more sleep, not being overwhelmed by tasks and information, whipping your office and files into shape, and using tools profitably. Maybe none of the individual changes were too huge, but you've been busy. By contrast, you're going to like the next three chapters—these tips and recommendations require less work! You can simply think your way through some situations, and they'll come out all right!

In Chapter 17, "Decision Making: Step It Up and Go!" you'll see why you're facing way too many decisions in a day, and you'll see that the more decisions you have to make, the harder it gets to make them. In Chapter 18, "The Art of Concentration," you'll discover a fundamental secret (oops! the title gives it away) for how to slow down the clock once and for all. In Chapter 19, "It Pays to Travel Light," you'll learn how to be on the lookout for the bells and whistles that over-complicate your life. Complexity is a tricky character. There you are, minding your own business, and before you know it, BOOM! Complications land on you like a ton of bricks, one at a time. You didn't even realize you were aiding and abetting the dumping. Once complications take hold, they spread like kudzu in Tennessee; beating them back becomes increasingly difficult.

Okay, enough pre-section banter. Here's a look at making big decisions in record time—and not making small decisions at all.

Chapter 16

Getting Adept with Mail and Correspondence

In This Chapter

➤ The old ways to transfer information and messages will still be around for a while

➤ How to save two-thirds of your correspondence time

➤ The good old Post Office is still worthwhile on some types of deliveries

➤ Employing a 31-day tickler file for timed responses

Mail moves the country, and ZIP codes move the mail—well, that slogan might have been accurate once. Regardless, most messages you receive—whether in the form of e-mail, faxes, or memos—will require your response.

The faster and easier you're able to respond, the better your day, week, career, and life will be—and the greater control you'll have over your time.

Options abound when it comes to speedily handling message replies. Let's check 'em out.

What Are You Sending, and to Whom?

If you're in sales (or another type of position where you initiate contact with potential customers), your mail and messages are proactive rather than reactive. You initiate them to get another party interested in your goods or services, although it's likely that most of the information you send to others will be in response to requests they've made or an obligation you need to fulfill.

Speedy Correspondence 101

I'll bet that too often correspondence that requires a prompt response falls by the wayside; you have to handle too many other things. Here's a secret to managing your time: When a response doesn't require formal business protocol (that is, when you know the other party well), or when the item merits only brief regard, remember that there are many ways to handle it quickly:

1. Some people use preprinted, plain-paper messages, such as, "Excuse the informality, but I feel it's more important to respond promptly than to offer a more formal reply that would take much longer."

2. Retain the return address information on the envelopes from the mail you've received. Thereafter, you can use this as your address label back to them and avoid having to engage your printer, copier, or label paper. Clip such addresses, or tear them out with the edge of a ruler.

   When I receive a package from someone, I clip the label from their package and attach it to the documents that came inside with a big paper clip or removable tape. When I'm ready to make a response, an address label to the other party is already available. (This will save you lots of time. When other people respond too slowly, often it's because they haven't devised a speedy reply system.)

3. Order a rubber stamper from your office supply store that says "Speed Reply." I have one myself; it's oversized and prints in bright red. When you receive a letter that merits a quick reply, stamp it with "Speed Reply," and offer your reply on the space at the bottom of the letter. Alternatively, you could print labels that say "Speed Reply" and simply affix them to the page.

   You have the option of faxing the letter (the fax machine treats deep, bold, red ink as black), or you could copy and mail the letter. Techniques such as these enable you to get a reply to the other party quickly and give you a record of the correspondence. Such a response is helpful to recipients as well; it presents their message with your reply. Think of how many times you've written to someone, the person responded, and you couldn't remember why you wrote in the first place.

4. If you're mailing a response, insert one of your own address labels to help the other party keep in touch with you. I enclose my address label with nearly all correspondence I mail. If you surmise that you'll write the other party again, include extra address labels.

   When you've successfully trained your correspondents to communicate adeptly with you, you both benefit.

5. Order a rubber stamp, or create a label that facilitates your fax replies as well. At the least include your name, phone, and fax number—your essential contact information. You could use the stamp on any correspondence you receive; it avoids using up the recipient's fax paper.

Often, when you receive faxes from a free-standing fax machine, the other party uses a full page to announce that a fax is coming, and then uses another page for a six- or eight-line message. The whole communication could have taken one-third of a page. When you initiate a labeling system, you let other parties know you respect their time and resources—and you keep your costs down.

And if you're using a fax/modem, the same principles apply. Keep your fax identification information concise and near the top of the first page. Keep your message brief; it makes a response more likely and keeps your transmission costs down.

6. For longer or more involved hard-copy correspondence, use the back side of the page you receive. Make a copy of the front and back for your own hard-copy files. Sometimes you can consolidate the correspondence you've received and do the same for what you send. For example, if someone sends you a two-page letter but you only need to respond to one key paragraph, simply clip that paragraph, include it at the top of your transmission, and reply below.

7. Feel free to number the points in the correspondence you've received and address each point in your reply. This cuts down on the time and energy it takes to reply. Otherwise, you have to quote chapter and verse in your reply.

When you number the points in the correspondence you receive, you can usually address everything in a one-page response. Formal responses that take two or more pages require copy-editing and tedious tweaking. They suck time out of your day and life faster than a vampire at a slumber party.

A Stitch in Time

Make a point of providing return address labels to your correspondents. Weeks later, you may begin to notice that you receive replies more promptly, and that the other party is using the address labels you provided. This tells you they've bought into your system.

Time Out!

Most professionals today indicate that they need more time to get their jobs done, often because of the correspondence they have to handle. Actually, that kind of thinking keeps you enslaved to the clock. More time is not on its way, and it's not the solution if you aren't operating efficiently.

Chronos Says

While business and organizational protocol may often call for formal responses, your mission (should you decide to accept it) is to offer efficient, informal responses, as often as appropriate.

8. Seek creative ways to use your fax machine, fax/modem, printer, and copier in combination to generate fast, appropriate responses to messages you receive; don't let correspondence pile up.

9. Design forms to handle routine communication. Better yet, see if someone in your office has already created one, or assign that task to someone. Many office-supply stores carry books with predesigned correspondence forms. They're worth the $10–$15; you're likely to save enough valuable time to pay for them the first day you use them.

Speed-Reply Options Abound

You've probably figured this out, but it's worth mentioning: Any time you want to respond to someone's message but you don't want a lengthy conversation, you can time your transmission to arrive when the person isn't in.

For example, if you're on the West Coast and it's 4:30 p.m., it's a safe bet that if you respond to someone on the East Coast by fax or voice mail, he or she won't be in at 7:30 p.m. to receive it. Your party will receive the fax the next day, which is fine with you because you didn't want to talk to anyone anyway.

It's also a good idea to order office supplies by fax so you won't have to stay on the phone and spell things out to somebody who writes at a blinding snail's pace. You won't have to worry that the other party will record my information incorrectly. A third- or half-page fax/modem transmission can present everything needed to convey in seconds.

The Post Office Is Still Good for Some Things

You already know about the express-mail services because you probably use them often: FedEx, DHL, Purolator, Roadway, Airborne, UPS, and others. But it still makes sense to use the U.S. Postal Service, despite all their troubles, if you know how to use the system effectively. Here is a brief, alphabetical description from the public information at the postal service regarding standard services. Following that is a description of services to safeguard, protect, and document your packages. Because the Postal Service is always changing their rates, I've left these out. You can call your local post office and, with any luck, can get somebody to give you the current rates.

Certified mail: This type provides you with a mailing receipt. A record of delivery is maintained at your receiver's Post Office. For valuables and irreplaceable items, the Postal Service recommends using insured or registered mail (they're coming up in this list).

Express Mail Next-Day service: This is the Post Office's fastest service. To use it, take your shipment to any designated Express Mail Post Office (generally by 5:00 p.m.), or deposit it in an Express Mail collection box. Your package will be delivered to the addressee by 3:00 p.m. the next day (weekends and holidays included).

First-class mail: This service is designed for letters, postal cards, greeting cards, personal notes, and for sending checks and money orders. You cannot insure ordinary first-class mail. However, additional services such as certificate of mailing, certified, return receipt, and restricted delivery can be purchased. If your first-class mail is not letter-size, make sure it is marked First Class, or use a large green-bordered envelope. First-class mail is actually the USPS's forte; the system is designed to move this category of mail most efficiently. A new generation of scanners can even read hand-addressed envelopes. Bar-coding makes first class mail even faster: Chances are your word processing system already contains a simple bar-coding procedure.

A Stitch In Time

The Post Office has more than 26,000 stations, and over 10,000 special Express Mail collection boxes in which you can deposit your parcels. Your letter carrier can accept prepaid Express Mail shipments when he or she delivers your mail. The Post Office can supply you with mailing containers (envelopes, boxes, and tubes) and the necessary mailing labels free of charge.

Third-class mail: Also referred to as bulk business or advertising mail, third-class mail may be sent by anyone but is used most often by large mailers. This class includes printed material and merchandise weighing less than 16 ounces. Two rate structures exist for this class: single piece and bulk rate. Individuals may use this class of mail for mailing lightweight parcels, and insurance can be purchased to cover loss or damage of articles.

Forwarding mail: When you move, fill out a Change of Address card in advance at your local post office. When possible, notify your post office at least one month before your move. First-class mail is forwarded at no charge. Magazines, newspapers, and other second-class mail are forwarded at no charge for 60 days.

Time Out!

Insurance won't protect you from all losses. No payments are made for sentimental losses or for any expenses incurred as a result of the loss.

Insurance: Insurance can be purchased up to $5,000 for standard mail, a certain maximum on registered mail, and a far lesser maximum for third and fourth-class mail. Insurance can also be purchased for merchandise mailed at the priority mail or first-class mail rates. With articles insured for more than a threshold amount, a receipt of delivery is signed by the recipient and filed at the delivering post office. The amount of insurance coverage for loss is the actual value, minus any depreciation.

Priority mail: This is first-class mail (more than 12 ounces and up to 70 pounds, with size limitations) to be delivered within two business days. (Rumor has it that P.O. workers are P.O.'d about this category of mail and deliver whenever they get the urge to, about every blue moon.)

Registered mail: The Postal Service regards this as its most secure mailing option. It is designed to provide added protection for valuable and important mail. Postal insurance may be purchased, for articles valued at more than $100, up to a maximum of $25,000. Return-receipt and restricted-delivery services are available for an additional fee. Registered articles are controlled from the point of mailing to delivery. First-class postage is required on registered mail.

Restricted delivery: Except for Express Mail service, you can request restricted delivery when purchasing return-receipt service. Restricted delivery means that delivery is made only to the addressee or to someone who is authorized in writing to receive mail for the addressee. Such mail addressed to officials of government agencies, legislative and judicial branches of federal and state governments, members of the diplomatic corps, minors, and individuals under guardianship, however, can be delivered to an agent without written authorization from the addressee.

Return receipt: This is your proof of delivery; it's available on mail that you send by COD or Express Mail, mail insured for more than $25, or mail that you registered or certified. The return receipt shows who signed for the item and the date it was delivered. For an additional fee, you can get an exact address of delivery or request restricted-delivery service.

Special delivery: You can buy special-delivery service on all classes of mail except bulk third-class. Delivery happens even on Sundays and holidays, during hours that extend beyond the hours for the delivery of ordinary mail. This service is available to all customers served by city carriers, and to other customers within a 1-mile radius of the delivery post office. Note that special delivery may be handled by your regular carrier if it's available before the carrier departs for morning deliveries.

Tickle Your Files for More Timely Responses

Chapter 11, "Filing: Your Simple Salvation," discusses setting up a file for each month and also creating a 31-day rotating tickler file. These files offer a home for things that you don't need to deal with immediately, or that are best dealt with at some future time (you know, like the turn of the twenty-second century!). To handle mail quickly, tickler files are just what the time-saving doctor ordered.

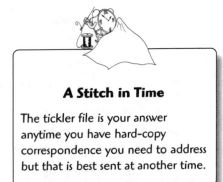

A Stitch in Time

The tickler file is your answer anytime you have hard-copy correspondence you need to address but that is best sent at another time.

Suppose you receive correspondence that doesn't have to be answered now. What are you going to do? Let it sit in the black hole known as your in-basket? Park it some place on your desk that is equally remote to a black hole? Create some new file for it that you never find again? All these temporary solutions are less than desirable.

While it may make sense to handle the correspondence now if it needn't be transmitted till later, do what you have to do with it and then park it in your tickler file. For example, if you receive something on the 5th that need not be mailed until the 15th (to reach the other party by the 19th), take care of it today while it's hot, fresh, and right in front of you. Seal it, stamp it, and put it in your tickler file for the 15th.

The electronic version of this technique is to type your e-mail message and then enter the date and time you want it submitted, or put it the Deferred mail box for sending when you choose.

You may recall that a tickler file is an ideal way to organize bills without paying them too early (which can cost you if you have an interest-bearing checking account) and avoiding penalties for paying too late.

Here are some other ways to use your tickler file for timed responses that save you time and help put you on top of things:

➤ Stash tickets to forthcoming events in the appropriate tickler-file date.

➤ Store coupons, discounts, and promotional items until you're ready to use them.

➤ Park items you want to read on your next plane trip in the tickler file for the day before your trip.

➤ Find temporary locations for notes, outlines, or other documents you'll want to have on hand when someone visits your office.

➤ Do the same for forthcoming group, department, or company meetings.

➤ Place any mail you receive but choose not to open now in your tickler file; choose a date that seems more appropriate for you.

➤ When you're waiting for someone's response, file a copy of your transmission in your tickler file or in a file labeled "Awaiting Response."

The Least You Need to Know

➤ Temporarily put down this book and order a long-life stamper that reads "Speed Reply" from an office supply store, or create labels using your PC and printer. Start using your speed-reply message on correspondence right away.

➤ Check out submitting legal contracts via fax. You can also become adept at negotiating via fax.

➤ Depending on what you want to send and to whom, the U.S. Postal System (for all its shortcomings) has a variety of services that may provide what you need.

➤ Set up a 31-day, rotating tickler file system so that when you have correspondence to handle but prefer to send it later, you have a convenient place to park it.

Chapter 17

Yes No Decision Making: Step it Up and Go!

In This Chapter

➤ The growing number of choices—and hence, decisions—you'll face

➤ When it's best to refrain from making a decision

➤ How more data can confound your ability to decide

➤ Using the power of your intuitive abilities

Decisions, decisions. Some are big; most are trivial. Any way you cut it, you're confronted by too many decisions—at work, at home, on the weekend, while traveling, when you wake, when you retire at night, when you're on vacation, and when you're with either friends or enemies.

Why are you facing more decisions? Is it because you're getting older and have more responsibilities? Is it because you have a bigger bank account (ha-ha)? Or is something else bringing on the change? As you may remember, Chapter 3, "With Decades to Go, You Can't Keep Playing Beat the Clock," discusses how anyone holding a responsible job may feel pressed for time; everyone's in the same boat.

Time Out!

The more information you're exposed to, the more choices you face and the greater the unrelenting pressure on you to choose.

More Choices Lead to More Decisions

In a world of 6 billion people and counting, more information is being generated and is sped your way by worldwide media and print coverage.

It's not hard to understand why you face too much information. Society spews it in abundance. For example, the White House is covered by 1,800 reporters! (You'd think maybe 300 or so could do the job....) When the media cover something they can sink their teeth into, they sink them deep.

When you go to the drug store to buy something as inconsequential as shampoo or skincare lotion, watch out. There are more than 1,200 varieties of shampoo on the market, and more than 2,000 skincare products. Choices abound in other arenas as well. More than 8,000 popular videos are available for viewing (more than 68,000 if you include management training, aerobic fitness, and how-tos). Three thousand books are published in the United States each week—more than 600 a day. Ten times as many radio stations exist today than when television was first introduced. If these examples don't indicate "choice overload," I don't know what does.

In his landmark book *Future Shock*, Alvin Toffler said that in the future too many choices will compete for your time and attention. He was right. Manufacturers engage in mass-customization to offer you products with whatever bells and whistles you want (and ads that make you want them). When Lee Iacocca was the chief executive officer of Chrysler, he converted all the company's car dealers to the concept of mass-customization. The customer comes in, orders a basic car, and then adds the specifics: tinted glass, whitewalls, automatic steering or power brakes, and several dozen other options.

Theoretically, with the perfect information, after having whittled down your search to the essence of your needs, you could purchase any product you seek. There's only one problem: You hardly ever receive even semiperfect information (at least in this life). So you're forever besieged by too much information—much of it conflicting—and it impedes your ability to choose. To win back more of your time, identify the big decisions and make them quickly. Start by determining which decisions are worth making and which are worth forsaking.

Separating the Wheat...

Think back to Chapter 5, "Okay, So What Do You Want?" and Chapter 6, "Supporting Your Priorities for Fun and Profit"; review the discussion on establishing priorities and goals. What you establish as important in your life is immediately linked to decisions that are worth making.

When something will have a significant impact in the area of one of your life's priorities, that's a decision worth making. Anything less than that is a decision worth forsaking—but I'm getting ahead of myself. Many people mix decisions worth making with those worth forsaking, treat them almost equally, and wonder where the time went.

If your boss requests that you make a decision, the situation is clear-cut. Nevertheless, decisions worth making are often conditional. If you're single and trying to choose between two likely mates, your decision will affect the quality of your life in the foreseeable future—and perhaps the rest of your life. The following are examples of decisions worth making:

➤ The choice of a spouse

➤ The choice of a home

➤ Major work decisions your organization requests of you

➤ Where you'll live

➤ With whom you'll associate

➤ What course of study you'll pursue

➤ Whether you wish to climb to the top of your organization or profession

Decisions worth making, while often conditional, are not always apparent. Consider the following five issues. Are they decisions worth spending any time on? It all depends. In the list that follows, mentally circle the decisions you believe worth making:

➤ The color of the next toothbrush you buy

➤ The next movie you see

➤ Whether to attend the next PTA meeting

➤ Whether to take your car in for a tune-up tomorrow

➤ What to eat for breakfast

Have you finished circling the items above? Good. So what are the right answers? As you may have guessed, there are none.

From the Chaff: Decisions Worth Forsaking

Decisions worth forsaking are always lying around. They ought to be easy to spot, but when you're faced with too many decisions anyway, your reflex action likely to be an attempt to grapple with all decisions.

1. **The color of the next toothbrush.** For most people this is a decision worth forsaking; it can't be that important. When might it be? If the decor of your home and bathroom is of utmost importance to you (don't laugh; it is for some people) then this becomes a decision worth making.

2. **The next movie you see.** It's likely you only go to movies you think you'll enjoy; when you see one you don't like, it is a mistake, but the earth doesn't tremble. If you consider movies as just a way to pass the time, then which one you see is not of paramount or universal importance.

   When would it be? If improving the cultural component of your life is among your priorities, and the movie is of the shoot-'em-up variety, your decision is clear: Don't go see it. Of the hundreds of movies you've seen in your life, how many have truly had a significant impact on your behavior and activities? Few, if any. Granted, seeing *Saving Private Ryan* may heighten your sensitivity to vital historical issues, but more often than not, choosing a movie is no big deal.

3. **Going to the next PTA meeting.** Your child's education or the betterment of your community is likely a high priority, so you would attend. If your child is doing extremely well in school, or if you're pleased about the school system in general, you could skip one meeting—or even a run of them.

4. **Should you put your car in the shop tomorrow?** Has your car been running poorly lately? What is the cost of you being tied up on the highway and not getting into work on time, and causing 10,000 people to snarl at you? Can you bring work with you to the repair shop, or can they give you a ride back to work quickly after your arrival? Is preventive maintenance part of your overall plan to be ready and stay on top of things? The more people who take care of their automobiles in advance of any failure of performance, the fewer breakdowns on the highway—which good is for everyone.

5. **What to eat for breakfast.** If you're already 32 pounds above your ideal weight and have no hope of ever getting back into shape, what you eat for breakfast tomorrow morning matters less than the longer-term health concerns you're facing. Go ahead and have that (one) honey-glazed doughnut with your coffee. If becoming the first octogenarian to visit the moon is a priority for you, then, once again, the choice is clear: Go healthy instead.

What's a *low-level decision*? When a coworker asks you where you want to go to lunch today, your response will most appropriately be, "You decide." Of the couple thousand times you've been to lunch, can you recall any significant impact related to your decision on where you went? Okay, so one day you met somebody you started dating. Another time, you learned something new. In general, there hasn't been much impact. Other examples of decisions worth forsaking include these:

➤ The park or playground where you'll take your children to play; let them decide.

➤ Whether to catch the news at 10 p.m. or not.

➤ Whether to get Del Monte frozen vegetables or Bird's Eye frozen vegetables.

➤ Whether to visit Colorado for five days or six.

You may be asking if there is any perceptible benefit to making fewer choices per day. To answer this question, I offer the following anecdote. In the 1980s, the Los Angeles Lakers, under Coach Pat Riley, would fly on chartered planes following their games; the players never had to wait. Each player had the same seat on every plane, bus, and cab. Magic Johnson said (in his autobiography *My Life)* that although this was a small thing, the players found it comforting and reassuring. Kareem Abdul Jabbar always sat across from James Worthy. Magic Johnson and Michael Cooper always sat behind Kareem. Magic said that after a long, hard game, he would jump on the bus or plane and know exactly where to sit. Riley took this low-level choice out of the hands of the players.

This sense of familiarity and comfort with one another undoubtedly contributed to the Lakers' cohesiveness as a unit—perhaps playing some small role in the team's five world championships during the 1980s.

Consider an instance of good manners in this light. When you go to a dinner party and the host has already assigned seating to the guests, it's an act of kindness. It reduces anxiety about who'll be in the chair beside you. This is a time-honored tradition from Walnut Creek, California, to the White House.

Don't Think—Act

If you find yourself overanalyzing situations too frequently, *relent*. You're a product of Western civilization: You've been trained from birth to collect all the data, statistics, articles, reports, and information you could lay your hands on before making a decision that involves the outlay of any sizable sum.

Time Out

Much of the data you collect may be redundant, reaffirming what you already know. Too often, you may unconsciously be collecting what you already know or believe, without seeing the data objectively.

When each individual in two groups of executives had to make a large purchase decision for their respective companies, the first group was armed with information—reports, data, statistics, and all that jazz. Understandably, each one used all the information to make the purchase decision.

The second group consisted of individuals who had no such data or statistics. They used instinct, or intuition, or whatever you want to call it. Weeks after the purchases had been made and each executive got to see the results, which group do you expect was happier with their decisions? (Well, okay, I did load the question a little to favor the second group.)

Honestly, though, you are more likely to have chosen the group that had the data and statistics. Moreover, if given a chance to be in one group or the other, you would have chosen to be in that well-informed group, wouldn't you? How could the second group possibly be happier? If you're 30 or 40 or 50 years old, everything you've learned in your life up to now is summoned when you make a decision. There's far more to instinct or intuition than is generally acknowledged.

There are also inherent traps in collecting more data on the way to making a decision. For example, the more data you collect, the likelier it is you'll get conflicting answers.

Sometimes the data that you collect is nothing more than a crutch. Or sometimes its only purpose is to cover your derriere (if the decision turns out unfavorably), by having an authority to cite: "It says right here blah, blah, blah."

Sometimes the data you collect is a substitute for taking action. Studying a decision is a classic way to delay making it. (The government has done it for years.) In all cases, whatever data or information you collect has to be applied.

More data is not always the answer, but what's the alternative? I'll deal with intuition in a moment. For now, here are some techniques for making big decisions in record time—and getting the answer you want with less effort:

1. **Three calls away from any expert.** If you can identify the single best person to call to start off your information search, you can get your answer within two more calls. Who's the first person to call? It could be your municipal or college library, an official of an industry or professional association, or an information service firm (such as market researchers). Perhaps you can find an expert within the government, or an editor at *Consumer Reports*.

2. **Finding the trailblazer.** Has anyone else already made a decision like this? If so, and if their circumstances are somewhat similar to yours, it would behoove you to learn what they have discovered. It pays to network with people in your field.

Later you can tap them for their experiences (abbreviated with the technical term O.P.E.: other people's experiences).

3. **Consensus building.** Can you assemble a group, hash it out, and base your decision on the consensus reached? In many instances this works fine. After all, you relied on the power of the group; if your decision crashes and burns, you can always point the finger at them (just kidding!).

4. **The answer will simply emerge.** This alleviates a lot of decisions. It's like the United States pulling out of Bosnia; often, as circumstances unfold, the decision that makes the most sense becomes apparent. If you suspect this might be the case, sit back and let time takes its course. The answer may become abundantly clear.

Rising to the Challenge: Decisions in the Form of Problems

Quite a few decisions you have to make are based on problems. Modern management theory holds that problems can be approached productively when you see them as opportunities or challenges. In *The Path of Least Resistance*, Robert Fritz suggests that you view problems as your best friends. It often works!

How does facing a problem help you get to a higher ground? This view of problem solving works best when you're dealing with minor issues, not extremes—rather than a hangnail, the death of a loved one. If the decision you face is a disguised problem, try treating it as your best friend or a teacher with wisdom to impart. You may dislodge something in your decision-making process and proceed more easily.

A Stitch in Time

If you come up with a decision that both addresses the immediate situation and provides long-term benefits, then you've got something.

Biographers have noted that Ben Franklin listed the pluses and minuses of one path versus another when faced with big decisions. Sometimes he gave weight to them; sometimes he didn't. While this is a basic approach to making decisions, listing your potential options on paper still beats merely weighing them in your mind; you can keep better track of them this way.

In *Feel the Fear and Do It Anyway*, Dr. Susan Jeffers suggests that when you encounter a decision that represents a hurdle or a roadblock, you need to let yourself feel all the emotions that arise. Are you uneasy? Quivering? Lightheaded? Is your stomach upset, are you trembling, or do you feel fearful? When you're honest with yourself about how you feel (namely, scared), initiate your decision anyway, Jeffers says. Often you're able to break through your fear and overcome the obstacle that loomed so large when you weren't being honest with yourself. (Hmm, sounds like it's worth a try.)

Use Your Inner Voice for Speed Decision-Making

Interested in the fastest way to make decisions? This involves using your instincts or intuition. You're already pretty good at this; you got this far in life and, hey, it ain't so bad. Write down your intuitive choice before making any final decision. Then, when enough time has passed to see the results of a more analytical decision, write them down and compare them to the results of your intuitive choice. As time passes, you'll begin to notice how frequently your intuitive choices were wise ones, and you'll find yourself trusting your hunches more easily and more often.

Chronos Says

When you get adept at trusting your intuition, you can bypass many reams of data and information that previously impeded your ability to choose. You can call upon your still, quiet, and faithful internal guidance system.

More Than Throwing Darts at the Wall: Intuition in Action

Do you have a dentist? How did you select your dentist? Did you open up the phone book and get the names of the 10–12 dentists nearest you, then call each of them, decide (based on the call) to visit five to seven, visit their offices, grill each one on billing procedures, background, expertise, competency of their staff, office hours, prices, and overall philosophy? Then did you whittle down the list to maybe two or three, call them back or visit on another occasion, and do some background checking for reputation, longevity in the community, and professional standing? Then, and only then, did you decide on dentist A? Or did you choose dentist B on the basis of whom your parents or friends see, where some referral service sent you, or simply the clever ad you saw in the phone book?

You probably used the latter method, picking a dentist by hook or by crook—and if that one didn't work out, you switched. In short, you used a combination of references and intuitive processes to come up with your dentist.

Why, then, do you overcomplicate so many decisions at work and in the rest of your life? When you base a choice on intuition, every cell in your body and every shred of intelligence you've ever accumulated are brought to bear. There's a lot going on behind the solutions you make.

New information is only going to hit you faster and faster as your life proceeds. You'll be able to absorb and use only a fraction of what you're exposed to. There's no time for exhaustive research on every consumer product you buy (ever try counting how many different ones you use?). You're going to have to trust your instincts.

A Stitch in Time

Pay attention to your small voice, you know—that little munchkin in back of everything that goes on all day. That's your intuition talking, and it's there to support you if you listen to it.

Suppose, on the other hand, you're considering whether to move to town A or town B. What factors would you logically consider? Try these out:

➤ Housing prices

➤ Taxes and demographics

➤ Schools

➤ Crime

➤ Community groups

➤ Family and friends

➤ Lakes, streams, and beaches

➤ Trails and mountains

➤ The business community

➤ Population density

➤ Education levels

➤ Nearby colleges

➤ Churches, synagogues, and mosques

➤ Road systems

➤ Major highway access

➤ Shopping

➤ Traffic patterns

➤ Deviant groups

You guessed it: There are dozens of factors you could analyze and compare. In the end, your decision would probably be based on some combination of data (though not too much) and intuition (probably a lot).

The Devil's Temptress: Procrastination

When faced with too many decisions, your natural inclination may be to procrastinate—or perhaps you fear making a mistake. Don't beat yourself up (that can be a way to delay action further); lots of people face this problem. Decisions that would normally roll off your back become more involved when there's too much on your plate—and chances are, there's too much on your plate. Here's a list of ways to break through the procrastination that stymies your decision-making process:

➤ **Face procrastination head-on.** What is blocking you? What is the real reason you don't want to choose? Write it down or record it on cassette. This exercise alone may dislodge something and help you decide.

➤ **Choose to easily begin.** Make a positive affirmation of yourself: "I can easily make this decision." This affirmation has power and is often enough. Elizabeth Jeffries, a Louisville, Kentucky-based speaker and a trainer for healthcare organizations, maintains a list of daily affirmations that help her make decisions she could otherwise put off.

➤ **Find the easy point.** Ask yourself, "What are three to five things I could do to progress toward the final decision without actually tackling it head-on?" Then initiate these "easy entry" activities. Often, they're enough to get you fully involved.

➤ **Set up your desk for a decision.** Set up your desk or office to enable you to focus on the decision at hand; ignore other (less important) matters. This might involve neatly arranging papers, file folders, reports, and other items. Working at a clear desk leaves only the issue at hand in front of you.

Probably 95 percent of your decisions will have only a minimal impact on your life; don't let the fear of being wrong shackle you unduly.

Comparison Shopping

When you need to make a purchase decision, sometimes all you need is a good set of questions to ask. Without further ado, here's a checklist of questions for making sound purchase decisions more quickly:

❏ Are there quantity discounts, economic-ordering quantities, or special terms?

❏ Are there corporate, government, association, military, or educators' discounts?

❏ Do they give weekly, monthly, quarterly, or seasonal discounts?

    ❏ Do they give off-peak discounts on odd-lot discounts?

    ❏ Do they offer a guaranteed lowest price?

    ❏ Do they accept major credit cards?

❏ Do they accept orders by fax? by e-mail?

❏ Do they offer a money-back guarantee, or other some guarantee?

❏ Do they have a toll-free 800–, 888–, or 877–ordering line and customer service line?

❏ Do they guarantee the shipping date? How do they ship?

❏ Do they offer free delivery? free installation?

❏ Will they keep your name off their mailing list (unless you want to keep up with special sales)?

❏ Do they intend to sell, rent, or otherwise transfer your name and ordering information to others?

❏ Are their shipments insured?

❏ Are there shipping and handling charges? Are their prices guaranteed? Is there tax?

❏ Are there any other charges?

❏ Do they have free samples?

❏ Are authorized dealer/repair services in your area?

❏ Are references or referral letters available?

❏ Are there satisfied customers in your area?

❏ How long have they been in business?

❏ Whom are they owned by?

❏ How long for delivery?

❏ Is gift-wrapping available?

❏ Does the product come with a warranty?

The Least You Need to Know

➤ From now until the end of your life you'll face *more* decisions—not fewer. Focus on decisions that advance your priorities and support your goals.

➤ Avoid making low-level decisions whenever possible.

➤ More data is not always the answer. Trust your instincts more often; they are there to serve you.

➤ If the decision represents a problem, see it as a friend and messenger. With that perspective, ask what the problem is helping you to do or overcome.

➤ Using a prepared checklist can enhance a purchasing decision. Feel free to copy the one given here.

Chapter 18

The Art of Concentration

In This Chapter

➤ The fallacy of doing several things at once to "save" time

➤ Doing one thing at a time and doing it well

➤ Your own interruption-management system

I'm willing to bet the farm that sometime in the last 48 hours, if not the last four hours, you engaged in some form of multitasking—doing two or more things at the same time. It's likely you've been working on a personal computer recently, and that while you were running the word-processing software, you may have been engaging the printer, a pop-up spreadsheet, and a calendar as well.

From the notebook PC that sits on your lap to the huge supercomputers that fill rooms, computers are well equipped to handle more than one task at a time. Human beings, however, are not computers, no matter what you may have heard. Stay tuned; this chapter will explore this case of mistaken identity.

Too Much to Do

When you're working with your PC, trying to answer the phone or open mail, trying to respond to the fax machine or the request from the next head to pop in your door, and whatever else you can add to this list—and when you attempt to entertain them all—you are attempting to engage in multitasking. It's a computer term, and there's a reason for that: It's a computer function. Unlike the computer, you're likely to do an unsatisfactory job when you multitask.

Time Out!

At the workplace and at home, trying to multitask ensures that you'll miss your day, week, and ultimately your life. I know people who are 40 years old who can't remember where their 30s went, and people who are 50 who can't remember where their 40s went.

Singling Things Out

All things considered, you work best when you focus on one thing at a time. On many levels you probably know this already, but when is the last time you practiced it? Probably not recently. It's too easy to fall into a familiar trap: "So much is expected of me, I have to double and triple my activities."

Nearly every message in society says it's okay—or necessary—to double or triple the number of activities you perform at once. You see advertisements of people talking on the phone while they watch television, or eating while they read.

The Urge to Urgency

Bob W., age 41, works for a large brokerage firm in the International Square building in Washington, D.C. He is friendly, successful, and always in a rush. He talks fast, moves fast, eats fast, and never lets up. Bob is hooked on multitasking. Many executives and career-climbers suffer from a misdirected sense of urgency stemming from far too many tasks and responsibilities. Certainly, it's appropriate to work more quickly than normal at certain times. It's a problem, however, when it becomes a standard operating procedure.

A Shared Burden

Research suggests that when you do two things at once, it's probably symptomatic of an ability (and burden) shared by the whole human species. That doesn't necessarily make it effective. The false economy of attempting to do two things at once is ingrained in a culture that rewards the workaholic, the 16-hour-a-day entrepreneur, the supermom, and the hyper-energetic high school student.

A Stitch in Time

Any time you undertake original or creative thinking—work with numbers, charts, or graphs; or writing, copy-editing, or proofreading—put aside all other tasks until you've finished. Diverting your attention is bound to result in far less than your best effort; often it leads to costly errors.

What's more, the mental and psychic toll you place on yourself in attempting multitasking (or in doing one stressful job for too long) can be harmful. Your brain can become overtaxed!

Consider the case of air-traffic controllers who have been on duty too long, had too many planes come in at a given time, and have the responsibility of keeping hundreds of lives safe by making the right decisions with split-second timing. It's no wonder that this is a high-stress, high-burnout position, one that professionals usually abandon at a young age.

Business Isn't Busy-ness

Researchers at the Medical College of Wisconsin have found that if you perform a task as simple as tapping your foot, you activate the primary motor in your cortex, a section of your brain. If your task is more involved, if it includes planning to tap your foot to a sequence (such as one-two, one-two-three, one-two, one-two-three), then two secondary motor areas in the front of the cortex are engaged. You are drawing upon more of your brain's functioning capacity.

Don't worry, your brain can handle it. The point is that when you engage in multitasking—such as attempting to watch TV while eating, or doodling while you talk on the telephone—your brain functioning changes to incorporate the extra activities.

If you want to do the best at whatever you're doing, allow your brain to concentrate on one activity—focus on one thing at a time. If it's a complex task, consider whether you're working on several parts of the same task or two different tasks. It sounds simple enough, but this advice goes against the grain of a society that tells you to do many things at once so you can "be more efficient." You see this every day: someone jogging down the road listening to a Walkman, or doing work or reading while eating lunch. People double their activities, as if that will make things easier and better.

I sometimes conduct a brief exercise with my audiences when speaking at conventions and executive retreats. I ask audience members to take out their watches and do nothing but stare at them for a solid minute. No one can do it! In this society, you're fed a message that emphasizes the importance of motion and activity. Merely reading, thinking, or reflecting doesn't look busy enough.

Chronos Says

"Men give me some credit for genius. All the genius I have lies in this: When I have a subject at hand I study it profoundly. Day and night it is before me. I explore it in all its bearings. My mind becomes pervaded with it. Then the effort which I have made is what people are pleased to call the fruit of genius. It is instead the fruit of labor and thought."
—Alexander Hamilton

Has the following happened to you? Somebody walks by your desk and, horror of horrors, you're reading! Maybe the person looks at you a little funny, or perhaps you feel a bit guilty because you're not "in motion." Yet studies show that informed people in executive positions need to read professional journals and reports for two to four hours each day. So to be as productive as you need to be, you often act in ways that run counter to what society tells you is "productive activity."

The Productive Potential of Doing Nothing

To reach your full potential, you've got to break out of the mind set imposed by others. Sometimes the best way to be productive is to sit at your desk doing nothing—at least nothing that looks like anything to people walking by. Reading or looking out the window in contemplation could be the single most important and productive thing you do in a day. Too often, you probably throw your time at tasks when you really need to reflect on them first.

What happens when you jump between different projects? It may feel "dynamic"—after all, you're exerting lots of energy. Yet there's a loss of productivity. You and a friend can test this easily at your desk or table. Decide on any three minor tasks in which the two of you can engage simultaneously. One task could be stacking pennies; another could be drawing 15 stars on a blank sheet of paper; a third could be linking paper clips. You each have the same number of items.

You and your friend start these tasks at the same time. You stack a few pennies at a time, make a few stars on a blank piece of paper, and link some paper clips, indiscriminately alternating between the three tasks. Meanwhile, on the other side of the table, your friend stacks an equal number of pennies to completion until there are no more. Then (s)he turns to making stars on a page and reaches 15. Finally comes linking the paper clips until they're all linked.

Who do you think will not only finish faster and easier, but will be in better shape mentally and emotionally? I'll bet on your friend who focused on the task at hand, took it to completion, then turned to the next one while you (ha-ha-ha) were bouncing back and forth between activities. You may have been more prone to errors, such as knocking over one of your stacks of pennies. Even if you were quite an adept task-juggler, you simply couldn't keep pace. The quality of your work was not as good. Perhaps your paper clips became tangled, or the 15 stars you drew on the page lacked a little artistic merit.

Multiply the effect of this simple test by the number of times you flip-flop between activities in a day or year, and it's easy to understand why you're not getting the best results from all that activity. Continually switching from task to task is just not as productive as staying on one job until completion.

Regaining Control

For today, give yourself the benefit of working on one thing at a time. You may have to switch gears when the boss comes in, when that important phone call comes through, or if you receive a fax that has to be acted on right away. When you switch gears, switch them entirely: Give your complete and undivided attention to the pressing issue at hand. Try it out. You might find that this is a happier, more effective way to work.

If you notice yourself falling into behavior patterns that resemble computerized multitasking, try these solutions:

➤ Take a 15-minute break once during the morning and once in the afternoon. That also means: Don't eat at your desk. Get away so you can recharge your battery.

➤ Invest in equipment or technology that offers you a significant return—that is, it pays for itself within one year or less, or it saves at least two hours a week of your time.

> **A Stitch in Time**
>
> The single best way to cope with a number of different projects is to begin working on one thing until its completion, and then go on to the next project, and then the next, until you are finished.

➤ Hold regular meetings with your team to discuss how everyone can be more efficient—without multitasking. Focus on the big picture of what you're all trying to accomplish. Often, new solutions to old problems will emerge, and activities that seem urgent can be viewed from a broader prospective.

➤ For a more human workplace, furnish your office with plants, pictures, art, or decorations that inspire creativity.

You Created the Situation

Robert Fritz says that when you are feeling overwhelmed or time-stressed, ask yourself, "Who created this situation?" The answer is usually *you*.

Of course, there are times when the boss lays a bombshell on your desk and you're asked to do more than usual. It's still your responsibility to head off this threat to your time. You need to invest in resources that will equip you to handle tasks that come your way, whether it's learning new software, learning a new language, or acquiring more training.

A System for Handling Distraction

In 1990, author Alvin Toffler told me that the workplace is a terrible place to get things done these days. With the distractions in your office, it's often better to work at the library, in the conference room, or on a park bench. This is especially true when you're doing conceptual or breakthrough thinking, when you need to have quiet space.

I was once consulting for a supervisor in Minnesota with six employees; he wanted to use his time more efficiently. He said his employees came to him with questions every couple of hours. That seemed harmless enough, but look at how it built up: If an employee asked a question every two hours, the supervisor got four from that person each day.

With six employees, that meant 24 questions a day, or 120 interruptions each week, resulting in disruptions of the manager's work three times each hour in a 40-hour week! I devised a system to help him cope with the interruptions and regain control of his time; I called it the "J-4 System." (The *J* was for Jeff. You can use your own initial.)

Simplifying Life the J-4 Way

I had the supervisor put the questions into four categories of manageability. The first distraction, J-1, was already answered in print and did not need a personal reply (it was in the company policy manual). The supervisor was then able to tell his employees, "Please don't bother me with J-1 distractions."

The second distraction, J-2, was a question that a peer or bookkeeper could answer; the supervisor did not need to be bothered with this type of question either.

J-3s needed only a straightforward, short answer of yes or no. Such questions required interaction with the supervisor, but not much—a quick phone call or a buzz on the intercom.

The final category, J-4 distractions, required the supervisor's input—he needed to answer them.

How many questions were at the J-4 level of importance? Even assuming each person asked two J-4 questions per day—60 interruptions each week—this would cut the number of interruptions in half! Almost immediately, the supervisor was able to better use his time and reduce his level of stress.

With this system, you'll gain greater control over your work, you'll find more time, and you'll feel more relaxed as that knot in your stomach begins to unravel. You'll even be able to do breakthrough creative thinking at your own desk.

The number of distractions—the things competing for your time and attention—is infinite. You're only going to have more distractions in the future, not fewer. To regain control over your life, learn to cope with distractions in new ways.

When Anxiety Tugs at Your Shoulder

I once heard anxiety defined as "the attempted unification of opposing forces." What majesty—this says it all! Anytime you're anxious, stop and figure out what opposing forces you're attempting to unite. Are you working on some low-level task when there's something far more important for you to give your attention to? You feel anxious. Your intuitive alarm system is ringing.

Your anxiety stems from your attempt to work on a low-level project (force #1) when you know there's something else that's more appropriate for you to be working on (force #2).

If you've been multitasking for a long time and suddenly attempt to switch to working on one thing at a time, guess what happens? You may feel a sudden increase in anxiety. It's like trying to kick an addiction to a chemical stimulant. You want to get off, and know you'll be better for doing it. But as you attempt to do without the stimulant, maybe you don't feel so good. The natural inclination is to get back into the addiction. So it is with multitasking—but what if that "dynamic" feeling is no more than an unproductive high?

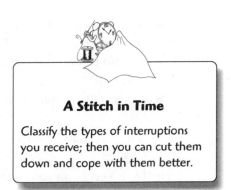

A Stitch in Time

Classify the types of interruptions you receive; then you can cut them down and cope with them better.

Let's Play Concentration

To become a master of doing one thing at a time, pick an activity you enjoy, where there's a high probability that you can engage in it without doing anything else. It might be driving your car with the radio off, reading in your favorite armchair without having any munchies, or just listening to music instead of banishing it to the background.

➤ Start with small segments. If you're reading in your favorite armchair, promise yourself you'll go 10 minutes without any munchies the first night. The second night, go 15, then 20, and so forth. Eventually you may get to the point where you can read for an hour or more without having to resort to snacks.

➤ If you're seeking to read, engage in conceptual or breakthrough thinking, or do some creative problem solving, find as quiet and comfortable a place as possible.

➤ If you're surrounded by all manner of tasks competing for your attention, identify the one that's most important to tackle, and stay with it until completion (or for as long as you can). If you're temporarily pulled away by something else, return to the important task at hand; again, stay with it to completion or for as long as you can.

➤ If you are paid to handle a multiplicity of items competing for your attention, practice giving short bursts of full attention to the task at hand before turning to the next thing demanding your attention.

Consider an airline reservation attendant in the middle of a high pressure situation. The approach is one person-and-ticket situation at a time; often the attendant doesn't even look up from the computer monitor. The same principle holds for a good bank teller, a good bus driver, or a construction worker walking on scaffolding five stories above the ground.

➤ Initiate personal balancing techniques: take deep breaths, stare out the window, see yourself as tackling the situation easily. Or try closing your eyes for a few seconds before confronting the task again. (More on this in the forthcoming chapters.)

➤ Observe the people in your organization who concentrate well. What do they do that's different from what everybody else does? Talk to them; learn from them.

➤ If it's necessary, bring earplugs to work. Use a sound screen if it helps. (See Chapter 8, "To Sleep, Perchance to Not Wake Up Exhausted.")

➤ Let others in on your quest to increase your powers of concentration. Mutual reinforcement can help.

➤ Practice using the interruption-management system discussed earlier in this chapter.

Okay, There Are *Some* Exceptions

For the most part, leave the multitasking to the computers. However, there are a few times when it's perfectly permissible to do more than one thing at a time—and most of these occur away from work. Obviously, at dinner with a friend or loved one you'll be talking and eating simultaneously, but that can be seen as one event (in some parts of the South, they call it "visiting," and it claims a person's whole attention). Generally, it's okay to drive and listen to the radio, cassettes, or CDs. The exception is when the decibel level is so high that your concentration is impaired (or you don't hear that ambulance).

Exercising with a Walkman isn't terrible, but it's not the greatest. At my health club recently, I was bemused to see a lady who was not only on the stair-climber with a Walkman, but she then opened a book and started to read. I almost asked if she wanted to chew some gum, to see whether she could do four things at once.

Physical exercise is ideally its own reward. Still, I know many people who use workout exercise tapes or get on a stationary bike while watching television. It seems to work well for them, so there's probably no real harm.

Other activities where it's okay to double up include the following: walking and talking with a friend, taking notes as you listen to a lecture, and talking to your lover while you're having sex (depending on your partner, this can enhance the experience).

The Least You Need to Know

➤ The more often you can get into the habit of doing one thing at a time, the better you'll do.

➤ The most accomplished people in history acted with urgency, but they were not in a hurry—they didn't walk faster, talk faster, or try to speed up other bodily functions.

➤ If you've been multitasking for years, going cold turkey and handling one thing at a time may cause anxiety. This is natural; you'll have to ease into it.

➤ Practice doing one thing at a time. Promise yourself you'll go for 10 minutes on a task the first day, 15 the second, and so forth.

➤ Most of the areas where it's okay to double up on activities are outside the workplace.

➤ You don't need to be entertained as much as you think.

Part 5
Managing Your Time in Special Situations

You've come along way, baby—ahem…Ms. or Mr., as the case may be. Wouldn't it be nice to apply much of what you've learned thus far to the very personal aspects of your life? Well, I for one think it would be—and since I'm the one writing this tome, I have a wonderful assortment of chapters for you next. All focus on making time for each other—as in a partnership, having some kind of life when you're a parent, carving out real leisure in your life, and (would you believe it) even considering taking a sabbatical.

If you've been thinking, "It sure would be nice have some kind of home life," you'll probably want to get started immediately. Alternatively, if your first thought is, "What's a home life?", you, too, are an excellent candidate for gaining great insights from the chapters that follow. Either way, you're hooked.

Let's start with the premise that you have a significant other. How do you carve out some time to be with him or her? Read on.

Chapter 19

It Pays to Travel Light

In This Chapter

➤ Streamlining your life leads to great things

➤ Taking stock of your priorities in life, one at a time

➤ How to pare it all down a little each day

➤ Make your personal systems simpler

Now you're making hay. So far in Part 3, ("Communicating at All Speeds") you've learned how to make big decisions in record time (Chapter 17, "Decision Making: Step it Up and Go!") and the magic of doing one thing at a time (Chapter 18, "The Art of Concentration"). Now you're ready to learn about merging and purging—clearing out what you don't need so you can have more of a "life" each day.

Merging and purging files (and other things you're hanging on to) is more than good housekeeping; it's an emerging discipline among winners in society today. It's essential because even with all the new high-tech tools, paper will continue to mushroom for the foreseeable future. When I speak to groups, I tell them that once you let go of all that stuff you're holding onto, you will experience the same reward as a good garage cleaning or unblocking that backed-up plumbing will provide. Freedom!

Conquering the Pack Rat Syndrome

Consider all you encounter in the course of a day, week, month, and year: faxes, memos, reports, newspapers, newsletters, bulletins, magazines, bills, calendars, promotional items—and that's just the beginning. How would your life be if you merged and purged these items on a regular basis as they came into your life? Well, for one thing, you'd have far more time. Why? Because accumulations by nature rob you of your time. First you receive them, then put them somewhere, look at them, move them, attempt to arrange them, file some items, discard others, try in vain to find the items you need, and then put up your hands and say, "I can't win."

You know you're hanging onto too much stuff, and it's slowing you down. When are the best times to merge and purge what you've retained? Try these on for size:

➤ Anytime you approach a birthday is a good time, particularly a zero-year birthday. If you're about to hit 40, this is one of the great times in life to get rid of the stuff you no longer need. Age 30, age 50, and age 60 work as well.

➤ New Year's is a good time, especially if it's the change of a decade, such as the year 2010.

➤ Merge and purge right after you've filed your taxes. If you procrastinate (and a lot of people do when it comes to taxes), not to worry. After you've finished filing, there are all kinds of benefits awaiting. For one, you can get rid of most receipts and documents from the tax year three years prior to the one you've completed. The law says you have to hang on to the forms filed, but not the nitty-gritty details. (If you've been audited, or if you anticipate problems with the IRS, that's a different story.)

➤ Spring-cleaning has traditionally been a time for clearing out the old and making room for the new. The arrival of fall (toward the end of the summer around Labor Day) works as well.

➤ Merge and purge when you move. There's no sense in paying the movers to haul stuff to your new location that you're never going to use anyway.

➤ When you change jobs or careers, you'll have to clean out your old desk at work. That's usually a given.

➤ Passing one of life's milestones—the birth of a child, the death of a parent, graduation, retirement, getting a major raise, and anything on that order—can often serve as a reminder to re-examine what you're retaining. Rearrange your affairs to accommodate the new you.

➤ Any time the spirit moves you is a good time to merge and purge.

➤ As you finish reading this particular paragraph, put down the book and actually go ahead and merge and purge in some area of your life. Make it an easy win, something you can tackle and master in 10–15 minutes.

Breaking it All Down

When you don't feel in control of your time, everything in your life may seem as if it's running together into one big blur. Thus the easiest way to approach merging and purging is to examine the most important compartments of your life one at a time.

Examine your desk and what needs to be there, then your entire office, then where you live, your car, and other important areas of your life. Here are some suggestions:

➤ Do you have a file folder, a notebook, or a magazine box holder where you keep all travel-related materials? This might include booklets on hotel and air fares, frequent-flyer numbers, passports, numbers for taxis and other transportation, and vacation club folders. I keep such phone and membership numbers in one long file on my hard disk; a print-out in a small point size tucks into my portable appointment calendar. Wherever I am, day or night, I have the information I need.

I've maintained such a list for more than 12 years now, and no one has ever gotten hold of it. The power and efficiency it gives me is awesome. Whether I'm at an airport, in a taxi, at a hotel, or in a phone booth, I have all the phone numbers, membership numbers, card numbers, codes, and everything else I need to stay efficiently in motion. Is this a fabulous time-saver? (Major, major hint: The answer begins with "Y.")

➤ You can undertake the same type of exercise in merging and purging items at your desk when it comes to key service providers, records related to your automobile, insurance forms and policies, banking information, and other areas where efficiency matters. In all cases, it takes a little time to merge and purge what you've retained and get it into a streamlined, highly useable form. Once you do, watch out—your efficiency level will soar.

➤ The same maneuvers can be undertaken around your office. What can be consolidated, reduced, eliminated, relocated, or donated? Is your office configuration serving you best? Do you need to move things (knowing what you now know) to improve your daily efficiency? Can hard-copy items be scanned to see if they're now on disk and you no longer need the hard copy? If you have four stacking trays, can you reduce the number to three? Do you even need an in-basket anymore?

➤ At home, if you maintain a desk or any type of home office, reapply all these methods and go a step further. For example, could you use a 31-day tickler file in your home desk as well as the one you use in your office? If you use scheduling software at work, do you need to update your system at home?

Can you consolidate family-related records so that you're in greater control? For example, all of Johnny's documents related to grade-school enrollment, immunization, early-school-dismissal policy, and summer camp could be put in the same three-ring binder. All records related to your car (purchase documents, registration, tax information, inspections passed, repair records, special installations such as a CD player, and so on) could fit into one file.

A Stitch in Time

It's better to keep your car records in your home office if that's where you make phone calls and payments concerning your car. You can always keep a back-up of much of the documentation discussed here, buried someplace deep in your car's trunk.

Time Out!

If you're high on the prospect of streamlining your life, then you've got to think about paring a little at a time; there is no other way. You already have a full-time job and a raft of responsibilities.

A Stitch in Time

An easy way to organize lots of little items is to use individual envelopes, small plastic sandwich bags, or clear zip-lock baggies. This enables you to see what's inside and keeps the items dry and together.

➤ Your car is also an important area of your life and, based on what may have accumulated, requires merging and purging as well. Can you get all your credit cards, library cards, and the like into a secondary wallet to be hidden someplace in the car? I do this rather than carrying a wallet with 25 different cards in it. Why? Because at any given moment, the only cards I actually need are my driver's license, one ATM card, and one credit card.

Anytime I might use one of the other cards, I'm usually with my car. By safely stashing the cards I would only use with my car someplace within the car, I free myself from carrying all of them. This has several time-saving advantages. One, you're less likely to lose a majority of your cards if you lose your wallet. Two, it's far easier to find your license, major credit card, and ATM card if they are the only ones you carry in your wallet.

As a safeguard you might want to copy all your credit cards and library cards on a copier, and keep a backup sheet at home and hidden in your car. (If cars disappear frequently in your neighborhood, skip this one!)

➤ I also find it a great time-saver to have all my maps in one place, within reach while driving. I use side pockets built into the driver's-side and passenger's-side front doors. You may use your glove compartment, a compartment between your two front seats, the trunk, or whatever space you have. Essentials such as car registration and proof of ownership stay snug at the bottom of my glove compartment.

Half the trouble of staying in control of your time is staying in control of your possessions. Let's face it, there's so much you have to keep tabs on that merging and purging could almost be a full-time job. If you're willing to occasionally kill one Saturday morning getting these systems into place, you'll find that the payoffs come back to you over and over again.

Discard as You Go

Don't attempt to tackle all arenas of your life on the same Saturday morning. Not only will you not finish, but the process itself may scare you away for a year or more.

Try these ways to cut down a little at a time without breaking your stride:

➤ Anytime you're waiting for someone at work, at home, or in your car, use the extra few minutes to pare something where you are. If you have to drive your children around town a lot, after a few days you ought to have your car's glove compartment and trunk whipped into shape.

➤ When you've finished a big project at work and you're not ready to tackle some other major, intellectual pursuit at the moment, pare your holdings as a form of transition. For example, if you recently finished a big report, can you now delete previous versions on your hard disk? Can you get rid of rough drafts and notes that are no longer applicable (items you'll never use again)?

➤ If your plans go awry because it's raining, the bridge is out, or the plane has been delayed for an hour, pare. Despite the availability of all manner of electronic gadgetry on airplanes, I know high-powered executives who will have none of it. Their seats in airplanes, they tell me, are among the few sanctuaries they have. It's where they get to open their briefcases and impose some order, merging and purging, updating lists, chucking what's no longer necessary, and getting that little office-in-the-air back into shape.

➤ The same holds true if you commute by rail or bus. Use the tiny moments of the day to pare. Instead of lugging around whole issues of *Forbes*, *Business Week*, or *Working Woman*, fly through them like wildfire and extract only the articles that look relevant. Leave the rest for the next passenger, or drop them at the next recycling bin. Stay light.

The Red Tape Demon

A stifling array of government laws and regulations hampers business, allowing the United States to support 70 percent of the world's lawyers, says Barry Howard Minkin in *EconoQuake*. Thus, it becomes vitally important for you, a mere pawn in the game of laws and regulations, to keep your own systems as uncomplicated as possible. It won't be easy; there is a pervasive tendency among organizations and individuals to over-complicate their lives. You can see its effects every time you fill out your tax forms.

Are the forms getting any easier to fill out each year despite the IRS's long-term commitment to simplifying them, or are they getting more difficult? Have you bought any property recently? Are there more forms, or fewer? Without question, there are more. Some states now have double the number they had 10 years ago.

Time Out!

All too often in the business world, if you can create a new reporting form, you do. Thereafter, it becomes difficult to eliminate. If anything, such forms get longer, more complicated, and more time-intensive.

If you're an entrepreneur, or if you supervise others, think about the last time you tried to fire someone. Is it getting harder or easier from the standpoint of completing paperwork?

Your mission, if you decide to accept it, is to examine the forms you've created in your organization, department, or venture, and re-examine them. What can be eliminated? Here are some immediate benefits you might experience from eliminating a single form:

➤ Paper reduction: Less ordering, fewer costs, less receiving, less handling, and less storing

➤ Reduced printing and associated costs: Less retrieving, less printer use, less electricity, and lower cartridge and toner costs (or lower outside costs if purchased from a printer or forms vendor)

➤ Reduced need for storage: Less collecting, less transporting, less storage space used, less employee time used

➤ Reduced distribution costs and labor: Less retrieving, less disseminating

You're not the only one who'll benefit from the elimination of that form. Here's what you'll be doing for the people who used to have to fill it out.

➤ Less writing, less handling, less ink used to complete it

➤ Less walking, less faxing, and less mailing or e-mailing because there's no form to have to submit

Finally, there are benefits for the people who used to have to process the form:

➤ Collecting: Less walking, less opening mail, less handling faxes

➤ Compiling: Less sorting, less calculating, less totaling

➤ Reporting: Less writing, less presenting, less mental energy expended

"No" for an Answer: A Parable

I was called once by a marketing representative from a well-established investment company. Usually I listen to them for a minute and then find a polite way to end the conversation. This particular caller seemed to know his subject well, so I listened and even responded. He talked about his company's various investment options and told me that he could send a brochure listing the 35 different investment vehicles available, plus his company's annual report and prospectus.

214

"Wait a second," I told him, "I have no interest in reading about 35 different investment options. Please, do me and yourself a favor by boiling down your information to a single page. Then send a paragraph on the three options that you think would be best for me." I also told him I was not going to read his company's annual report, so there was no reason to send it.

If I liked what he sent me on the single page, I could always get the annual report at another time. I told him that while I'm an MBA, am certified as a management consultant, and have worked with hundreds of companies, "I'm not fond of reading prospectuses, so please don't send that either."

A Stitch in Time

Now would be an excellent time to sharpen up those skills you've learned for dealing with junk mail and managing your correspondence. Chapter 9, "Volunteering a Little Less—and Liking It," and Chapter 13, "Are You a Slave to Your Beeper?" will give you a refresher course.

At the end of our conversation, I repeated to him that I only needed to see a single page with the three investments he thought were best for me—and perhaps one slim brochure about his company.

Several days passed, and I forgot about the call. When Monday's mail came, I noticed a thick package from his investment house. I cringed. I opened it, and voilà: a brochure on the 35 investment vehicles, an annual and a quarterly report, the company's thick prospectus, and other useless brochures and fliers. I grabbed the pile and tried to rip the whole thing with one flick of my wrists, but it was too thick. I tossed it and (rest assured) did not become a client.

If that broker had sent me what I asked for, who knows—I might have made his day.

Paper Reduction as an Art Form

Here's an artist with vision to not over-paper society. While most artists consider the destruction of their work a tragedy, as reported in *Time* magazine, photographer Brett Weston always considered it a necessity. Best known for haunting semiabstract nature studies in the tradition of his famous father Edward, Weston vowed for years to destroy his negatives so that others could not make new prints from them after his death. On his 80th birthday, Weston kept his vow. Surrounded by friends and family, he tossed hundreds of negatives into the living-room fireplace of his home in Carmel, Calif. Art historians and photography curators were horrified. The Center for Creative Photography, a photographic archive in Tucson, even sent a representative to Weston's home in an unsuccessful effort to persuade him to change his mind. Weston insisted that he was merely limiting his legacy to work fashioned by his own hand. "Nobody can print it the way I do," Weston explained. "It wouldn't be my work."

Keep Only What You Use: The Replacement Principle

When you boil it down, uncomplicating your own systems is synonymous with getting into a replacement mode. When you take in something new, something else has to go. Table 16.1 offers some everyday examples of non-replacement policies (left column) contrasted with replacement policies (right column).

Table 19.1 The Replacement Principle

Non-Replacement Policies	Replacement Policy
Your child's collection of videos grows to beyond 50 as you buy or copy the classic and latest hits.	You decide with your child in advance on a total number of videos (s)he can have. Each new one means replacing an old one.
Your file cabinet keeps growing until you need to buy another.	Your files stay the same size; for each item you add, you discard one.
You keep old equipment in closets and storage bins, thinking it'll come in handy.	As soon as you buy new equipment, you donate the old equipment to a charity and get a tax deduction.
You've collected books for years and now have no hope of reading what's on the overflowing shelves.	You retain only books of continuing or sentimental value, scanning or copying key pages of most of the rest, then giving them away.
You have a 6.2 gigabyte hard disk, and are considering getting more disk space.	You don't need more disk space be-cause you prune your disk of outdated files at least once a month.
You have an unread collection of annual reports and other items from investment houses.	An investment firm sends you an annual report; right away you replace last year's.
Your clothes drawers and closets are filled with items you haven't worn in years.	There's plenty of space in the house for clothes you actually use; you give the rest to charities.
Your record collection spans many shelves and is covered with dust; you hardly ever play them.	You sell, trash, or donate those LPs and buy a few "greatest hits" CDs you know you will play and enjoy.

If you're not constantly reducing what you hold onto, you're at the mercy of an era that keeps throwing more at you than you can respond to. Seize control of your time—merge and purge and then go splurge!

The Least You Need to Know

➤ Merging and purging what you're retaining is an emerging discipline among winners in society today.

➤ The best times to pare are a birthday, a change of year or season, one of life's milestones, or anytime you have the spirit to do so.

➤ Pare a little at a time; biting off too much may tempt you to think the situation is hopeless, when it's not.

➤ Examine your work environment to determine what forms can be eliminated. It all counts.

➤ Uncomplicate your own systems by not volunteering to be inundated by junk mail and irrelevant stuff; rely on the replacement principle.

Chapter 20

Time for Each Other

In This Chapter

➤ Being connected takes cooperation

➤ Exhaustion overrules vibrant relationships

➤ Men have needs, too

➤ Making your relationship Job One

Jacqueline Taylor, age 42 and name disguised, is the new chief executive officer of a manufacturing company that produces home security devices. Her responsibilities include heading four divisions, managing six affiliates, maximizing shareholder value, reporting to the board of directors, and keeping the operations profitable. It's her core belief that the primary way to manage your time most efficiently is to stay completely focused on what you want to accomplish.

An Orderly Existence

Taylor begins work the moment she rises, which is 6:15 sharp every morning. She's already mapped out the night before what she'll tackle that morning. She spends the first three hours at home, then proceeds into the office for a 9:15 arrival. She departs from work at the end of the day when she feels satisfied with what she's accomplished. This could be anywhere from 7 p.m. to 10 p.m.

In Command and on Course

"I am passionate about my work," she says, "and ruthless about how I allocate my time. If somebody wants to present a plan that is not in alignment with my objectives, I don't devote a second to it. I steer them in another direction, don't schedule a meeting with them, and don't give them any encouragement."

"I can't remember the last time I had a business lunch, because in my mind, they take too huge a chunk out of the middle of your day. Most times, I have a salad and a slice of pizza, or a bowl of soup right in my office. Of course, there are important reasons for connecting with others. I'm not saying that networking is trivial. So I schedule to meet people occasionally for a light dinner after work, or for tea or coffee after that."

Ms. Taylor, as you might have guessed by now, has never been married and does not have children. By the standards of most, she also has no social life. She doesn't do errands, she doesn't shop, and she doesn't cook. There's practically no food in her kitchen, and if anybody ever dropped by—although nobody ever would—she'd have nothing to offer them.

She's got a routine worked out that maximizes her time—one that's become comfortable for her. (It wouldn't work for most of us, however.) For us, there are other people, other interests, and other demands beyond our jobs. In this chapter you'll learn how to make certain that you have the time you need to accommodate all aspects of your life. In particular, we'll address the dynamics of couples—married or not, with children or not—and discuss how they can carve out some time for each other. In the chapter that follows, we'll tackle the more involved notion of carving out time while maintaining effective parenting. Focusing on the traditional man-wife couple, let's first consider common elements of the woman's perspective.

If You Live Alone, Time Management Is Relatively Easy

It's relatively easy to manage your time if you choose to live the existence Ms. Taylor lives: no significant other to converse with, make plans with, or accommodate. Sure, you'll face your work and domestic challenges, but by comparison to those who have a meaningful relationship with someone else, managing one's time is far less of an issue.

Being Connected with Others Takes Work

Let's talk turkey. By that, I mean the realities of having a relationship with a significant other. Couples who have a tight relationship continually put energy and effort into it. It doesn't seem to happen by chance, although some blessed individuals have personal

220

chemistry that seems to jibe with one another to the nth degree. Even among those lucky couples however, if you were to stop and analyze their day-to-day and moment-to-moment communication patterns, you'd see that there's a high degree of listening, cooperation, and respect for one another's schedules.

The Allure of Work

Most women today hold a job outside the home in addition to maintaining the brunt of household responsibilities. Studies show that although they're not likely to 'fess up to it flat out, many women would rather be at work than at home.

Sociologist Veronica Tichenor from the University of Michigan says that women are actually putting in longer hours at the office than ever "because they enjoy it." Yet, no matter how many hours they put in and how much money they make, they're still doing most of the housework because they want to or feel they have to. This includes even top female executives.

It seems that by the mid '90s, both men and women discovered that work does have its appeal.

Part of the appeal of work is that there are indicators nearly every step of the way to let you know if you're on track, meeting the quota, or turning a profit. You get evaluations, you get performance appraisals, you get raises, you get promotions. What corollary is there in your home life? How do you know when you're a good partner, spouse, or lover?

What You Need Is a Wife

Some working women come to the conclusion that they would have a wonderful life if they had the equivalent of a "traditional wife" who stayed at home, kept the house in order, took care of the kids, cooked the meals, and handled all the errands. This is only an alternative for the ultra-rich; however, most women still do the housework, no matter how demanding or exhausting their work might be.

Many women confided to Tichenor that regardless of their achievements in the workplace, they still feel a strange and strong need to be regarded as excellent home-makers. If you're a woman, you probably already know and feel this on many levels. If you're a man, I hope you read this section closely, because it's going to be the key to your carving out time for one another.

Chronos Says

"A woman's responsibility for her family is a 24-hour task. Her time plan is a plan for living. There must be time allowance for the necessary work of the household, such as food preparation, serving, cleaning, and laundering. Family obligations, however, do not cease with the completion of the technical work of the home. There are children to be trained, supervised and enjoyed; the interests and activities of other adults in the family group must be shared; time for civic interests as well as for social activities and obligations must enter into the larger concept of time management for the housewife."—Irma Gross and Mary Lewis, *Home Management* (1938).

Many women fall into this syndrome, but as Irma Gross and Mary Lewis recounted back in 1938 in the book *Home Management*, "...the wise homemaker still will not let the interests listed above make such inroads upon her time as to unbalance her living in terms of health and personal development." They recommend that there be "time for rest, sleep, recreation and hospitality, together with sufficient leisure to pursue some phase of living that will keep her emotionally stable and intellectually alert."

Stamped into Their Souls

This 1938 book admonished its female readers that if their housekeeping was too disorganized, it could "interfere with the development of the various members of the family and their happiness of association."

From this—and a ton of other books and studies one could dredge up from 1938, before, and even after—it's easy to see why women have an ingrained notion that they have sole responsibility for the utter and complete management of the household. And while they appreciate any help others provide, regardless of what else is going on in their life, they often regard the state of their home as akin to the state of their being. (Guys, are you reading closely?)

A Little Cheating Never Hurts

In recent years, particularly among executive women, there's been movement towards maintaining outside services to help manage the household. Among those who can afford it, there's less reticence to bringing in a nanny, a cleaning crew, a gardener, a window-washer, and various delivery services. Women today buy prepared food for a dinner party, whereas in previous years they'd never think of it.

You already know my view on using outside services! Use them to the max! Where is it written that your guests will leave unsatisfied because your food was catered rather than personally prepared by you? Come on! Where is it written that paying someone else to take care of a task you'd prefer not to do, and to free up hours for you in which you could earn more per hour than the person you're paying, is somehow unholy?

Take Your Pick: Me or the Rest of the World

In 1990, when I was writing my 18th book, *Breathing Space: Living and Working at a Comfortable Pace in a Sped Up Society*, I made the strong suggestion that the crunch of too many things competing for one's time and attention was actually keeping couples apart from one another. Now, a decade later, it's abundantly clear that that's the case!

All the tasks, attention-diverters, and stimuli in your external environment, all but guarantee that you'll have nothing left for your partner. You can be physically there, you can talk the talk, and you can go through the motions, and you can even semi-deceive yourself that you're succeeding.

To be *there*, however, in a physical, mental, and emotional sense, and to offer the complete essence of your being, requires that you begin to disengage from the mountains of minutia that are already over-complicating and glutting the lives of most adults in society.

Overwhelmed and Emotionally Spent

The highest divorce rates on earth are generally in the more complex, technically sophisticated societies. It doesn't take some enchanted reasoning to understand that the nuances of what it takes to fan the flames of a relationship can't be given short shrift. It can't be afforded only the remnants of what's left of you after the over-information society has buffeted you for yet another day.

A Stitch in Time

If you're in a committed relationship, every time you accomplish something through delegation, through reliance upon the services and efforts of others, you potentially free yourself up on both a physical and emotional realm to be more of a partner to your partner. Got that, pardner?

Time Out!

Do you really want to be with anyone when you're exhausted? Do you want to be with a partner who's exhausted? If you're both exhausted, will that be of value to either of you?

Anyone for a Deck Chair?

Taking traditional and minuscule measures to free up some of your time and being, such as occasionally retaining outside help, is like rearranging deck chairs on the *Titanic*. It's been a while since you had meaningful time for and with each other, and if you feel the integrity of your relationship slowly starting to unravel—and if you value your relationship highly—to stay with the sea analogy, it's time to launch all ships.

➤ Delegate any task you possibly can.

➤ Let go of perfectionistic standards that keep you mopping floors when you should be making love.

➤ Carve out at least a few minutes of uninterrupted time for each other every day—and several hours every weekend.

➤ Ask for help.

➤ Turn off the TV an hour earlier than normal, or don't turn it on to begin with.

➤ Schedule dates on your calendar.

➤ If both of your jobs allow for it, schedule unhurried lunches.

➤ Take 10-minute walks together after dinner.

➤ Leave nice notes around the house.

➤ Read a joke book together.

Men and Relationships

In many ways, the 1990s was a decade of male-bashing. Males were seen as:

➤ Neanderthals

➤ Hot-blooded animals

➤ Uncouth detractors of society

➤ War-mongers

➤ Pumped-up athletes

➤ Exploiters of women

➤ Child-support deadbeats

➤ All of the above

In some circles, including male circles, men are regarded as the fundamental reason why societies are breaking down. After all, men aren't interested in relationships, raising children, or staying for the long haul. Men have a good time and then they leave. Let's face it, you can't trust men. If you find one you can trust, you're among the lucky few.

What About My Needs?

The problem with the above kind of banter, beyond the obvious, is that it presupposes that an entire sex is wrong! From an evolutionary, biological, and cosmic perspective, how can a sex be wrong? Men have needs, men have aspirations, men have desires. A man in a relationship has needs, aspirations, and desires.

Seeing Each Other Anew

I had the opportunity to counsel three couples as part of a feature story to be run on the front page of the *USA Today* lifestyle section. One of the couples was a minister and wife. The wife lamented that with the growing congregation the minister tended to, she had less and less time to spend with him. Even Friday and Saturday evenings, which traditionally had been date nights for them, were now taken up by the minister's routine visits to sick or hospitalized members of the congregation.

Most of the minister's visits lasted only 20 minutes, but by the time he got back, the magic of the evening was on the wane. I suggested a tactic to them that they found to be curious but rich with potential.

A Stitch in Time

Whether you've been in your primary relationship for 10 years or more, or 10 weeks, a quintessential activity in making the relationship work and carving out time for each other is to look anew at your partner, to see what it would take to connect with and be with your partner on the highest level.

A Return to Date Night

Hereafter, she would accompany him in the car on Friday and Saturday evenings whenever he called upon the sick. Because most of his visits were 18–20 minutes in length, she could literally sit in the car and read a magazine or listen to the radio or tape player while he made his visit. When he was through and got back into the car, they were both there, dressed and ready to go. The night was still young and held great potential.

I caught up with them several months after they put this plan into practice. It worked from the first Friday evening on.

Seeing Hidden Opportunities

By examining the responsibilities and activities of your partner, actually comparing calendars, and applying a high dose of creative thinking, you may surprise yourself as to the amount and quality of time you can carve out for one another.

I had a girlfriend who was studying for the CPA exam. Her preferred method of studying was to go to a university library, with all her books and paraphernalia and a few snacks. She'd find a big table in the corner and camp out for hours. In the past, this was a lonely if necessary undertaking for her. Few of her previous boyfriends found this to be enticing. I, on the other hand, thought this was pretty close to heaven. I was always working on new outlines for speeches and researching for books and articles.

Oh, what fun to be able to go to the library with someone who was equally intent on getting a whale of a lot of work done, while being together. We would work for 50 minutes and then take 10-minute breaks walking and talking. Then we'd get back to work and repeat the process. When it was done, we'd go out for pizza. I got more done during those sessions than I'd ever have imagined. She passed her CPA exam, on her first try!

The Relationship Is Job One

Everything discussed in this chapter thus far leads to the fundamental notion that, for a relationship to work in these harried times, it must be the most important element in each partner's life. If the relationship comes in second to work, chances are that the vibrancy of the relationship will dwindle.

Uh-Oh for Gung-Ho's?

If you're a gung-ho, world-beating, career-climbing overachiever, this doesn't mean you have to mute any of your goals or aspirations, or be something you weren't intending to be. Plot your career strategy in the context of being in a committed relationship. This will work, and by jove, the most successful people on the planet routinely have strong and committed relationships. It's no coincidence. They draw strength and sustenance from this relationship. Many report that it actually gives them a sense of freedom.

Conceived in Heaven, Actualized on Earth

What are the hallmarks of a relationship in which couples steadfastly make time for each other without ignoring the other aspects of their lives? Foremost is respect for each other. During the early part of a relationship, when you're in rapture with one another, it's easy to show high levels of respect. After all, you're practically bending over backward to be on your best behavior.

Once the initial rush is past (or the honeymoon is over)—and for some people this can be 18–24 months or longer,—many partners begin taking each other for granted. This is so even if one had sought the right relationship for years!

Here are some ideas on how respect is played out among couples who intend to make time for each other:

➤ When some time opens up for one partner, the other partner is immediately called to see if there's a match in terms of available time with each other. The relationship continues to come first.

➤ They go out of their way to ensure that they understand one another. They talk, debate, or argue until they've cleared up an issue. They don't broad-brush over differences, but work toward an understanding. The longer they are together as a couple, the more adept they become at this.

A Stitch in Time

Try what other successful couples do at close of day: Each recaps what the other did that was particularly pleasing. "I greatly appreciated your coming to the office to drop off the package." Or, "I like the way you cheered me up when nothing seemed to be going right for me earlier today."

➤ They continually validate each other, telling each other what they appreciate about one another, finding the good in one another, and positively reinforcing one another as often as they can.

➤ All the while, they acknowledge and recognize each other for the little things that each of them does. They also express their appreciation in no uncertain terms.

➤ They are reassuring to one another. They have learned to accept each other's weaknesses. They know that no partner comes without weaknesses, and while it's easy to love the facets about someone else that please us, accepting the whole person is a much more challenging task.

➤ They're devoted to one another. They don't allow other people to come between them; in fact, when approached by outside potential partners, they end that relationship and then report the occurrence to their mate.

➤ They convey a strong sense of caring. They leave notes to each other all over the place. They send e-mail messages, leave phone messages, and leave unannounced, small gifts in odd locations so that the partner encounters them when it's least expected.

Time Out!

Do you know anyone who professes to be in a committed relationship but in reality has given it short shrift? Take a good, honest look at yourself—if this description fits you, it's time to reorganize your priorities before your relationship is damaged.

➤ They recognize that no matter how busy they are with their careers and other activities, keeping the relationship alive takes work. Each is committed to devoting the time and energy to keep their relationship alive, and each partner knows it.

Notice how, in this roster, winning couples carve out time and attention for each other almost automatically as they proceed each day. So, when the relationship is foremost in each of the partner's lives, time for each other materializes in ways that doesn't happen for couples who knowingly or unknowingly assign secondary status to their relationship.

A Potpourri for Thee

If you're convinced that you can make time for each other and you're ready for action, here's a potpourri of strategies and techniques to get your relationship back on to the high road.

Calling All Baby-Sitters

Start calling everyone in the local community shopper newspaper who advertises baby-sitting services. Also post your own ads. Your assignment is to develop a roster of 8–10 baby-sitters in the local area so that you're never at a loss for one when you need one. Also enlist grandparents, relatives, and anyone nearby who could possibly serve in the same capacity. You don't want your relationship and indeed social life to hinge upon your ability to get a baby-sitter on any given evening. That would be dreadful. You want to comfortably be able to rely on a bevy of baby-sitters should you and your spouse feel the need to take the night off.

One Fine Day: Pick an Evening

Set aside one night per week as a mini-date night. This could be having a light workout together, cooking on the grill, strolling through a mall, playing Scrabble or cards, or anything other than watching television or a movie (too much focus on the screen and not on each other).

While the Kids Are Enrolled

If you have children—the topic of the next chapter—plan to have time together while your kids are attending various classes or activities. Plan to drop them off together, spend the first few minutes seeing what they're doing, then taking off for a walk or whatever, and coming back to be with them for the last few minutes as well.

Encounter an Encounter Group

Investigate some of the local marriage encounter groups popping up in many areas. These are usually weekend affairs in which you're able to forge stronger marital bonds through improved communication and understanding.

One couple commented that these encounters offer a safe, relaxing, pensive atmosphere that enables couples to talk quietly and privately to each other about their lives and relationship. Neither partner has to feel lonely or bored, and these weekends help to revive the spark and romance.

Bed Down at a Bed and Breakfast

Married with children or not, head for a bed and breakfast every couple months to renew your spirits. Such lodgings are available in almost every county throughout the country. They usually charge less per night than a hotel and offer quieter, more intimate surroundings.

Accent the Little Things

Many family therapists agree that having mom and dad head off for a weekend to have some time together is actually healthy for children. Kids need to know that their mom and dad can have fun together, without them.

If you simply can't get away, or don't want to, make a big deal out of walking by the lake, playing some favorite songs, having a picnic in the backyard, thumbing through your photo albums, going to brunch at that four-star hotel, or even making something together such as furniture.

Rediscover the Holidays

The next time Valentine's Day, Memorial Day, or even Columbus Day rolls around, rediscover the fun you had as a kid, and share it with your significant other. On Valentine's Day, cut out hearts and creatively inscribe them. On Memorial Day, visit a grave site, a historical place, or a monument to those who made the ultimate sacrifice. On Columbus Day, or any other of the lesser-celebrated holidays, get into the spirit of what originally made that day special.

Time Out

Don't knock marriage encounter groups until you've tried them. Couples who attend say that the experience has been rejuvenating for their relationship or marriage.

A Stitch in Time

Traditions between couples and within families are often under-rated. By making the most out of recognizable dates on the calendar, you establish the potential to do it again and again.

Establish Non-holiday Family Traditions

Don't just celebrate birthdays, *celebrate birthdays*! Also, do something very special for your anniversary, or the anniversary of the initiation of your relationship, the anniversaries of graduations, promotions, relocations, and special achievements in each of your lives. Mark these on both your calendars way in advance, so there's sufficient notice that these special occasions will be treated as such.

Chronos Says

Joe Jeff Goldblatt, Ph.D., is Dean of George Washington University's Graduate Program in Special Events. Goldblatt says, "Life is a special event." To truly have time for each other, celebrate all the special events you can in your lives.

Only for the Brave

Here is a strategy that's certainly not for everyone, but it's worth mentioning. According to the U.S. Small Business Administration, a husband and wife are co-owners or have roughly equal roles in directing operations in 800,000 small companies throughout the United States. For such couples, their marriage and their business become the cornerstones of their lives.

Most couples in such arrangements agree that while starting and flourishing within a business is difficult, it's that much more difficult when your spouse is your equal partner. Hence, you learn to compromise quickly, communicate on the highest of levels, drive over the road blocks, and move on.

Upping the Stakes

It's even more challenging if you run the business out of your home. Nevertheless, for some couples, this is just what the relationship doctor ordered. It's okay if your business is 90 percent of your lives, just as long as you don't make it 100 percent. Couples who successfully operate businesses learn to create boundaries for themselves, develop outside interests, and establish independent identities however often they are together throughout the week.

One business counselor denotes that such couples can create unwritten but highly effective operating guidelines that enable their relationship to flourish despite the additional challenges they assume in running a business.

On the Fly

Many couples in love and in business prefer, however, to simply deal with what comes up on the fly. The ebb and flow of being in a relationship and making a go of a business venture requires a high degree of flexibility. One entrepreneur confesses that if he and his spouse would have to write everything down between them, their business would come to a standstill.

If such an arrangement sounds a little risky, take heart. I know more than a dozen couples involved in their own business venture, and all are doing quite well. In fact, in most cases, the success of the business far exceeds what either one of them could have achieved on their own. With business success comes profits, and from that often comes the ability to travel, buy creature comforts, and endow each other in special ways.

Who knows? You might like it.

The Least You Need to Know

➤ If you're alone, it's relatively easy to manage your time.

➤ Most women today hold a job outside the home in addition to maintaining the brunt of household responsibilities. Many accept domestic help when offered but still want to stay in control.

➤ As a potentially successful partner to another person, are you willing to learn about your partner's needs, aspirations, and desires? To what degree are you willing to meet them?

➤ Hidden opportunities to be together exist no matter what workload one or both partners face.

➤ Celebrate the occasions in your lives, big and small, at every opportunity.

Chapter 21

Tips for Parents

In This Chapter

➤ The family in flux

➤ Good parenting means sacrifice

➤ How fathers can pick up some slack

➤ Planning for family events

No institution in our society has undergone such rapid transformation in the past two to three decades as has the family. In the early 1900s, four out of five households included children. Today, only one in three households have children. Amazingly, half of all households are comprised of families that have no children under age 18, all of which means that fewer adults today are involved in parenting than any time in this century.

Concurrently, more than 50 percent of all children will spend some time during their upbringing in a single-parent home. One child out of three is born to an unmarried mother—and among African-American children, two children out of three are born to an unmarried mother. Married or not, most mothers are now employed. Most families require two incomes to reach their desired standard of living, thus putting single-parent families in financial straits.

Finally, divorce rates in America continue on at about 50 percent of all marriages, and the likelihood of divorce increases with each remarriage. It has been estimated that less than 7 percent of the population represents the traditional, intact, two-parent family for at least the years until the child or children are age 18. With fewer adults involved in parenting comes an increased resistance to support services and programs designed to help children.

Against this backdrop, is it any wonder that being a parent today is potentially more challenging than in previous generations? In this chapter you'll learn tips for managing your time despite the daily obstacles you may face.

Chronos Says

"It's hard enough today just defining the family, let alone capturing its needs or trying to meet them.... What are the boundaries of the family? Who is in and who is out? When does a family start—at cohabitation, at marriage, or at parenthood? When does it end—at separation, at divorce, at remarriage, or at death? And how does it normally progress, with or without parenthood or with or without living together?"—Dennis K. Orthner, *Parks and Recreation*, March 1998

The Times They Are A-Changin'

The *Times Picayune,* based in New Orleans, asked parents to call in their suggestions for keeping the flame burning amidst the stress and pressure of child-rearing. A staff writer reported, "We received a whopping five phone calls, two e-mails, and one letter—a far cry from the plethora of responses we typically receive on other parenting issues. The lackluster reaction to our question—which we asked three times—tells us one of two things: either couples didn't want to share the intimate details of their love lives or, worse, there were no details to share. Given the hurried lifestyles of today's families, I'd guess the latter."

If you're parents of newborns, it's almost a given that for the first two or three years, you'll be sacrificing your time and body in devotion to your baby. Some couples have an arrangement where one keeps working outside the home, while one becomes the primary caregiver, usually the woman, but in a growing number of cases, also the man.

The key to effective parenting and to maintaining control of your time is essentially to sacrifice yourself for roughly the first three years so that your child is reared in a wholesome, nurturing, reinforcing atmosphere. This affords you the greatest opportunity for raising a brighter, more alert, healthier child. Fortunately, the things that good parents traditionally have done to raise their children remain relatively the same.

➤ Read to your child.

➤ Hug, cradle, and comfort your child (especially important).

➤ Nurture your child in every way, by talking, playing, or just noticing what he or she is doing.

Bucking the Stereotype

One of the heartening developments of parenthood in the last decade or so is the trend among some yuppie-age fathers to become more involved in their children's lives. One St. Louis-based accountant commented, "It's a wonderful thing to be able to see your own children grow up." Many surveys now indicate that young fathers value being fathers as much as anything else in their lives and careers.

Table 21.1: What Men Want

84 percent	Being a good father
74 percent	Having a close spousal partnership
67 percent	Being healthy and fit
53 percent	Being socially responsible
52 percent	Achieving balance with work, family, and social life
47 percent	Having good friends
30 percent	Making good money
27 percent	Career advancement

Source: Consumer Survey Center Poll, conducted for Slates/Levi Strauss August 1996

Why this movement arose is not abundantly clear. It may be because of the increases in divorce, the rise of dual-career marriages, or perhaps the fact that many fathers didn't have the kind of relationship with their own father that they had hoped for during their childhood.

Some psychologists and sociologists believe that the woman's movement has had much to do with the expanded roles that some men now play in the lives of their children. Regardless of the underpinnings, the trend is a healthy one and appears to be picking up steam.

Concentrate on Your Children

Whether your child is 3 or 13, there's a common denominator to ensuring that you're most effective as a parent: offering your attention. Offering your complete attention also helps to make most effective use of time you have together.

The Future Starts Here

Giving your complete attention to your child sets up future scenarios in which your child will feel confident and at ease when you're not around. He or she begins to learn that sometimes Mommy or Daddy has important things to do and hence can't give them any attention. But, when Mommy or Daddy does give them attention, it's complete and undivided.

If you want to raise an insecure and unconfident child, stay preoccupied all the time whenever you're with your child. That'll do the trick in a hurry.

Kids Learn Around the Clock

How are you when you're not playing with your kids but doing something else that sends them messages? How about the way you serve dinner?

➤ Do you start and stop?

➤ Do you talk on the phone?

➤ Do you go upstairs to do something?

➤ Do you pull clothes out of the laundry?

Now here's a more probing question. Would you act like that in front of company? If not, then why do you do so in front of your kids? The message that you're giving your children is that there's so much to do in life that you can't keep up if you simply sit there at the table with them. That, in turn, tells your children that such an existence will be theirs as well.

Chronos Says

If there's one part of the day when you want to be sure to give your children undivided attention, make it dinner. Serve them, and then sit with them for the whole time. Talk to them, just like in the old days, as your parents did for you or, if that's not the case, the way their parents did for them. Give them a strong, clear message that the pace of the world has little effect on your family's ability to have a complete, engaging dinner with one another.

The Over-Activity Trap

You hear it all the time—one parent talking to another about little Josie's spate of activities. She takes karate lessons, is on the soccer team, plays piano, and has a big part in the school play. Jason's on the tennis team, is taking trombone lessons, is a traffic monitor early mornings at school, and is on the student council.

I Overdo it, Therefore I Am

Increasingly, we transmit our predisposition toward over-engaging in activities to our children. It's not enough to be a kid anymore, to do your homework, get good grades, have some friends, and leave it at that. Too many children of yuppie parents have become yuppie juniors. They're occupied every moment of the day, are in a frenzy to get what's next, and have little time to reflect, or to be a kid.

A quick, but not easy, way to carve out more time for your children as well as for yourself (because you're usually the one schlepping them all over creation) is to help them decide which highly desirable, enjoyable, fun-filled activity they will *not* engage in for at least the current season. So they belong to one less team, or so they don't take such-and-such lessons for this fall. Is the quality of their life likely to diminish? Of course not! If anything, it may improve.

Chronos Says

A study at Cornell University found that children from birth to age 18 spend an average of 7.5 hours per day with both parents when the father works outside the home and the mother does not. This is only 23 minutes more per day than the children of mothers who work outside the home during the child-rearing years. The study also indicated that men whose wives work outside the home offered 40 percent of the parenting responsibilities compared to 35 percent for those men whose wives stayed home. In other words, whether the wife works outside the home or not, the men's parenting responsibilities were nearly the same!

Kids Need Balance, too

Where is it written that a kid is supposed to become fully accomplished in all manner of endeavors by such-and-such an age?

I'm not knocking the value of engaging in activities that one enjoys, that will make one more effective as a human being, and that serve others. Nor am I pooh-poohing the value of having a child learn something that he or she may not otherwise have gravitated to on his own/her own. I'm talking about the fine balance between engaging in some activities and being over-booked. You know exactly what I'm talking about!

Balanced Parent, Balanced Kid

While we're on the topic of helping your children to reduce scheduled activities, how about cutting back on some of your own? Are you the little league coach, the scout master, and the fund drive chair? Are you doing more for your community than for your kids? What's behind your over-volunteerism? Are you feeling that you're not whole and not complete? Do you have the erroneous notion that others are keeping score?

Noontime Isn't for Lunch Anymore

One of the not-so-sly ways that men and women are taking care of personal business at work so they can free up more time when they're headed home is to eat lunch before or after lunch at their desk, and use the lunch hour to take care of errands. Many parents and women in particular are banking, shopping, visiting the dry cleaners, and taking care of other errands in the middle of the work day.

A Stitch in Time

The U.S. Bureau of Labor Statistic indicates that married couples with children under 18 where the husband is the only income-earner represent 8 percent of the United States population. So, for all you working parents out there, here's a motto: Do what you can, when you can, as best you can—and then you get somebody else to do the rest.

Rather than lamenting how little time they have to be with their children, many parents are opting to upgrade the quality of the time that is available, and taking care of errands at lunch supports that cause. As a result of what I call creative time-shifting, many parents are actually able to spend as much time with their children as those who do not work outside the household.

Recognize the value of enjoying a leisurely lunch break on some days, and saving yourself some precious time by running a few pressing errands on other days. Either way, you're reducing the possibility of getting short-changed during your day.

Getting the Kids to Pitch in

A growing number of parents, particularly women, find that effective parenting today hinges on your ability to get your kids to pitch in with chores in one form or another. At the least, kids need to be responsible for keeping their own room orderly. From about age 6 on, this should be an everyday habit. Until then, you'll probably have to help them.

Since my little girl, Valerie (now age 8), was 3 years old, we've practiced what I call the replacement principle, which we present in Chapter 19, "It Pays to Travel Light."

In a nutshell, whatever you add to the room merits one other thing being removed. Add a new video? Sure. Which one do you want give up?

What a Combination: Kids and Homework

Harris Cooper, professor of psychology at the University of Missouri, says, "I'm discovering that there's a growing variation in the amount of homework. In general, it seems it has become necessary to motivate students to do homework. In addition to the whirlwind of social, cultural, and sports activities, many children aren't receiving the proper parental support when it comes to homework. Among those children of parents who both work, either the parents are too pooped to help, or feel guilty and give the child too much assistance—and end up doing most of the homework."

Your role as parent? To encourage your child to do his or her own homework in a timely manner as it's assigned. To help out when needed, but not to end up doing the homework.

Chronos Says

As a rough guideline, about 15–20 minutes of homework per day is appropriate for children up to grade 2, about 30–60 minutes a day for grades 3–6, and up to two hours for junior high. In high school, assignments can vary widely, but beyond three hours may tax even the most ambitious students.

For all the blabbering about homework in the United States, in comparison with Europe and Asia, American children have it made in the shade. A 1991 study conducted by the U.S. Department of Education of 13-year-olds indicated that American kids actually do less homework than their counterparts in other countries. Only 31 percent of kids in the United States have more than two hours of homework daily. This contrasts with other countries as listed here:

Table 21.3: Homework: U.S. Kids Versus the World

United States	31 percent
Taiwan	44 percent
Former Soviet Union	52 percent
France	55 percent
Spain	62 percent
Ireland	66 percent

The same 1991 study conducted by the U.S. Department of Education revealed that 22 percent of children in the United States watch five or more hours of television daily. This compares unfavorably to other countries:

Table 21.4: Watching Television: U.S. Kids Versus the World

United States	22 percent
Former Soviet Union	19 percent
Spain	11 percent
Ireland	9 percent
France	4 percent

Encouraging Johnny to Compete Academically

When it comes to helping your children with their homework, here are some effective guidelines:

➤ Set a regular time every day when homework is expected to be done. Also establish ground rules as to what takes place during this time. For example, no television sets, CDs, or other forms of electronic intrusion shall invade the homework place.

A Stitch in Time

Research shows that behavior that's rewarded is repeated. If you want to get your children into the habit of doing homework and doing it well, frequently reward them for the good behavior that they exhibit—and, preferably, directly after they exhibit it.

➤ If you haven't already done so, set aside a desk or table in one of the rooms in your home so that your children will have a regular place in which to do homework. Assemble supplies such as pen and pencils, magic markers, crayons, scissors, rulers, note pads, dictionaries, and anything else the child will need to do his or her homework and to know that you are fully supporting his or her efforts.

➤ Be available to offer helpful suggestions and guidance, but as mentioned, do not do your child's homework. Give clues so that your child proceeds down the right path without actually giving the answer.

➤ Offer lavish praise when a child has completed a difficult math problem or has written a nifty book report.

The False Lure of PCs

Don't suspect for a minute that having a computer in your child's life will enhance his or her ability to do homework, or to have a more rewarding childhood experience. Make sure your child knows the basics first.

"Rather than take over kids' lives, computers should add a new dimension," says Barbara Bowman, president of the Erikson Institute for Advanced Study in Child Development based in Chicago, Illinois. A program on animals, for example, is much more meaningful if your children have already visited a zoo or petting farm. Don't allow a virtual experience to be the substitute for a real experience.

If your child is old enough to be doing homework on his or her computer, that's a different story. Writing papers, doing research, and solving problems can all be enhanced by a computer. Obviously, you run the risk of having the child use the computer for anything but homework, so it's important to provide some periodic monitoring.

Connecting with Your Kids on a Higher Level

Homework or not, raising bright, happy, well-rounded kids requires effective communication, much like having a rewarding marriage or primary relationship. In a survey conducted by Roper Starch Worldwide, the following rather dismal data was generated among parents of students ages 10–14:

➤ Some 58 percent of parents and 73 percent of kids say they spend less than one hour a day in conversation. About 46 percent of kids and 27 percent of parents say they spend less than a half-hour a day in conversation with each other.

➤ Most parents underestimate their child's maturity level and have misconceptions about what's important to them. Parents believe the top priorities for their children are having fun, being with their friends, and looking good. Children report that their top priorities are their future, their school work, and family matters.

➤ Twenty percent of children say it's easy to talk with their parents about things that matter; 26 percent say it's somewhat to very difficult to talk about such things. All the rest report that it is somewhat easy to talk about such things.

➤ Fifty-seven percent of kids report that their parents don't always give them a chance to explain; 51 percent of parents feel that their kids don't always give them a chance to explain themselves.

Stay in Touch, or Lose Touch

Against such a backdrop, how do you stay in touch without spending oodles of time but nevertheless conveying to your kids that you care? Among a variety of options, try these:

A Stitch in Time

Listening doesn't have to be a formality. Often, your child will open up to you while you're walking along, driving the car, or raking leaves in the backyard. As you develop a bond and rapport with your child, the times in which you can open up to one another may begin to happen more spontaneously.

➤ Start to convey trust at an early age. If your children know that you listen to them, they'll begin to open up to you about everything in their life, even when confronting issues such as problems at school, drugs, or sex.

➤ Flat-out ask for their opinions. Who in this world isn't pleased by being asked for their opinions? Your children, among everyone else, will feel particularly pleased. You can ask them about big things or little things, it doesn't matter.

➤ Let them have their say. It's a bad habit for you to anticipate what someone is going to say, let alone finish the end of their sentences for them. You wouldn't do this at work, so don't do it with your children. Give them time to explain themselves, and make it more time than you would afford to an adult.

➤ While you're letting them explain, also pay attention to their body language and emotions. Are they holding anything back, is there something they'd like to say but are not saying it well, is there something they want you to draw out of them?

Coordination Is the Key

Whether a mother and father, a mother alone, or a father alone take major responsibility for rearing and directing the affairs of their children, coordination is vital. One mother of three comments that she always reviews her week in advance on Sunday evening, even if it's only for 5–10 minutes.

When you look at the week as a whole, there are fewer surprises, fewer time crunches, and less anxiety. I liken this to the business executive or entrepreneur who uses spreadsheet software to precisely determine the company or department's cash flow analysis for, say, the coming 12 months. When you're able to plot all the cash inflows versus all the cash outflows and gain a reasonable portrayal of what the cash balances will be at the end of each month, you're far less likely to get caught short.

So it is with parenting. If you merely get up each day and try to determine what it will take to get you and your children through the day, it's likely that you're going to run into some major snags. Your time horizon wasn't broad enough. A peek at the next week affords you a better opportunity to manage the pace with grace.

Some family counselors believe that multiweek, month-long, or multimonth planning is even more desirable. As you plot out dates of birthdays, time off from school, other family celebrations, kid's lessons, and other start and stop times of schedule events, you gain a much broader picture of who needs to be where, when, and supplied with what.

The Super Planners

One effective parent says that he prefers to do family planning as much as two years in advance. He's frequently asking his children's teachers and school administrators the dates of certain events so that he can plot them on his calendar and ensure his attendance or participation.

In many cases, he laments, he has to force the dates out of others, because they haven't mapped out their activities that far in advance!

Overestimate the Time, Nearly Every Time

The more accomplished, effective, and intelligent you are, the more likely you are to fall into a time trap. Your optimism combined with resourcefulness leads you to believe that certain tasks will take x amount of time. If it turns out they take 1.2 or 1.3 times your estimate, you're frustrated because things never seem to be completed based on your own perceptions of how long they should have taken.

So, it makes sense to overestimate the time that task or activity will take, particularly when in relation to your children. Then, if you finish on time or in advance, you'll feel far less frustrated.

Time Out!

"People sometimes feel that everyone else is accomplishing more than they are, but that is usually because they overestimate what others do and underestimate what they themselves do," says Windy Dryden, professor of counseling, Goldsmiths' College, London.

Over-Schedule Less, Live More

If you've fallen into the trap of over-scheduling your child and underestimating the time both of you will expend on activities (least of which is chauffeuring!), undoubtedly you'll be perpetually frustrated. If you—and, by extension, your child—have the wherewithal to schedule less and be more generous in your scheduling, you're apt to lead more serene, less hectic lives. You'll certainly have a greater chance of enjoying the few activities you choose.

Positive Strokes for Positive Folks

Laura Woloch, owner of Peak Productivity Consulting Group in Boulder, Colorado, learned to give herself positive strokes for what she did accomplish as a mother. She might have had as many as 33 things on her domestic to-do list, but she began to realize that it was more realistic to choose three priorities to accomplish for each day.

"At the end of the day, I felt quite successful if I completed those three items. I didn't overload myself, beat myself up at the end of the day, or feel guilty for not having accomplished more. I was actually able to relax," she says.

Time Out!

Many psychologists agree that the mother's acceptance, or lack thereof, of a potentially caregiving father plays a dramatic role in whether the father is successful. Some mothers lament that they are highly desirous of having the father play a more prominent role in raising the children, yet they don't fully understand the power that they have to make this happen.

Sharing and Caring

If you're fortunate enough to be in a true parenting partnership with your spouse, both you and your children stand to benefit. While there are no hard-and-fast rules as to what equal parenting caregivers are supposed to do, here are some ideas:

➤ Alternate who gets up earliest on selected mornings to take care of breakfast and help the kids get dressed and ready for school.

➤ Alternate who gets up first on the weekend.

➤ Divvy up household chores according to personal preference or inclination—or, to remain completely egalitarian, based on a rotating schedule.

➤ Alternate who reads or plays with the kids. Alternate who chauffeurs the kids. Schedule who will serve as baby-sitter when the other parent needs some time away for work or non-work activities.

➤ Maintain equal contact and address information, including doctors, dentist, coaches, teachers, and so on.

➤ Log in equal hours when it comes to emergencies, when the children are sick, or when, for whatever reason, one of the parents needs to break out of work.

Where Does All This Leave You?

When you look at your household calendar and it appears as if it's practically filled to the brim with kids' activities, take a second look and see how many of those activities you initiated of your own free will, how many you actually participate in, and how many you actually enjoy. There's no use playing the martyr or the perpetually sacrificing parent. You'll end up resenting your kids and their activities, and they'll feel it in spades. So, how do you create the win-win scenario? Here are a couple ideas.

Find a Buddy, Buddy!

Suppose your child plays in the little league, whether it be baseball or soccer, whether for boys or girls. When you attend such functions, perhaps you meet with another parent whom you befriend. Sitting in the stands, you both watch the game and have enjoyable conversations. It's one way to maintain a friendship, be a parent, and have a life.

When it's Okay to Double Up: The Exception

You've already discovered that I'm not a big fan of doubling up on activities because you don't tend to experience either to their fullest, and because the process itself seems to accelerate the pace at which life is passing. However, in some instances you can take your child to an event and at the same time can read or take care of some light paperwork.

In Cary, North Carolina, there is a play center called Amaze= N= Castles. My daughter wants to go all the time; we average about one visit per month. During those visits, she darts into the maze, where she runs, jumps, climbs, swings, slides down tubes, throws balls, and exercises in every way. The 90 minutes or so that she's there, I sit at a table and handle paperwork.

I look up every time she calls, and periodically look to see what she's doing when she doesn't call. Meanwhile, for 90 percent of the time I'm able to take care of my stuff. I am completely present in both the drive up and drive back, in getting her started, and in playing together in the arcade section of the facility. Undoubtedly, you have corollaries in your life.

Stage a Mini-Workout

My daughter is also interested in a variety of activities that don't interest me. She likes to attend the gymnastics meets at the University of North Carolina. There are four events at these meets, including the balance beam, vaulting, the uneven parallel bars, and the floor exercise. Because the event is held in an 8,000-seat gym—and because 7,600 of the seats are open—we're able to sit where ever we choose.

She watches intently. I watch as well and at the same time stretch, do light calisthenics, engage in isometrics, and in general get a mini-workout during this time. As the teams exchange places on the floor following different events, we sometimes move around in the stands, which gives us walking exercise as well. The longer the meet lasts, the more of a mini-workout I get. Alternatively, I could do light walking, bring a hand gripper and strengthen my hand and arm muscles, or bring a variety of other exercise aids that I could use right in my seat.

Tube it Together

If your child frequently clamors to watch videos (and what child today doesn't?), choose videos that you would enjoy watching as well. There's enough G- and PG-rated videos around in which both of you could find interest. Among these are various categories: historical biographies, comedies, period pieces, sci-fis, and musicals (largely from the 1930s).

Learn as Your Child Learns

My daughter tried skating once and was thrilled by it. She decided it was worth pursuing and wanted to take lessons. When her mother brought her to skating lessons, her mother decided to rediscover skating for herself and took private lessons while Valerie was in a group lesson elsewhere on the ice. It's amazing sometimes how rewarding it can be to rediscover pieces of your own childhood.

The Least You Need to Know

➤ In the first three years of a child's life, complex changes occur in the brain that lay a foundation for the child's whole life.

➤ The common denominator to effective parenting is the ability to offer your complete attention to your child.

➤ Encourage your child to do homework in a timely manner, and help out when needed—but don't do the homework.

➤ Convey trust at an early age. If your children know that you listen to them, they'll begin to open up to you.

➤ You don't have to over-schedule your child. Start over-estimating the time both of you will expend on activities.

Chapter 22

Time Out for Leisure

You want leisure, you need leisure, you may even crave leisure. Yet most people have an odd relationship with leisure—Americans, in particular. At least four times in the 20th century, Americans have questioned the central reality of work and struggled with this strange and frightening concept of leisure time; in fact, "it's not a place we're really comfortable with," says Benjamin Hunnicutt, a professor of leisure studies at the University of Iowa. Hunnicutt questions whether work will ever be anything but the No. 1 activity in our cultural hierarchy. If anything, he believes it's the closest thing to a modern religion.

There's no disputing the value of having sufficient leisure in your life. You instinctively know when you haven't had enough, and seek it out with the relentlessness of a sperm trying to fertilize an egg.

Blurring the Boundaries

Whether or not it is human destiny to socially evolve into a world that is increasingly difficult in which to live, insights on finding leisure abound. You can chart a new course, one to which perhaps the masses will someday gravitate.

Executives and entrepreneurs in industrialized societies have been attempting to accomplish more in the same amount of time by engaging in activities at a fast pace, doubling up on activities (shazam!), or giving less focused attention to activities. On top of that, they're attempting to time what otherwise would be leisure activities with greater precision. This doesn't lead to the experience of true leisure—rest, relaxation, regeneration, and renewal. Rather, it makes leisure much like everything else—moving too quickly, having too many stimuli, and being over too soon.

Watch Words

To define **leisure** as time away from work is to sadly misunderstand the concept. One group of researchers defined it as that which is worth your time and attention, given that you otherwise face a minimum of limitations and/or responsibilities. It sounds a little clinical, but what it means is rewarding activity free from work and preoccupation with work.

When the boundaries between work and personal time blur, it creates the perception that you have no leisure at all. As I wrote in *Breathing Space*, if you attempt to force-fit leisure between periods of otherwise frenzied activity, your leisure is bound to suffer.

Most people cannot start and stop on a dime—they can't one minute be working hard, and the next moment be totally engaged in some relaxing, rewarding activity. Human nature being what it is, we all tend to need some transition time.

Chronos Says

In 1986, 33 percent of Americans polled called leisure "important," compared to the results of a similar poll in 1997 wherein 57 percent called it important. In the same 1986 survey, 28 percent of Americans polled said society needed to put more value on free time and stop emphasizing work. Eleven years later, that figure rose to 49 percent.

What People Are Missing Because They Don't "Have Time"

➤ Coming together for dinner as a family

➤ Making homemade dinners, baking bread

➤ Baking traditional Christmas cookies, even with prepared dough

➤ Making gifts (and handmade Victorian valentines)

➤ Spending holidays together

➤ Sitting around with the family when it's not a holiday

➤ Relaxing and feeling at ease during family reunions

➤ Going on excursions together

➤ Going to church or to temple (maintaining one's spiritual life)

➤ Going for a leisurely Sunday drive

➤ Attending cultural events (the opera or an exhibit at the nearby gallery)

➤ Dressing differently for different occasions

➤ Letting children be children (such as playing ball and not being rushed from one experience or activity to another)

➤ Putting children to bed with storybooks

➤ Reading the Bible or other religious books with your children

➤ Teaching with natural subjects, such as pond water and wildflowers

➤ Learning mother's recipes

➤ Learning to play a musical instrument

➤ Sewing one's own clothes

➤ Writing letters

➤ Planting a garden, then eating or canning the produce

➤ Exercising or taking leisurely, relaxing strolls

➤ Relaxing at a spa

➤ Reading a literary novel or epic

➤ Maintaining etiquette

➤ Starting a hope chest for one's daughter

➤ Courting

➤ Drinking brewed coffee

Chronos Says

When the U.S. troops began returning from World War II, they were assembled in large numbers, consigned to ships, and over several months slowly sailed home. The time on board enabled them to reflect with one another, decompress, and mentally and emotionally prepare themselves for reintegration into civilian society. When they returned, many were greeted by parades and celebrations. Not everyone had a smooth transition, but the probability of reintegrating into a peacetime existence was heightened because of the nature and duration of the transition time.

Conversely, U.S. troops departing from the Vietnam War came home one at a time. They came via jet planes that transported them in less than 24 hours from a hellish environment back to the world they had left. There was little or no transition time, no camaraderie with people who had shared a similar experience, and no time to mentally and emotionally prepare for re-entry into the civilian world. Most were not greeted as heroes or given celebrations. Consequently, Vietnam-era veterans had the most difficult time reintegrating into society of any class of American veterans.

Build in Some Slack, Jack

I've found that building slack into my schedule is as critical as anything. Having some time when nothing is scheduled—some whole days where it's not critical for me to do anything—is essential for my overall health and well-being. It helps me renew myself so that when I return to more vigorous pursuits, I have more internal resources at my command. Building slack into your schedule allows you to get back in touch with your own natural timing.

Sometimes to handle challenging tasks under stringent time lines, you need to slow down a moment or two to get back in sync with your own rhythm, your own nature, and your own way of being. Hence, leisure gives you the ability to speed up when you need to.

Build in pockets of leisure here and there throughout the day and week to keep yourself in balance. For example, if you have a flight scheduled weeks or months in advance, mark on your calendar that the plane will be departing 10 minutes before it actually will. Guess what happens when it's time to take your flight? When you get to the gate, you realize that you have an extra 10 minutes.

Fun Excuses for Not Being Obsessed by Time

➤ I'm not late; I'm incredibly early for the next day.

➤ I had to find a baby-sitter for my inner child.

➤ Be on time? That's just what you'd expect me to do.

➤ Didn't Einstein say time was relative?

➤ Mentally, I was here 20 minutes ago.

➤ Oh, I'm just being fashionable.

➤ Sorry, I had to stop and smell the roses.

➤ Isn't the universe expanding?

➤ I'm not late; I'm chronologically challenged.

➤ I haven't figured out the big hand/little hand thing.

➤ According to the VCR, it's only 12 o'clock.

➤ I was hypnotized by the weather channel.

➤ One of my multiple personalities is a late sleeper.

➤ Somewhere, it's got to be a national holiday.

➤ I'm having a bad hair day.

➤ I'm trying to make our time together more precious.

➤ I just finished my first novel, and I'm thinking of reading another one.

➤ It's a leap year.

➤ I blame myself.

➤ It's true: I'm late, but I'm still worthy.

➤ I had to wait for my mood ring to turn red.

➤ This is not really me; it's my evil twin.

➤ You missed me? You really missed me?

➤ To err is human, to forgive divine.

➤ I'm not a morning/afternoon/evening person.

➤ I'm protesting the oppressive nature of clocks.

➤ I don't feel tardy.

➤ I thought you might need some time without me.

➤ I was just trying to make you look good.

➤ What's a few minutes between friends?

➤ Actually, I'm on time; I wanted to feel how the other half lives.

➤ I decided to take the road less traveled.

➤ Why do we need labels? Can't we rejoice that we're here?

Source: Honda Civic Corporation

All of a sudden, you have time to collect yourself, arrange your luggage, take a drink of water or go to the bathroom, get balanced, and feel good about what you're doing. Such opportunities are available all the time—it's just a matter of how you handle your affairs and prepare your schedule.

Preparing For Leisure?!

The notion of *preparing* for leisure may seem a little foreign to you at first, but it makes excellent sense.

The last time you took a big vacation, you marked it down on your calendar. You may have reserved airline tickets or hotel reservations. Undoubtedly you discussed the event with others in your family or with friends. You made plans, wrote notes, and spent money, all in preparation for this time away. Mentally and emotionally you geared yourself to the reality that it was coming. The same process is advantageous when it comes to experiencing leisure on a daily basis.

A Therapeutic Commute

Following World War II—through the 1950s as suburbs started to spring up—and during much of the 1960s, the commute at the end of the day reasonably provided the mental and emotional transition time vital to enjoying one's time at home. The roads weren't so crowded. You could get a seat on passenger trains or subways.

Soon commuting became a chore, then highly burdensome, then stressful—and now, for some, a prompt for outbreaks of rage and even violence. Today the commute for most people does not serve as a valid transition time between work and leisure. For many, it represents a daily ordeal. See Chapter 6, "Supporting Your Priorities for Fun and Profit" for commuting tips.

A Stitch in Time

In his book, *Your Body Doesn't Lie,* Dr. John Diamond claims that classical music offers the right syncopation to get your body back into a more natural alignment. If you don't like classical music, put on something else that's relaxing for you.

Transforming Your Monster Commute

Suppose you *are* stuck in a daily arduous commute. You hate it—every morning you crawl along at a snail's pace down that interstate highway that is nothing more than a moving parking lot. However long it takes you to arrive, you perceive that it's three times as long. How do you turn such an experience into more productive time, one in which you're prepared to actually have a life the rest of the day?

Make sure that you *condition* your car: Use the time to check that your air-conditioner works, close all the windows, then put on a cassette or CD that you truly enjoy.

Make the interior of that car or, if you use mass transit, the personal space around you as supportive as you can. For some that means simply closing your eyes, for others donning earphones connected to a Walkman, for others reading, and for yet others staring out the window.

Getting Serious About Having More Fun

If you're serious about having more leisure in your life, then chances are high that it's a topic that demands your earnest attention and initially you're going to have to be vigilant about it. It takes guts to buck the norm in a society of frenzied, exhausted overachievers.

It's all too easy when immersed in such an environment to believe that's normal and acceptable. This is the underpinning of Dr. Erich Fromm's work. A noted psychologist and author, Fromm made the observation decades ago that you may not be crazy after all—it may be society. It seems to me, especially after looking around today, that he was right on the mark.

Here, then, is your mini-plan to effectively take time out for leisure—leisure that you want, need, and deserve.

If You Build It Into the Calendar, It Will Come

As discussed earlier, when you go on a big vacation, you mark it on the calendar and go through all kinds of supporting behaviors to ensure that you take off as scheduled. I'm suggesting that you treat lower-level leisure episodes—the week-to-week and daily kind of stuff—with the same vehemence.

Put low-level leisure time on your calendar.

➤ Look forward to it.

➤ Dwell on it.

➤ Talk about it.

➤ Make plans around it.

➤ Revel in it.

Never mind if this seems a little obsessive, because it's likely to be at first. Once you start treating leisure as an important component of your health and welfare, you won't have to be as vigilant. For now, make a commotion about it.

Stay on Course

Leisure activities do not represent built-in excuses for you to cancel or reschedule them. You need to treat them with the same reverence that you presently exhibit with key prospect appointments or, heck, trips to the IRS auditor's office.

Okay, every blue moon—and blue moons appear rarely—there are compelling reasons why you need to change your schedule. So, every now and then, you can shuffle some items around on your calendar.

Stay Focused

When it's time for the leisure activity to commence, be there, experience it, and get immersed. Allow for this activity to be as important as any other. Let go of your left brain, eyes-on the-clock, is-this-helping-my-career predisposition. If you're shooting baskets, shoot baskets. If you're hiking, hike. If you're meeting with the stamp club, meet with the stamp club.

If you find yourself wishing you were someplace else or attempting to do other things than the leisure time you've scheduled, then change your leisure activity; perhaps you've picked the wrong one. Don't, however, shortchange how much time you devote to leisure.

Guilt, Guilt Go Away

I know some people who feel guilty when they work long hours because they feel that they should be with their kids, their friends, or someplace else. Conversely, they feel guilty when they're with their kids, friends, or someplace else because they feel they should be working more.

Table 22.1: Sun, Sea, Sand, and Electronic Leash

The Duracell Company's Ultra Battery division conducted a study to determine what people take with them on vacation:

94 percent	Bring cameras, CD players, camcorders
38 percent	Bring cell phones and beepers
18 percent	Bring a notebook PC, palmtops, and electronic organizers

When they take a vacation, they're overly concerned with what's going on back at the office. When they take a walk, they're too concerned about the voice mail and e-mails that might have come in while they were out. Precious reader, there's no way you're ever going to experience leisure and all its intended benefits if you feel anxious about what else you could be doing or what you're missing, or if you feel guilty about spending the time at all.

Creative Leisure

If you're single, your options for getting sufficient leisure abound. Depending on your work situation, you can take off at a moment's notice. You can take advantage of holiday weekends or perhaps go whole hog and explore the possibility of going on sabbatical (the topic of the next chapter). If you're married—and particularly with children—having leisure for yourself and having leisure for your family can be much more of a challenge.

The trend in America in the last decade and a half or so has been toward more frequent but shorter vacations, often boxed around holiday weekends. If you use the contrarian approach and take your time off when the rest of the world isn't, then holiday weekends are a good time to stay at home and let everybody else compete for highway lanes and parking spaces.

In my book *The Complete Idiot's Guide to Reaching Your Goals*, I list a wide variety of possible goals in various categories such as social, leisure, and lifetime goals. Following is but a small subset of the lists contained in that book, with some extended explanation.

Learn How to Meditate

Every town has someone who can teach you the fundamentals of meditation. Indeed, there's really nothing to learn. It's more a matter of sitting still. Many expect that something is going to happen, but alas, this is not the case with meditation. You don't move from point A to point B. You meditate to meditate—it is its own reward.

If nothing happens, fine. You don't sit down to have a particular thought or realization. You simply sit. One of the wonderful aspects of meditation after you've become "a veteran," is that the benefits accrue each time you meditate.

A Stitch in Time

In the midst of even a big, noisy family, you can carve out 15–20 minutes for yourself sometime during the day, perhaps at 5 a.m.! Thereafter, you'll be more calm when you are with your family, and on any trips you may take.

Join a Renaissance Festival

If there's a group in your town that re-enacts periods in history, check it out. Many people say that they have loads of fun at such encounters, whether they be Renaissance festivals, Civil War re-enactments, or Colonial re-enactments.

Join a Choir or Chorus

Maybe there's an opportunity for you within a local group, or at your place of worship, to open your mouth and make a "joyful noise." Through the ages, singing has been beneficial to one's health. After all, you have to breathe more deeply, expand your lungs, and exercise your lower facial muscles.

Time Out!

You probably want to get involved with a group that meets either weekly or every two weeks, as opposed to more often. Otherwise this can end up being a drain on your time or energy.

A Stitch in Time

How about writing poetry? You may have tried it when you were high school. Think about how much more wisdom you have acquired, and how that could impact your ability to get poetic. No one is saying that you have to try to get the stuff published, or even show it to anybody else. Perhaps you just keep it in a log or journal for your own edification.

Once you've found a group that meets at an interval that is comfortable for you, many benefits await. You get to open up that creative space in your brain that you haven't tapped recently. Most groups choose songs that are among the world's favorites. You get to participate with others who potentially are at the same place in life as you— or who are at the same place as you at least for those few moments during the week.

Do Some Creative Writing

Maybe you couldn't stand writing in high school or college. Maybe, like me, your teachers and professors marked up your papers so vigorously that you were dissuaded from writing for a couple decades. Nevertheless, you have the opportunity before you, either by turning on your PC or simply taking out a pen and paper, to let your creative juices flow.

How about a short story? Some well-crafted short stories are less than 100 words. Could you write one?

Collecting Churches and Cathedrals

No, you don't have to become a multi-millionaire and start buying up buildings. I'm talking about visiting buildings or natural settings that inspire you. My mother, who was not Christian, used to "collect" cathedrals. When she was in a town and saw pleasing architecture, she'd stop and focus on it, or sometimes go in and marvel at the statues or stained glass.

I do the same when I pass a scenic lake or happen to be atop a hillside. These are tiny moments of leisure that have a cumulative effect if approached as the true gifts that they are.

Teach a Course in Which You Are a Master

I know, as soon as you read this, you said to yourself, "Oh brother, that's just what I need to add to my schedule: a course to teach!" Read on.

When you teach a course where you're already master, there's no heavy work involved on your part. You don't need to read up or prepare a lot of notes or outlines. Particularly if you're teaching in an adult education or university extension, you can walk in and let the sparks fly. The reward comes in your ability to share with people who want to benefit from your wisdom.

Chronos Says

It's been said that you don't learn while talking to others; you learn only while you listen. But that's not entirely true. Sometimes you say things in new ways, or you say things that you didn't know you were going to say, and you actually learn as a result of your own articulation. When you're teaching a course, you're really opening yourself up for the chance to learn: As students ask questions, pose their views, and offer insights that represent new ground for you, you are learning as well.

Start a Card Group

Did you used to play cards on a regular basis? I did in college. We played poker on Wednesday and Sunday nights. I played more for the fun and camaraderie rather than for any meager earnings (as it turns out, I lost $85 in the course of one semester). Many people who once played pinochle, bridge, or canasta are surprised and pleased to find that the joys of card games quickly re-emerge. This is especially so when you're playing against others on your skill level and with people you like.

Researchers tell us that playing cards, filling out crossword puzzles, playing Scrabble or Boggle, and engaging in other such activities helps to keep you mentally alert and mentally sharp, especially as you get older. There's no need for your cerebral powers to decline.

A card group is easy to arrange. You only need three other people—and if you have a spouse or significant other, perhaps only two other people. Hence, that means just one other couple. How easy can it get?

A Grander Notion

Some people like to combine their leisure time with intellectual improvement. Maybe you're one of them. Have you ever considered educational travel? This is when people travel to a location with the primary purpose of learning something that's directly related to the location. So, if you go to Stonehenge, or the pyramids, or the Falkland Islands off the coast of Argentina, you act as both tourist and student.

A Stitch in Time

Educational travel makes perfect sense. You study archeology, the environment, art, architecture, or natural history by actually being onsite and examining subjects in their original location or natural condition. Educational travel allows you to immerse yourself in whatever it is you're studying and come back a better person.

The Smithsonian Institution in Washington, D.C., routinely offers educational travel. Such trips are cited within the first couple pages of each issue of their monthly magazine the *Smithsonian*. Other institutions offer them as well, primarily universities, conservation societies, and even some professional associations.

If you suspect that this type of vacation might be your "chicken soup for the soul," read on. Chapter 23, "Not for Everyone: Taking a Sabbatical," gives you more ideas on how to support such a quest.

Some Parting Ideas

Here are some additional ideas on how to make the most of your leisure:

➤ Start a policy of receiving only magazines that either make your life simpler or that amuse you.

➤ Only take airplane trips on vacation that are one-flight, non-stop. Anything else taxes you in ways you don't need to be taxed.

➤ Go the store and buy bubble bath today, even if you're not sure exactly when you'll use it.

➤ Install a hammock in your backyard. Never mind when you think you'll actually use it (see the advice about bubble bath).

➤ Take on new friends who engage in leisure activities that you find very alluring and who will teach, guide, train, and include you in their activities.

➤ Open your home more frequently to others via parties, receptions, meetings, and brief visits.

➤ Find others in your town who like to play in ways that you like to play.

➤ Frequently take walks in shopping malls, along city sidewalks, down nature trails, and anyplace else you feel safe.

➤ Go to the library one evening a week, and read whatever magazines appeal to you. Join a monthly book review discussion group.

➤ Buy a joke book, learn some card tricks, practice impersonating others, or learn juggling.

➤ Take an impromptu weekend trip to someplace you haven't visited.

➤ Consider taking up a sport you've never attempted, such as golf, archery, hiking, or snorkeling. Or take a class on crafts, be it wood, pottery, metals, ceramics, leather, stained glass, jewelry, or woodworking.

➤ Become an amateur geologist, going on your own "fossil" hunts. This could be as simple as finding rocks and breaking them open, or looking for petrified shark's teeth, troglodytes, or minerals embedded in stone.

➤ Buy a telescope and start watching the sky.

➤ Train a hamster, a gerbil, a cat, or a dog.

➤ Get on the committee that sponsors a festival, holiday parade, street fair, or exposition.

➤ Take a course in handwriting, calligraphy, or sketching.

➤ Visit one new restaurant a month—or, if the spirit moves you, once a week. With your spouse or significant other, go to a restaurant much earlier than usual some evening, linger over drinks, linger over appetizers, linger over the entree, linger over dessert, and take your sweet time leaving as well. By the time you're out of there, the world will have changed. So will your attitude.

The Least You Need to Know

➤ Leisure means enjoying rewarding activity free from work and preoccupation with work.

➤ Recognize the value that transition time plays in improving the quality of your leisure.

➤ Do something bold (for you) to rediscover leisure, such as meditating or teaching a course in which you are already a master.

➤ Educational travel can change your perspective about the world; check it out.

➤ Linger long at dinner when you feel like it.

Part 6

Own a Peace of the Mental Rock

You're making great progress! You're all the way up to Part 6. When you first bought this book, you worried that you might not make it this far, didn't you?

Yet, you've made great strides. In Part 1, you learned specific techniques for making the most of your day. In Part 2, you learned about the importance of controlling your environment, getting enough sleep, whipping your office into shape, filing, and using the tools of technology. In Part 3, you discovered some innovative ways to stay in touch with others without overloading information intake capacity. In Part 4, you refined your capabilities further by learning to make decisions quickly, practicing the art of doing one thing at a time, and lightening the load by merging and purging. In Part 5, you rediscovered that there is such a thing as a home life, a life away from work.

Now it's time to move into that wondrous and potentially serene arena—your head—to discuss goals for peace of mind. This is where you learn to become a master of winning back your time through deciding to live in real time, catching up with today, dropping back and punting, and realizing that the best is yet to come.

Get ready for the stratosphere. Fear not—you are ready. First up is making the most of your day (as opposed to having your day chew you up and spit you out).

Chapter 23

Not for Everyone: Taking a Sabbatical

In This Chapter

➤ Getting some major time off now and then

➤ Making your vacation your employer's idea

➤ Surviving a sabbatical's early days

➤ How others handle it

Now we move on to that rarified air about taking a sabbatical from work. Maybe you're thinking that if ever there was a chapter in this book that you could skip, this is going to be it. If every cell in your body rebels at the notion of taking a sabbatical—"Where could I ever find the time?" or "Who can afford it?"—then all the more reason for you to peruse this chapter.

A Time for Every Purpose Under Heaven

Your life, the life of all creatures on earth, the earth itself, the solar system, the Milky Way, and the universe (did I leave anything out?) are governed by laws. Some laws are readily apparent, such as laws of cause and effect, laws of gravity, and the laws of motion. Somewhere in the big book of karmic order, it surely says that ever so rarely you need major time off. Forget all the logical explanations as to why this is all but impossible, and stay with me.

Live Long and Take Time Off

As we've seen in earlier chapters, chances are you will live longer and work longer. The longer you work, the greater the odds are that you need time away from work.

If the need for income, to watch over Jason and Jennifer, or simply to feed Fido were not issues, could you mentally and emotionally bring yourself to the point of acknowledging that a month or three months away from work is something your inner and outer being desperately craves?

Even if you can't foresee the possibility now, hold on to your hat—there may be a sabbatical in your future.

Time to Renew and Refresh

Upon returning from the Andes Mountains in South America, one man from Sacramento remarked that it was about 15 days before he actually realized how long he was going to be away. His 90-day sabbatical started with one week in a cabin in Wyoming with no TV and no phone. He promised himself at the outset that he wouldn't bring his notebook computer, so e-mail was not available.

He did phone home every couple days to make sure the place was still standing. Otherwise, this was to be a time of deep, personal reflection, renewal, and even restoration of the parts of him that he feared were all but lost.

Anyone for Sabbaticals?

Professors and other faculty members at colleges and universities have long been privy to the benefits of taking a semester-long sabbatical, with pay, every six to seven years. With a little planning and forethought, many university professionals extend their sabbaticals by taking a second semester off, usually without pay, hence racking up 8–12 months away from the ivory tower.

Corporate sabbaticals, the kind in which you're much more likely to be interested, tend to be a tad shorter. Three months would be a long time; two months or one month is more like it. They're also likely to be unpaid.

The Employer's View: Some Compelling Reasons

Why would a company offer sabbaticals at all? Isn't it a hardship to have a key employee leave for months at a time? What if he or she is a member of a team?

Many valid reasons exist as to why companies offer sabbaticals. Sabbaticals are provided as a recruiting tool to attract top talent or as a reward to keep valued employees. Competition for talented employees in some industries is vigorous, and companies will do what they can to retain the best.

Chronos Says

Some companies offer paid sabbaticals with the provision that the time off be used for some specific purpose, such as community service, learning, or travel. A 1996 poll taken by The Society for Human Resource Management in Alexandria, Virginia, found that 23 percent of its 829 respondents offered unpaid sabbaticals, and 5 percent offered paid ones. Granted, the sample included some schools and universities.

Conversely, some companies use sabbaticals as a way to facilitate their downsizing plans. A senior public relations manager at AT&T commented that "AT&T expects that a number of people will not return, a situation that would ease the need to downsize."

At AT&T, more than 1,500 employees have taken unpaid sabbaticals in the last six years—while still retaining other job benefits such as health care insurance—and leave with the promise of having their job when they return. Many companies believe that sabbaticals offer key employees a way to learn, grow, and ultimately be more valuable to the firm. Indeed, the probability of most people bettering themselves and bringing new skills and perspectives back to the workplace has proven to be a bonanza.

And sabbaticals are an international phenomenon. In the United Kingdom, the number of organizations offering sabbaticals increased from 18 percent in 1990 to 25 percent in 1997, according to a survey by Hay Management Consultants. A study by the Institute of Personnel and Development found that 13 percent of employees are now entitled to sabbatical leave, although far fewer actually take a sabbatical.

All Kinds of Options

Often companies grant sabbaticals to employees who will be engaged in job-related study or research. A lesser number of companies grant them for employees simply seeking rest or vacation, and still a slightly lesser number for non-job related study.

Some firms maintain a policy of one week's extra leave for each year of service. So, if you've been working for someone for six years, you're entitled to a six-week sabbatical. More organizations realize that as the nature of work intensifies, and as the number of hours logged in by management staff increases, the notion of taking a break beyond annual vacation time is of great benefit to both employer and employee.

Gimme a Break

One worker returning from a sabbatical said that he hadn't previously taken a break during his professional career. When he returned to work he had far more confidence and energy, hence benefitting his company. Being away for a while was refreshing and rejuvenating. "The sabbatical gave me a chance to take stock, put things in perspective, and be clearer about what I wanted out of life," he says.

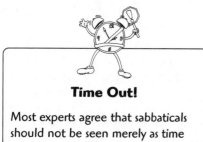

Time Out!

Most experts agree that sabbaticals should not be seen merely as time off to recover from a variety of stress-related maladies.

Rewarding Techies

If you're a techie, your odds of taking a sabbatical are high. Silicon Valley companies such as Apple Computers and Intel—who compete fiercely for top talent, and where many employees devote their bodies, minds, and souls to the job effort—increasingly are offering sabbaticals as part of their bait.

Reward for Intensity

Employees at Genentech, a bio-technology company in San Francisco, California offers full-time employees a sabbatical of six continuous weeks with full pay and benefits beyond their annual vacation time, starting in their seventh year of employment. Judy Heyboer, head of human resources at Genentech, says, "The sabbatical program is one of several awards given to employees in acknowledgment of the high level of intensive work and commitment required at Genentech." In essence, in exchange for a high level of commitment, Heyboer says, "We give back the incentive of a more significant break than is typically offered."

Hire the Best and Reward Them Well

Another human resources director commented that the greatest challenge his company faced was attracting and keeping good people. If you can't find and keep good people, then your problems start to multiply. He went on to say that balance is an important part of everyone's life: "We don't celebrate 80-hour work weeks around here. In fact, we think the person who has to work like that is, in the long-run, not very smart."

Getting Your Mind in Gear

One of the biggest benefits of a sabbatical is the basic acknowledgment that you're going to experience a long time away from the job. That, in itself, can result in favorable physiological and psychological benefits. If you know that six months from now you'll have three months off, you can plan your affairs accordingly and perhaps pace yourself for the six months as well.

You want to approach your time off on an even keel. Remember, the sabbatical is not for attempting to overcome extremely stressful job-related maladies. That needs to be taken care of while on the job.

Mowing Down the Obstacles

On your way to achieving the mind-set that you, too, can take a sabbatical, you may need to overcome some mental obstacles. The common ones are having enough money, caring for kids, and making a smooth transition back. Let's mow 'em down in order.

I Don't Have the Money!

The more time you have before a sabbatical, the more time you have to plan your finances accordingly. Your daily expenses when not working are actually far less than when working. You don't have the commute, the corporate lunch, the dry-cleaning costs, and a variety of other nickel-and-dime items that add up to many dollars in the course of a week.

A Stitch in Time

Some employers fear having employees go on sabbaticals because they believe employees will use that time to look for new jobs. Data doesn't bear this out, however. And if you and your employer always have the opportunity to engage in long-term thinking regarding what you'll do when you return, you can increase the probability of a smooth reconnection.

You can wear more comfortable clothing—and wear it more often—eat less expensively (and probably eat more healthfully), and forego expenditures related to keeping up with the corporate Joneses. You can walk and bike instead of taking a car.

If you opt to travel during your sabbatical, consult a few traveler's guides from your local library so you can find relatively inexpensive lodging all over the world. You can also engage in vacation club or home-swapping programs, and hence pay no more for lodging than you would otherwise. If you're going on a paid sabbatical, then you've got it made in the shade.

What About the Kids?

What about them? If you have young children, and you're their primary care provider, chances are you can't take a sabbatical. Or, maybe, you can bring them along.

If your children are a little older, perhaps there's a neighbor, relative, grandparent, or semi-willing spouse who'll grant you the month or two months you need to get away from it all. Perhaps they'll do it in exchange for you doing the same for them some time. Maybe they'll do it for you out of the goodness of their hearts.

If you have no children, you have no excuse.

Chronos Says

While it might be emotionally difficult to spend one month away from your children, ultimately it could be an enriching experience for everyone concerned. You can stay in touch by phone and e-mail, if you so choose. Your children will gain a different perspective on life without Mommy or Daddy around for the relatively brief time you're taking off. They may actually appreciate, respect, and love you more upon your return! Now, wouldn't *that* be a triple bonus?

Won't I Be Out of Sync at Work?

Will a couple months away put you behind when you finally step back into the office? In today's overinformation society, no one has a long-term lock on what's coming down the pike next. In many respects, the two months or so that you're away will be an advantage because of the newfound perspectives that you'll gain.

You can quickly catch up on the corporate memos and scuttlebutt. That'll take maybe half a day. A coworker can bring you up to speed on any new programs or procedures in a couple hours here and there, and this type of learning is likely to be more efficient than learning things on your own, had you been there all along.

Chances are, within one week of your being back, you won't feel as if you've missed out on anything. You're more likely to feel as if your time away was too brief, like a distant dream.

Breaking Away!

Here's a brief action plan to help you make leaving a reality. Go back and review Chapter 1, "I Know I Can Finish Most of This (If I Stay Late)." This is where you learned the vital steps for clearing out of the office at a normal time at least one day per week, and then escalating it to more than one day. Much of the same philosophy applies here.

It Can Be Done!

You have to adopt the fundamental notion that it can be done; you *can* take a month or two or longer away from work. Having done that, now pick the actual time. It's no good to have a vague date: *Someday* never comes. If you keep postponing the time when you'll take a sabbatical, the chances are it will never really happen. One obligation after another will creep up, and any windows of opportunity will close right up.

If you're on the Internet, visit sites offering insights and reflections on sabbaticals. Any of the major search engines (such as Yahoo, Altavista, HotBot, and Excite) offer a variety of Web sites at your disposal. Also, log onto dejanews.com and see what people are saying in the newsgroups about sabbaticals. You'll gain lots of insights and observations in a hurry, and these may help improve the quality and nature of your sabbatical.

Time Out!

The likelihood of you taking a sabbatical is directly related to your ability to set a firm departure date, put away a tidy sum (if it's a non-paid sabbatical), and announce to all of significance in your life that it is going to happen. Other than that, you're not even whistling Dixie.

Okay, I'm Going!

Now that you're firmly committed, here are the steps to make it happen:

1. When you've picked the date, actually mark it on your calendar. Then circulate a memo, e-mail, or what have you to coworkers, staff, peers, and anyone else. Break the news to your family as well, if applicable.

2. Set up a savings plan with your employer, bank, or other financial institution so that a specific (and sufficient) amount will be extracted from your paycheck each week, in anticipation of building to a sum that will see you through.

3. Secure with your employer that all benefits still accrue.

4. Talk with your boss about the plans he or she has for you upon your return. Build in some slack time so that you can get up to speed without feeling overwhelmed on the day you come back. Print an actual memo in writing as to what your tasks and responsibilities will be that first week, for the second week, and thereafter. Then file it away in a place where it will be secure.

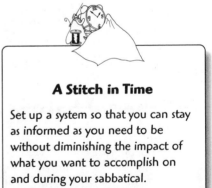

A Stitch in Time

Set up a system so that you can stay as informed as you need to be without diminishing the impact of what you want to accomplish on and during your sabbatical.

5. As the magic time approaches, start sending out a reminder of your time away to all correspondents. Some require only an e-mail. Some require an e-mail and a postcard. Some require everything.

6. Arrange with staff support, your family, and all others how you want messages to be fielded, mail to be allocated, and other correspondence to be handled in the event that your sabbatical is one in which you will not be directly privy to these communiques.

7. Plan a mini-celebration, both at work and at home on the day of or a few days before your actual sabbatical begins. This will give everyone a vivid message that you're departing for a while. Have everyone attend, and really whoop it up so that everyone has the message clearly stamped in their brains that you are not going to be here for the next two months.

8. Get your other affairs in order, should something out of the ordinary happen to you during your time away. Update your will, pay bills in advance, ensure that certain minimum sums are in various checking and savings accounts, and so forth.

9. Install appropriate messages on your voice mail, answering machines, and e-mail so that people who didn't know you were going to be away for a stretch and who try to get in touch with you aren't left thinking that you're ignoring them.

10. Identify what you need in terms of clothing, implements, and so forth. If you'll be traveling, look to consolidate as much as you can, using the smallest containers and lightest objects. If you have a specific mission for your sabbatical, such as doing research or volunteering in some capacity, identify in advance as many of the supplies and other tools you'll need to facilitate your efforts. Make checklists, checking them once and checking them twice.

11. Get a complete health checkup so that you leave with a clean bill of health, or at least the cleanest bill of health that you can. Visit your eye doctor, your dentist, and any other doctor with whom it makes sense to have an appointment.

12. If you'll be traveling by car, take your car in for a complete tune-up.

Let the Sabbatical Begin!

On that first day, when you don't head into work and your routine is different, you'll probably feel good. Over the next couple days, if you're at home, you may feel rested. You get to clean out the freezer, take care of the minor inconveniences that you let slide during the interim, and feel in command of your home.

If it's not a stay-at-home sabbatical—that is, if you're on the road, almost from the opening day, you'll experience what the stay-at-home types experience by about the sixth or seventh day: "My goodness, this really is different."

Here's a list of do's and don'ts to help you along during these first few impressionable days:

➤ Do allow yourself to get extra sleep. Everyone needs some, so there's no use pretending that you don't. However, after a couple days, your need for extra sleep should diminish.

➤ Do allow yourself to try new foods.

➤ Do take a multi-vitamin every day.

➤ Do be open and responsive to new viewpoints, ways of thinking, and ways of accomplishing things.

➤ Do allow yourself to explore, wander, or simply do nothing.

➤ Do feel free to keep a pen and pad or a pocket dictator nearby to capture whatever thoughts strike you.

➤ Do allow yourself the opportunity to just *be*.

➤ Don't fall into the trap of trying to make every day and every moment "productive."

➤ Don't let your exercise routine slide.

➤ Don't be concerned if you feel out of sorts, out of sync, or just plain out of it.

➤ Don't feel guilty about the work and people that you've left behind.

➤ Don't second-guess yourself about whether you should have taken the sabbatical. The benefits may not appear for a quite a while, perhaps not even until the sabbatical's over.

Tales from Beyond

Following are scenarios of people who've taken sabbaticals, what they've experienced, and what they had to say. The names have been changed to protect the innocent, but the experiences and insights are real.

Business Ideas Abound

Albert forsook his job in Richardson, Texas, for eight weeks to rediscover himself and some of his interests. He used to enjoy several hobbies, but he had all but ignored them for the last 10 years. Taking up old hobbies lasted for about three days, whereupon he started looking for new business ideas. As the weeks passed, he became excited about opportunities he uncovered.

When the sabbatical was over, he decided not to return to his company. A distinct number of individuals will consider alternatives to current employment during sabbaticals only because of the dynamic nature of the economy. Let's face it: With change bursting forth every day in the form of new software, new communication capabilities, and new ways of serving others, the opportunities are almost boundless.

Albert's experience is not an anomaly. One executive recruiter from New York remarked that as much as employers may not like it, the sabbatical is an ideal time for a person to assess where he or she wants to go in life, what kind of work they want to be doing, and, for some, to actually make plans to begin on a new path. She went on to say that the sabbatical offers people a marvelous opportunity to update their resumes, interview with other companies if they so choose, and actually latch on someplace.

The funny thing in Albert's case was that before taking his sabbatical he really had no plans other than to return to his original company. He was sincerely looking forward to the time to rediscover himself and his hobbies. Yet, as those notions quickly passed, he found his energy rising each day, and he explored the new possibilities for his life and his work. If this turns out the be the case with you, then look at it as simply aspiring to the inevitable sooner rather than later.

The Barrister Lays His Soul Bare

Richard was a partner in a law practice outside New York City. He put in so many billable hours over the past six years that he saw himself age more rapidly than he ever imagined he would. He finally got to the point where he knew he had to take some time off, and his partners agreed. For him, the money was no issue. He had saved more than enough to take a good three months off and not even think twice about it.

The big issue with Richard was actually making the break—not going in to work on that first day, that second day, that third day, that first week, that second week, and so on. About two weeks into his sabbatical, he noted that the change of pace was finally refreshing. He viewed his time away as a mid-life crisis of sorts, but under control, with no real downside.

"I had a marvelous opportunity to change my routine, rediscover other aspects of my life, and then return to what I'd been trained to do," he says.

Although he also had not planned on it, Richard found himself reading about law, from philosophical and ethical perspectives during his time away. At first he thought to himself, "This isn't really an activity I should engage in, after all. I'm on sabbatical." But then he thought "Hey, what the heck, this is what my time off has led me to."

His reading turned out to be rewarding for him. He rediscovered why he was initially attracted to the field of law. He also pledged to be more ethical in every way, both in his personal practice and in his daily life.

"I was able to spend some time contemplating what type of attorney I wanted to be and what type of practice I wanted to run. When I got back, I was automatically making more effective choices about what types of cases to take on, how to spend my time, and how I would act toward clients, peers, and the entire cast of courtroom characters I routinely encounter."

In Richard's case, he did have a backlog of work waiting for him when he returned. But by bringing on some extra help and pacing himself accordingly, he was able to handle it without making it into any type of ordeal. In addition, because he returned with more energy and enthusiasm for his practice, the extra work didn't seem as burdensome.

"Nearly all my clients were completely understanding of my quest to take time off. In fact, some of them were downright gracious about it."

Pedal Power

In her early 40s, Ellen decided to bike her way across the Midwest during her time off. She had long been a bike enthusiast and was eager to embark on a trip that would enable her to bike for hours and days on end. Of her three months off, she biked for all but about two weeks of it.

"It was great being on the open road, just me and my bike and the slimmest pack of gear and supplies I could bear to take with me. I'd stop and use hostels when I could find them, YMCAs, college dorms, and occasionally a Motel 6. In two weeks, I felt my body begin to return to my more youthful, slimmer self, although I'd never really gotten too far out of shape. The spring in my legs was amazing. I reduced my waist by an inch and a half, and other parts of me by even more.

"You know, when you're biking, even for a few hours just on the weekend in the middle of your normal work life, you get to think great thoughts. When you bike for hours on end, your mind will take you places faster and further than your wheels ever can. I started to think about all the things I wanted to do with the rest of my life, the kind of relationships I wanted to have, the kind of work environment I wanted to create.

"I knew when I got back everything wouldn't go exactly according to plan, but I was able to achieve some pretty significant and highly rewarding changes in many areas of my life.

Would Ellen do it again? In a heartbeat! In fact, she's planning to start clumping her vacation time with other holidays and accumulated leave so that she can get a few weeks solid off at a time every year to go biking.

I'm Not Eccentric!

Buddy was wary of taking time off for a sabbatical because he was sure his boss as well as coworkers would think he was a slacker, someone who was giving less than his professional best. Unfortunately, all during his month away, he fretted over these concerns. He traveled in Europe during the time, and rather than fully experiencing the continent, he maintained a dual existence, half there and half someplace else.

When he got back to the office, he was surprised to find that no one, from his immediate boss on down to the support staff, regarded him with any glimmer of disdain for having taken the time off. Among many, the opposite was true. They wanted to know everything about his experience, what he did, how he felt, whether he would do it again, and so on.

As time passed, Buddy began to view his time off in a different light. The actual rewards for having been away began to accrue long after he was back. It's a shame he couldn't have fully embraced his experiences in Europe while he was there, but you do what you can with where you are, when you are. As a result of his experience, he'd like to take another sabbatical, perhaps in a year or two, for longer than a month. Now if he can just figure out how to work the details of getting away for that long, he'll have it made.

Chronos Says

A survey conducted by the International Foundation of Employee Benefit Plans found that a third of all American companies will soon have sabbatical policies in place, including companies such as McDonald's, Nike, and Time Inc. The larger your organization, the greater the probability that some sabbatical policy is already in place. The terms may differ greatly from one organization to another, from as much as six months off with full pay in some organizations, to an indefinite time off without pay in other organizations, so you won't know until you investigate.

Really Getting into the Flow

Jessica spent 12 years working as an exercise physiologist in Chicago and knew that it was time for her to take an exotic adventure. Clearing away four months for her first sabbatical, she traveled literally to the far reaches of the globe.

In Argentina, she met a man who longed to open his own equipment rental shop. There was a great need in his village, and the plan made perfect sense. She remembered that man, and when she returned to Chicago, she actually raised enough money to get him started.

As she put it, the object of taking time away is to expose yourself to different corners of the world. If you simply step off of a train, a plane, or a boat with the knowledge that you'll return in a week or two, you never get into the rhythm and the flow of anyplace else. It's when you're someplace else for weeks on end, with no thought of going home, that real life begins to unfold. You connect with other people. You experience new points of view. You want to help; you want to be involved.

"It all seemed right for me. It was as if the cosmos was saying, 'This is what you need to do now.' When you get back, unquestionably, there are some readjustments you have to go through. You're kind of in slow motion compared to everybody else. But so what? You've added a dimension or two of your life that simply didn't exist before you took off."

Quiet! Hemingway at Work

Like many people in the work-a-day world, Marisa longed to write the great American novel. With tremendous discipline, it would be possible to write on evenings and weekends, but on top of everything else she was doing, she never quite found the time. Once she was able to take six months off, without pay, from her Atlanta-based employer, she knew exactly what she would do from the first day on.

That first day, she expected to start on her novel with a flourish. But she found herself procrastinating, sharpening pencils, adjusting the Venetian blinds, and so forth. After about two and a half wasted days of fits and starts, she began writing. The words poured onto her PC screen. She wasn't concerned about the time because she knew she had days and weeks to work at her craft.

"There's a wellspring of creativity that opens up when you know you don't have to trudge back into work the next morning," she said. "Just me and my screen, that's all I really needed."

How about you? Are you finally inspired to take control of your time in a way that a small but growing number of others are beginning to discover? I certainly hope so. Happy time off!

The Least You Need to Know

➤ You may live longer and work longer than you currently envision, hence the greater need for time away from work.

➤ Some companies offer sabbaticals as inducements when hiring top talent.

➤ Approach your time off on an even keel: The sabbatical isn't for overcoming stressful job-related illnesses.

➤ Sabbaticals come in many varieties from educational travel, to working in another profession, to pursuing your hobbies, to doing nothing in particular.

➤ You may feel disoriented the first few days—and even weeks—once the sabbatical begins.

Making the Best of Your Day

In This Chapter

➤ Are you the prisoner of preoccupation?

➤ What *real* time is, and what it's like being there

➤ Twelve measures to help you live in *real* time

In your quest to keep pace with all that's thrown your way, it's a good bet that you're frequently preoccupied. You don't enjoy lunch because you're worried about what needs to be done in the afternoon. You don't enjoy the afternoon because you're thinking about how you have to pick up your child, get across town to attend a meeting, and then get back. You don't enjoy the evening because it goes by too fast. You don't enjoy the morning because you're always in a rush, concerned about getting to work on time. Perhaps that's the *old* you because the first 23 chapters have actually sunk in. I hope so.

Real Time: A Primer

How would your life be if you could tackle problems and challenges as they arise? What would it feel like to engage in conceptual thinking whenever you wanted or needed to? What would you feel like if you had a sense of control and ease about each day? The short answer: You would be living in *real time*.

From Start to Finish

A program planner at the National Institute of Health in Bethesda, Maryland, carries a task to completion instead of leaving it for later (when it might be one of a growing pile of tasks, requiring additional effort). He finds that even if it doesn't "feel good," sticking with the task at hand is one of the most effective ways of staying in real time and getting things off his desk, be it fielding a phone call, returning correspondence, or working on a budget.

An executive with the North Carolina Travel Association finds that one of her core strategies for effectiveness is to take phone calls when they come in (as often as possible) rather than letting them pile up. In essence, she uses the technique of completion to focus on the task at hand, pause, answer the phone, handle the call, and resume work. She's honed the ability to switch quickly from one task to another—and each is the *one* task she's engaged in at the time.

By taking phone calls as they come in, she can interact with the caller to resolve the issue, often within the duration of the call. "When you let the number of return calls you have to make build up beyond a certain level," she says, "you ensure that you won't get back to all the callers, and you're going to procrastinate when it comes to calling many of them."

She also finds it useful to deal with mail and papers that come across her desk as they arrive, but she concedes that this isn't always possible.

You may know people who live in real time, or who at least live out significant chunks of their lives in real time. Who are these people? If you know someone who stays in shape, who has the time to take a phone call, and who actually knows each of his or her children's friends by name, you've got a clue. The person who volunteers for and takes an active role in community organizations is probably living in real time.

The Big Twelve

Going for completion, handling phone calls as they come in, and finishing the task at hand are worthwhile achievements—and these elements of life are within your reach. Examine the following 12 components of living in real time, with the realization that each of these are within your grasp.

1. Leave home in the morning with grace and ease. As you know from Chapter 11, "Filing: Your Simple Salvation," you can manage the details beforehand. Take care of as many things as possible the night before so that in the morning you have only to get bodies out the door. No need for a mad rush; you've got everything ready to go.

2. Focus on the important issues facing your organization, your department or division, and your job or career. As you learned in Chapter 6, "Supporting Your Priorities for Fun and Profit," you have to pay homage to the issues that you

identify as important in your life, and you must have the strength to ignore the also-rans. Magically, when you take care of the important things, the others fall into place.

3. Handle and deal with the day's mail upon arrival, keep piles from forming on your desk, and handle phone calls within 24 hours. If you practice the techniques discussed in Chapter 12, "Neat and Uncomplicated Tools to Manage Your Time," and Chapter 13, "Are You a Slave to Your Beeper?", your skills will be enhanced in all these areas. No need to be inundated by the mail; no piles accumulate on your desk; there's no snarl of phone calls to get back to.

4. Enjoy a leisurely lunch. You know the importance of completing tasks so that when you go to lunch, you're *at lunch*. You get to chew slowly and carefully. You give up reading the newspaper and focus on the food in your mouth. Old sensations may return. You actually enjoy your lunch, digest your food better, do better back on the job, and have a vastly improved gastrointestinal outlook. Can you beat it?

   One manager with American Express in Phoenix insists on having lunch away from his desk. By getting away from the office, he is able to recharge his batteries. He feels that when you stay at your desk too long, every task competing for your attention, whether big and small, seems too urgent. By getting away at lunch time, he is able to stay focused on the big picture. He can return to the office with newfound energy.

5. Depart from the workplace at normal closing hours, and feel good about what you accomplish each day. This is straight from Chapter 1, "I Know I Can Finish Most of This (If I Stay Late)"; leaving the workday on time and feeling complete is the single most important step you can take toward permanently winning back your time. Ask yourself, "What do I need to accomplish by the end of the day to feel good about leaving on time?" You'll hardly ever leave defeated or in a bad mood.

6. Have sufficient and up-to-date health, life, disability, and automobile insurance coverage. If you want to live in real time, this is part of the overall picture. Following the discussion of priorities in Chapter 5, getting adequate insurance to protect you and your loved ones is bound to support your overall priorities.

7. File your annual (and any quarterly) income taxes on time. For one recent tax year, the IRS reported that more than 40 percent of taxpayers filed for extensions; they did not need to send in their completed tax returns until August 15 or, in some cases, October 15. You, on the other hand (once you've decided to live in real time), recognize that taxes are a necessary evil and will always be levied. You set up a tax log at the start of each year with room for each legitimate deduction, where you can file receipts and documentation. Perhaps you buy software such as Turbo Tax or Quicken that helps you complete your tax returns on a timely basis.

8. Take time to be with friends and relatives. People, not things, count most in this life. By remembering your priorities and supporting goals, and by becoming adept at making decisions, you gain the power to carve out time in your schedule to ensure that you don't short-change the people who are central in your life.

9. Stay in shape and at your desired weight. When you observe the bodies of most individuals, you can see the results of a losing tug-of-war with gravity. Body parts seem to be unduly influenced by gravity (such as drooping), but this doesn't need to be the case. Health and fitness experts say that working out for as little as 30 minutes a day four times a week can keep you comfortably fit. As I observed in my book, *Breathing Space: Living and Working at a Comfortable Pace in a Sped-Up Society*, if you're too busy to stay in shape, you're too busy!

10. Make time for hobbies. On the way to losing your time, did you abandon enjoyable activities that were a part of what made you who you are? I thought so. Revisit that stamp collection, garden, hiking club, or whatever you let slide. Living in real time means enjoying your most rewarding hobbies and pastimes regularly.

11. Participate monthly in a worthy cause. As you learn in Chapter 9, "Volunteering a Little Less—and Liking It," it's not possible to give your time and attention to all worthy causes—or even to many. Your life is finite, regardless of how long you live. When you pick the one or two that matter most to you and take action, you feel good about yourself and about how you're spending your time.

    Some factors that increase the probability of your paying homage to these causes include: not having to travel too far to participate, enjoying your coparticipants, and getting a psychological boost (an internal reward) and recognition for your efforts (external rewards) when you participate.

12. Drop back at any time, take a long deep breath, collect your thoughts, and renew your spirit—the focus of the remaining chapters.

Ready, Set, Actualize

It's one thing to have lists of all the items you're going to do, but lists alone are useless unless you take action.

Several of the ways to live in real time discussed in the preceding section may appeal to you. Suppose you wanted to actualize #9, staying in shape and at your desired weight. How would you actually succeed?

From Chapter 5, "Okay, So What Do You Want?" and Chapter 6, you learn that any goal you set needs to be specific and time-related. One of the first things you might do is commit to working out regularly and determine what you'll weigh by a certain date. From Chapter 17, "Decision Making: Step it Up and Go!", you learn that you don't need to surround yourself with reams of data and analysis before taking action. Although some information may be worthwhile, your intuition is up and running. Use it, too.

Plan your changes gradually. In the first week, you could decide that you'll no longer eat in your car. In the next few weeks, you'll stop eating when watching television. Thereafter, you might substitute skim milk for whole milk, stop putting butter on your potato, and so forth.

After you pick one of the 12 measures of living in real time (or some other measure that's important to you), create a 6-, 8-, or 10-step action plan. Based on the measure you choose and the particular circumstances of your life, your plan will be different from someone else's. The keys to making your plan work are to follow the goal-reinforcement techniques discussed in Chapter 6, some of which are briefly summarized here:

➤ Seek others with goals similar to yours.

➤ Post reinforcing statements and reminders in view.

➤ Record affirming statements on cassette.

➤ Determine any cash outlays in advance.

➤ Take bite-size action steps.

➤ Have someone waiting to hear of your progress.

➤ Envision yourself succeeding.

➤ Plot your plan on the calendar, starting from the end date.

➤ Build in some flexibility.

The Least You Need to Know

➤ To make your whole day go better, strive to make your morning routine a calm one—it'll have an impact on the rest of your day.

➤ Take time to be with and enjoy friends and relatives, and to re-engage in your hobbies. These are strong indicators that you are in control of your time.

➤ Devise a realistic action plan that ensures you will master one of the important measures of living in real time. Then take on the rest.

The Lost Art of Relaxation

In This Chapter

➤ Who is holding the whip over you?

➤ When you're in motion, it's easy to *feel* productive, but true productivity is measured by results

➤ Lingering at crucial moments throughout the day helps reclaim control of your day

➤ Overly hard-driving types are rarely as productive in the long run as those who pace themselves

Once you realize what it means to live in real time—and how far you've strayed from the mark—there are several things you can do to begin to catch up with today (or at least this week). Many are deceptively simple, but don't let that obscure the powerful results they offer.

Whip, Whip, Who's Got the Whip?

As I travel around the country speaking to organizations, I am struck by the number of people in my audiences who seem perpetually overwhelmed. The irony is that these people could take breaks throughout their days and weeks, but they don't. The biggest obstacle to winning back your time is the unwillingness to allow yourself a break.

A Stitch in Time

Seven hours and 50 minutes of work plus 10 one-minute intervals of rest or reflection in a work day makes you more productive than does eight solid hours of work.

I spoke to one group of executives and their spouses, and learned from many spouses that their executive husbands or wives simply do not allow themselves to take a break. Paradoxically, increasing evidence indicates that executives will be more effective if they pause for an extra minute a couple of times each day. This can be done every morning and afternoon—when returning from the water cooler or restroom, before leaving for lunch, or when returning from lunch. And that's just the short list.

To insist on proceeding full-speed through the day without allowing yourself 10 minutes to clear your mind all but guarantees you'll be less effective than those who do. Even the people who already perceive this need do not let themselves meet it.

Staying Competitive

The Motorola Corporation discovered the hard way that a little instruction here and there didn't educate their employees the way they had hoped. It certainly didn't stick with their employees. Motorola now has its own university with its own staff of 300 instructors and a $60 million annual budget. They have also developed in-house programs and long-term alliances with local colleges.

Why such elaborate procedures? To help the organization stay competitive. Similarly, for you to stay competitive, you need to pause periodically throughout the day—every day.

Some of the most productive and energetic people in history learned how to pace themselves effectively by taking a few "time outs" each day. Thomas Edison would rest for a few minutes each day when he felt his energy level dropping. Buckminster Fuller often worked in cycles of three or four hours, slept for 30 minutes, and then repeated the process. He found that in the course of a 24-hour period, he would get far more done than if he had followed traditional waking and sleeping patterns. While this approach isn't for everyone it worked for Bucky. By giving himself rest at shorter intervals, Fuller was able to extend his productive hours.

Remember, for most people, the time when they are least alert is between 2:00 a.m. and 5:00 a.m. Highest alertness is between 9:00 a.m. and noon, and between 4:00 p.m. to 8:00 p.m. Your alertness will vary depending on your own physiology and inclinations, as well as on the hours of consecutive duty, hours of duty in the preceding week, irregular hours, monotony on the job, timing and duration of naps, environmental lighting, sound, aroma, temperature, cumulative sleep deprivation over the past week, and much more.

Clarity in Idle Moments

You'd think that entrepreneurs, running their own businesses and managing themselves, would be more inclined to take strategic pauses throughout the day—after all, they're in charge of their own schedule. Too often, it isn't necessarily so; the temptation to overwork can be ferocious. Conversely, if you work for others, perhaps a large organization, you may erroneously believe that pausing for the total of 10 strategic minutes throughout a work day could somehow jeopardize your standing. This misconception is unfounded.

A Stitch in Time

The CEOs in many top organizations routinely take naps at midday to recharge their batteries. They have executive assistants who shield them from the outside world, take their calls, and arrange their schedules while they snooze.

If you are not the CEO of a large organization, the thought of being able to take a nap in the middle of the workday may seem like Nirvana to you. Yet, the 10 strategic minutes I have recommended provide a similar benefit. If you can't take a flat-out nap, 10 strategic minutes may be your best alternative.

Laugh at Life

How many times do you actually let out a good laugh during the day, especially during the work day? Five-year-olds reportedly laugh 113 times a day, on average. However, 44-year-olds laugh only 11 times per day. Something happens between the ages of 5 and 44 to reduce the chuckle factor.

Once you reach retirement, fortunately, you tend to laugh again. The trick is to live and work at a comfortable pace and have a lot of laughs along the way—at every age. When you proceed through the work day without humor, the days tend to be long and difficult. Part of taking control of your life is being able to step back and look at the big picture, being able to see the lighter side of things. Some of your worst gaffes eventually evolve into the things you pleasantly recall—or your best ideas! Pros who survive, laugh.

Letting Go of Anxiety

When she was 5, I told my daughter, Valerie, that my sister is a doctor—but not a doctor of the body, a doctor of the mind. Valerie promptly asked, "Does she check your mind by opening your head?" I told her no. Valerie then asked, "Do you make an appointment to see her when your mind hurts?" Out of the mouths of babes! I said yes. Valerie finally said, "Sometimes my mind hurts when I cry too much." And so it is with grown-ups whose minds hurt when they try to *take in* too much, *work* too much, and *be* too much.

285

You have to let go of the anxiety that comes from walking past the rack with hundreds of issues of magazines. You need to let the stress subside when you walk into a bookstore to pick out one book on your topic from the 80 available, or when you receive so many sales promotions, discounts, and bonus offers in the mail that you can't read all of them, let alone absorb or take advantage of them. Let them pass.

Reclaim Your Time Today and Tomorrow

The "Winning Back Your Time" Worksheet in this chapter includes nine activities: four at work, three after work, and two during vacation time. Each of these activities has a "Lately," a "Short-Term Goal," and a "Long-Term Goal" category. In the Lately column, enter how many times in the past month you have actually done each activity. In each Goal column, enter how many times you would like to, say, take a slow and leisurely lunch. In the Short-Term Goal category, for example, you could indicate two times per week.

Be realistic when recording what you have been doing. Be reflective in the short-term goal column, marking down what you can realistically achieve. Be visionary in the long-term goal column, marking down what you would ideally like to achieve.

Worksheet for Winning Back Your Time At Work: Today and Tomorrow

Time	Lately	Short-Term Goal	Long-Term Goal
Extra minute taken daily			
Leisurely lunches per week			
Hours per week in non-rush mode			
Full weekends you take off per month			
Days per month using alternate way home			
Days per month you have fun on the way home			
Days per month tele-commuting from home			
3- or 4-day vacations you take annually			
Week-long vacations you take annually			

In the weeks and months ahead, review your chart weekly for reinforcement. You need to be taking breaks such as these throughout the day, week, and year. I don't know who else is going to tell you this, and I don't know how you're going to make yourself do it unless you systemize the procedure.

The advice to take periodic breaks seems so simple, yet you may find it difficult to put into practice. It reminds me of lyrics from that song by The Who, "I'm Free"

> *If I told you what it takes to reach the highest high, / You'd laugh and say that nothing's that simple. / But you've been told many times before, / Messiahs pointed to the door / And no one had the guts to leave the temple.*

What You Need Is New Routine

Sometimes, in the quest to catch up with today, shaking up some of your time-honored routines can help:

➤ **Get up one hour earlier.** Several decades ago, the concept of "late night" (11:00 p.m.) news was unknown. People went to bed at 9:30 or 10:00 p.m. Once people began staying up for the late news, the networks began running late-night talk shows. As a result, the entire population is staying up later than the previous generation.

➤ **Work on the porch of your house instead of in the office.** As you've learned throughout the book, when you change your venue and the scenery, you open up new vistas. Alternatively, work under a tree or by a pool during nice weather. Being near nature opens up a way of viewing things that you cannot get in the office. When working in a natural, tranquil setting, you'll gain peace of mind in your otherwise-hectic work routine. When you do this for some of your tasks (especially tasks that require conceptualization or creative thinking), you'll be more productive than ever.

As the author of more than two dozen books, I find that I proofread much better on the porch or in a swing than when I'm at my desk. Begin to identify the places in your life that are welcome retreats to go and work—a library, even sitting in your car in a shopping center parking lot. When you change where you're working, you can benefit immensely and immediately.

➤ **Drop the unproductive 80 percent of your activities.** The Pareto Principle (the "80/20" rule) states that 80 percent of your activities contribute to only 20 percent of your results. The remaining 20 percent of your activities contribute to the other 80 percent of your results. Take a hardware store for example: About 20 percent of its stock accounts for 80 percent of the revenues; the remaining 80 percent of the stock accounts for only 20 percent of the revenues.

The key to successful retailing is identifying the 20 percent producing the bulk of the revenues. A smart store manager knows to place that 20 percent where it's most accessible, and put the rest where it won't get in the way. As you learn in Chapter 6, you need to identify which activities at work (and in your personal life) support you and bring you the best results. Have the strength to abandon activities that don't benefit you—get rid of that unproductive 80 percent.

➤ Ask for input. Have you ever gone to lunch with a colleague and begun discussing ways to approach your work more effectively? After a few minutes, you're both deep into the conversation, coming up with all sorts of great ideas. However, when the waiter comes to take your order or bring your check, what happens? The conversation dies down.

When you both go back to work, those ideas are often forgotten or put on a back burner. If you consciously schedule a meeting for the sole purpose of letting the creative sparks fly, you'll grab control of your time and have some of the most productive sessions you've ever had.

I meet with a mentor once a month in his dining room. At a cleared table, we sit across from each other with a tape recorder, discussing problems and issues that face us and ways we can overcome them. Each of us keeps a copy of the tape, takes it home, and makes notes on it. We capture those ideas instead of letting them die.

Chronos Says

When you come in contact with other people, you're exposed to whole new worlds—their worlds. When you interact with another person, you get the benefit of his/her information, in addition to your own.

Look for other ways to shake up your routine for the insights and breakthroughs that may result. Every day and every moment holds great potential.

Can You "Slow Down" Time?

You may be thinking, "Yeah, if each minute holds so much potential, how come they still race by so fast?" The way you experience time passing each day is based on your perception. You can slow down time if you choose. How? Whenever you feel you're racing the clock or trying to tackle too much at once, try this exercise:

> *Close your eyes for sixty seconds and imagine a pleasant scene. It could be in nature or with a loved one. It could be something from childhood. Let the emotions of that place and time predominate. Get into it! Give yourself more than a New York minute for the visualization to take hold. Then open your eyes and return to what you're doing. What you're working on is not quite so bad; the pace at which you are now working is not quite so feverish.*

One effective method for catching up with today is periodically deleting three items from your to-do list without doing them at all. Before you shriek, consider that much of what makes your list is nonessential. If you can eliminate three items, in most cases it will have no impact on your career or life, except for freeing up some time for yourself in the present. Nice gift.

Get Back (Where You Once Belonged)

Think about flying on an airplane. You have a window seat, and it's a clear day. As you gaze down to the ground below, what do you see? Cars the size of ants. Miniature baseball diamonds. Hotels that look like Monopoly pieces. Life passing by.

The same effect can take place at the top of a mountain or a skyscraper. As often as possible, when things seems to be racing by too fast, get to higher ground for a clear perspective. If you're among the lucky, perhaps you regularly allocate time for reflection or meditation. If you don't, no matter—there are other ways to slow it all down. After the workday, really listen to relaxing music with headphones on and with your eyes closed. A half hour of your favorite music with no disturbances (and your eyes closed) can seem almost endless. When you re-emerge, the rest of the day takes on a different tone.

Let Rover Help

If you have a dog or cat and do not consider it a drain on your time, here's a little something about Rover or Mittens that you may not have known. In recent years, as reported by *U.S. News & World Report*, scientists have found proof for what was only suspected: Contact with animals has specific and measurable effects on both your body and mind. The mere presence of animals can increase a sick person's chances of survival and has been shown to lower heart rates, calm disturbed children, and induce incommunicative people to initiate conversation!

A Stitch in Time

The exact mechanisms that animals exert to affect your health and well-being are still largely mysterious. Scientists suspect that animal companionship is beneficial because, unlike human interaction, it is uncomplicated. Whatever the reason, having pets works to reduce stress. Puppy, anyone?

Animals are nonjudgmental, accepting, and attentive; they don't talk back, criticize, or give orders. Animals have a unique capacity to draw people out.

Some folks find watching fish restful. Even if you only have goldfish, sometimes simply staring at them in their silent world can help slow your pace.

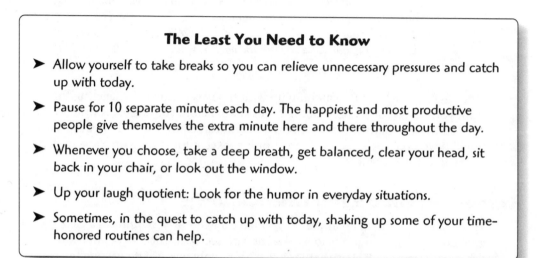

The Least You Need to Know

➤ Allow yourself to take breaks so you can relieve unnecessary pressures and catch up with today.

➤ Pause for 10 separate minutes each day. The happiest and most productive people give themselves the extra minute here and there throughout the day.

➤ Whenever you choose, take a deep breath, get balanced, clear your head, sit back in your chair, or look out the window.

➤ Up your laugh quotient: Look for the humor in everyday situations.

➤ Sometimes, in the quest to catch up with today, shaking up some of your time-honored routines can help.

Chapter 26

When You Just Gotta Get Away

In This Chapter

➤ It's getting harder (and hence more crucial) to take a break from your normal work routine

➤ Retrain and recharge yourself on cue!

➤ How to get new references in your life

➤ How about a personal sabbatical?

Can you withdraw from the maddening crowd? I'm talking about going whole weekends without doing anything, taking true vacations, and spending evenings sitting on the porch, as the late John Lennon said, "watching the wheels go round and round." These are not lost arts. Nevertheless, if you've spent too many anxiety-ridden days in a row—say, 10 years' worth—or maintained some monomaniacal quest to fill up every minute with meaningful or worthwhile activities, your task is cut out for you. This chapter can help.

Who Sped Up This Merry-go-round?

The great paradox of being an ambitious professional functioning in an information-ridden society is that you tend to keep doing what you're doing. If you're working too long, trying to keep pace, and taking in more and more information, the impetus is for you to keep doing that—even when it isn't satisfying or healthy.

Anyone can fall into this trap—it's human nature. As your responsibilities mount at work, you may actually find yourself dreading the notion of taking a vacation because of all the work that would pile up when you're away. (Sound too familiar? Thought so.) Entrepreneurs, in particular, find it hard to know when to drop back and punt.

Author and historian Arnold Toynbee once said, "To be able to fill leisure intelligently is that last product of civilization." He is right on target; an increasing number of people have problems in this area. In fact, I could go so far as to say that the concept of leisure time is on the rocks. As I discussed in *Breathing Space: Living and Working at a Comfortable Pace in a Sped-Up Society*, it no longer means "total hours minus work hours."

True leisure—when you get to enjoy rewarding activities, free from work and preoccupation with work—is absolutely vital.

Do the strains of the work week prompt you to place great emphasis on your weekends and other days off? If you seek to relax but are hounded by pressures, it's hard to get legitimate rest, even when you've got the hours to do so.

Regaining a Little Sanity

Hope springs eternal, and I know that you have the ability to change. When I was in Boston visiting my best friend, Peter Hicks, I saw on his den wall the "diploma" he received in kindergarten. It was there as a kind of joke. I was in the same kindergarten class and had saved mine, too. His was fading. Perhaps he had exposed it to the sun. When I mentioned that I still had mine, he asked if I could make a clean copy and send it to him so he could reconstruct his original.

Back home, while I was looking for the diploma, I also found my first-grade report card. This is one of the lifetime treasures that you don't chuck. Not having looked at it for years, I eagerly flipped it open.

A Stitch in Time

People *can* change, especially you. What's more you can change in positive, dramatic ways.

Individuals Can Change

In those days (right after dinosaurs ruled the world), report cards came in booklet form. The teachers actually hand-wrote both the letter grade and the comments at the bottom. As I looked at each of the grades, I smiled, "A, B, A, A...." Then I got to arithmetic and saw the "C."

I didn't remember being bad in arithmetic. In fact, I led my high school in SAT scores for math. I looked down at the bottom where the teacher had written, "Jeff has a good understanding of arithmetic fundamentals, but he rushes his work and sometimes makes careless errors." I was aghast. Here I was, decades later, still making the same kinds of errors!

I resolved then and there to be more methodical in my work, whether it related to numbers, writing, or speaking. And I can report that since then, I have become much more astute.

Society Can Change

I am happy to report that all of society can change for the better, too. In late 1989, I sent a proposal for a book entitled *A Layman's Guide for Saving the Planet* out to an editor at Warner Books. This book would tell readers how they could walk through their homes, room by room, and be more environmentally responsible. The editor sent me back a rejection letter saying he thought the proposal and book had great merit, but the editorial staff at Warner felt that no one in America realistically would change their "cozy, comfortable lifestyles."

Four months later, another publisher released the book *50 Simple Things You Can Do to Save the Earth*. It quickly became a worldwide best-seller, endorsed at the highest levels of business and government, including the White House. Several other environmental books quickly followed, many of them doing quite well.

Since then, many organizations, including state and local governments, have initiated environmentally sound policies. Many recycling centers were created. People began to recognize the value of recycling newspapers, tin cans, plastic, and other materials. It turns out the editors at Warner were wrong. People *can* change. You can change.

Here are some suggestions for periodically abandoning the rat race, starting with small steps:

1. Give yourself permission to go a whole weekend without reading anything, as mentioned in Chapter 24, "Making the Best of Your Day."

2. Decide to put your home phone answering machine on "answer," flip the ringer off, and don't play back any messages until the next day.

3. Collect all the magazines piling up around your house, and give them away to a retirement community, library, or school.

4. Go ahead and schedule that spa treatment you've been dying to take.

5. Exchange photos with a friend you haven't seen in years. Mail your friend two or three photos of you and the family, and receive two or three in return, or spend one Sunday afternoon writing or calling friends and relatives with whom you've lost touch.

6. Unplug your phone each Friday night. Banish the beeper.

Time Out!

When you force-fit leisure between barrages of constant frenzy, the quality of your leisure is going to suffer. For that matter, so are you.

7. Get schedules of your favorite professional or amateur teams, and mark on your calendar the appropriate dates to sit back and enjoy the games.

8. Visit a botanical garden to enjoy the variety of flowers; let your sense of smell, rather than your eyes and ears, dominate.

9. Attend the graduation ceremonies of your local high school, even if you don't know anyone who's graduating. Recapture the spirit of what it's like to complete an important passage in life.

10. Pick up a bouquet of fresh flowers at the grocery store or flower shop and display them somewhere in your home.

11. Walk around your yard barefoot, the way you did when you were a kid. Feel the grass between your toes. Stick your feet in dirt or in a puddle.

12. Visit a historical monument and let yourself become immersed in the challenges that people of that era faced.

13. Attend a free lecture some evening about a topic outside your professional interests.

14. Sleep late.

All About New References

In one of his monthly "power talks," infomercial king and best-selling author Tony Robbins explains why it's important for you to constantly get new references in your life. Robbins explains how people can easily fall into the same routines, travel to work the same way, and believe that the world is exactly the way they see it. The new references come from field trips you can take yourself, such as going to a small museum, a seniors' home, a circus, a dairy farm, a soup kitchen, a daycare center, a municipal court, an open-air market, or any other place you find intriguing, inviting, or awaiting your help.

These references give you a different perspective on the world, and ultimately on your own life. All of them represent small steps—it's not like I'm asking you to take a week away from your job or go hiking in the Himalayas.

What new references will you incorporate in the next week or month?

Replenishing the Energy Well

The value of periodically abandoning the rat race—or at least your personal rat race—is that it gives you the opportunity to recharge yourself. Think back to Chapter 7, " Money Comes and Goes—Time Just Goes" (on the value of getting more sleep)—what it would be like if you could recharge yourself like a rechargeable battery? What if you could have that old zip and zest or a twinkle in your eye when you came in to work? What if you could have the stamina to put in a full work day but still leave with lots of energy?

Legendary late-night TV talk show host Johnny Carson chose Robin Williams and Bette Midler as his last guests. Why these two people, of the thousands of possibilities? Many actors and actresses, comedians, and other types of entertainers would have given their eyeteeth to be on this celebrated show that attracted tens of millions of viewers. I brought this question up with friends; after tossing about several possibilities, we came up with what has to be the answer:

➤ Robin Williams was about the highest-energy male Johnny Carson could have had as a guest.

➤ Bette Midler was about the highest-energy female Johnny Carson could have had as a guest.

Both performers exude energy. As a showman, Johnny Carson learned quickly that what you offer to your audience *is energy*. So it is with you and your career. What you offer to your employer, employees, customers, or coworkers is energy.

How can you recharge yourself and rev up your energy level, if you're not willing to occasionally drop back and punt? Do you think Robin Williams, Steve Martin, or any other seemingly manic comedian can charge ahead at full throttle all the time? No way.

Time Out!

How can you possibly exude high energy if you plow ahead day after day at the same old grind, short-changing your sleep, short-changing your rest, and perhaps never taking any true vacations?

A Stitch in Time

The more positive energy you offer, the greater your returns in terms of the wages you earn, the business you generate, or the synergy you achieve.

Fifty Days Away

Fifty Days Away—that's what Joe Kita, a writer for *Men's Health* magazine, took to recharge and renew himself (it's also the title of an article about his experience). Kita feels that even if you get three or four weeks of paid vacation a year, you're probably finding it difficult to take merely five consecutive days off. He arranged his life so that he could take 50 days away from work (see Chapter 23, "Not for Everyone: Taking a Sabbatical"). He found that this near-retirement experience enlightened him in a way that didn't typically happen during one- or even two-week vacations. Here's a summary of what happened:

1. He started dreaming again. After a few days, away he was having incredible dreams, as if he was directing major motion pictures. He found it amazing that all that dream activity was somehow quite restful. He'd wake feeling fresh and alive. During this time, he learned that everyone dreams every night. When you get highly restful sleep, and as much as you need, your dream-rich REM periods last longer; you wake up feeling more refreshed.

2. He lost track of time. With little reason to look at the clock or even at the calendar, time began to slow down. Kita said he felt like a kid again. After years of seeing his life speed by almost without control, the days began to pass at a gentler pace. He walked, rather than drove, to the store.

3. His memory returned. Being saturated with so much information had a dampening effect on his memory. He remarked that people today are bombarded with more daily intelligence than J. Edgar Hoover ever encountered. When the shelling subsides, even for a short period of time, your memory can spring back in full bloom.

4. He became more thoughtful. Kita recalls that during his hectic working time, he never truly read anything—he scanned. He never saw anything—he glanced. During his time away from the rat race, he began to chew his food and digest it properly. He even began to taste it.

5. He became calmer. He began to notice that he was more patient with his children. He was able to listen to his wife. He found that, in general, he was more tolerant in dealing with others.

6. He was able to re-divert energy. He discovered what amazing things he could accomplish with a little time off. He painted his entire house, analyzed and restructured all his investments, and even cleaned out his T-shirt drawer.

7. He gained new perspective. He began to see that few jobs in this world carry life-or-death consequences. He discovered that it's productive to be unproductive sometimes. He gave up feeling guilty about occasionally doing nothing.

8. He rediscovered sex. The biggest obstacles to the sex lives of working men (and women), says Kita, are lack of time and fatigue. Because he had enough time now—and he wasn't tired—his libido returned. Such a life.

Are there any downsides to staying away from work? Yes—you might lose a bit of your self-worth. What you do at work is often tied to who you are as a person. Predictably, you may start looking forward to going back to work. After all, you chose your work and remain at it (at least I hope you do) because you're good at it and well suited to it. You get strokes from it as well as income.

Establishing Your Kick-Back Routine

When you feel ready to live life at a more leisurely pace, whether or not you're taking time off from work, signs appear. You wake naturally without an alarm clock and have time to reflect each morning. If it is a work day, you leave the office on time at the end of the day, engrossed with what you'll do next, without any thoughts of work.

If you're ready to drop back and punt but aren't quite ready to take a huge chunk of time away from work, here are some things you can do now to ease the throttle back on the pace of your life:

➤ Play with your child for hours on a Saturday afternoon, without any concern for time.

➤ Eat dinner early in the evening, and have time to take a stroll or whatever you feel like doing.

➤ Resubscribe to the local community theater's fall series—and actually attend.

➤ Re-engage in one of your hobbies (as discussed in Chapter 22, "Time Out for Leisure") with renewed enthusiasm.

➤ Make a new friend about once a month. From where? Who knows? They start showing up because you've allowed time for it to happen.

➤ Book a cruise or a cross-continental trip, maybe for the first time or the first time in years.

➤ Volunteer for a charitable or civic activity in which you've long wanted to help but, until now, have not taken action.

➤ View a sunrise at least once a month, and maybe even once a week. Also, view many, many sunsets each month.

➤ Frequent some of the area's best parks. Occasionally feed the ducks.

Signs of Slippage

As the chapter comes to a close, here's a list of indications that you have let things slide a tad too long (and had better reread this chapter closely):

1. You're daughter is an intern at the White House and you're not concerned.

2. You hear the word Whitewater in the news and think it's about rafting.

3. You heard something about a sequel to *Titanic* but forgot that the ship was real, sank to the bottom of the sea, and two-thirds of the passengers died.

4. You recently drove to the local record store only to find that they no longer sell records.

5. You're on the last notch of your favorite belt, and it's still way too tight.

6. You're looking forward to going to your 10th high school reunion, when you realize it's actually your 15th (or 20th!).

7. You're not only eating lunch at your desk, but you're starting to eat dinner at your desk.

8. Your boss keeps asking you to take a vacation.

9. Your wallet is twice as thick as your index finger.

10. Your kid sees you walking up your sidewalk and asks, "Can I help you, sir?"

The Least You Need to Know

➤ No matter how many hours you've put in over the last several years, you can retrain yourself to approach your work and time in more rewarding ways.

➤ Everyone needs to recharge themselves, especially you. When you're recharged, you have more energy and all your relationships go better.

➤ You need a vacation. Start planning a real one now.

➤ You can initiate many small steps, even before taking time away from work, to achieve a more leisurely pace; you can play with your child for hours on a Saturday or subscribe to the local community theater series.

Chapter 27

The Future's So Bright, I Gotta Wear Shades

In This Chapter

➤ Life is a marathon, not a sprint. Are you wearing the proper running shoes?

➤ The world will become more complex—what are you going to do about it?

➤ Control is a personal choice

➤ You can make profound choices by which to steer your life

Whether you're 28, 38, 48, or somewhere in between, it's time to start looking at your life as if the best years are yet to come, for indeed they can be coming. Sure, you'll get a little slower with each advancing year, but you have the ability to put together all that you've learned in each decade (this is sometimes referred to as wisdom). Perhaps you'll be even more prudent with your time. More than 100 years ago, in his essay "The Feeling of Immortality and Youth," British essayist William Hazlitt said, "As we advance in life, we acquire a keener sense of the value of time. Nothing else, indeed, seems of any consequence, and we become misers in this respect." That may be true, yet as you learned in Chapter 2, "Time Flies Whether You're Having Fun or Not," you probably have more time left on this planet than you think.

In for the Long Haul

Regardless of your age or how much time you have left, anytime is a good one to practice measures for winning back your time. You may even find it rewarding to revel in your current age—it holds so much potential. Marlee Matlin won the Academy Award for Best Actress at age 21; the late Jessica Tandy won it at age 80. The U.S. Constitution was written by men who were, on average, 40 years of age—when the life expectancy was barely 40. Sure, there were some old-timers like Ben Franklin, but most of the founding fathers were young by today's standards.

James Michener didn't write his first novel until age 42. He produced one best-seller after another until his death at age 90. As I hit the big four-oh, I started to feel a little uncomfortable about the passing time in my life. Now, at nearly 50, for some reason I feel more at ease about how I use my time. I found it comforting to look up the birth dates of notable people who are about the same age as I am:

01/09/51	Crystal Gayle
01/09/51	Stevie Wonder
01/12/51	Rush Limbaugh
01/13/51	Jeff Davidson!
01/30/51	Phil Collins
02/15/51	Melissa Manchester
02/15/51	Jane Seymour
04/10/51	Steven Seagal
07/05/51	Huey Lewis
07/08/51	Angelica Houston
09/09/51	Michael Keaton
10/07/51	John Mellencamp

When Elvis was my age, he'd been dead for six years! (Unless, of course, you've sighted him recently....) Some people take up marathon running in their 50s; some people take it up in their 60s. Become comfortable with your current age, and recognize the vast potential you have with all your remaining years. Alice Cornyn-Selby, a prolific author and speaker from Portland, Oregon, uses two powerful key phrases with her audiences:

1. "I have now come to the end of my life and I'm disappointed that I didn't...."

   How did you finish that sentence? Whatever came up first is probably something you want to do right away. No use putting it off any longer, because it bubbled up to the surface immediately.

2. "I have now come to the end of my life and I'm glad that I...."

   What did you come up with this time? Was it the same issue that you addressed in the first statement? Was it something you've already accomplished? When you begin to look at the opportunities that await and those you can create, all the rushing about that came before and the times you felt you were missing your life can begin to melt away as you head in the direction that will give you deep satisfaction.

Put It in Perspective

As you've learned in this book, the more often you can feel complete about your accomplishments, the more energy, focus, and direction you'll have. All things end, whether poorly or wonderfully. Whether they take a few seconds or an astronomical epoch, every event has an end. For example:

Everything Ends

➤ 100-watt light bulb's life	750 hours
➤ Columbus's first 1492 trip	70 days
➤ Car muffler	2.5 years
➤ Car water pump	3.5 years
➤ U.S. presidential term	4.0 years
➤ Skylab's time in orbit	6.2 years
➤ A year on Jupiter	11.9 years
➤ The Cold War	43.5 years
➤ The Soviet Union	61.9 years
➤ Your life	??? years
➤ Human organs	115 years
➤ The 100 Years War	116 years
➤ The Crusades	196 years
➤ The Holy Roman Empire	841 years
➤ Cro-Magnon Man	30,000 years
➤ The Jurassic Period	64 million years
➤ Dinosaurs (Mesozoic Era)	165 million years
➤ Earth before *homo erectus*	4 billion years
➤ Sun's remaining life	5 billion years

You can use completion-thinking to get caught up with this moment, feel good about everything that's transpired thus far, and energize yourself for what's ahead. In *The Fountain of Age*, Betty Friedan closes with a remarkable paragraph:

> *I am myself at this age. It took me these years to put the missing pieces together, to confront my own age in terms of integrity and generativity, moving into the unknown future with a comfort now, instead of being stuck in the past. I have never felt so free.*

New Goals for a New You

So, what kind of completions can you realize about your own life? What kind of goals do you want to make, given the fact that today represents a new opportunity to reclaim your life? Not like that trite old phrase, "Today's the first day in the rest of your life," but with a deeper realization that you can be in control.

The following is a set of new goals you might want to entertain. These aren't ones that traditionally make achievers' lists, but they can be important to the quality of your life.

1. *Weight.* What weight do you want to be at one year from now or five years from now? What size waistline do you want to have? Do you want to become as fit as you've been in the past? It's possible, but it's a choice you'll have to make first.

2. *Blood pressure.* I'll bet you never thought of this. Would you like to get your blood pressure down to 120 over 80? What foods and habits are you willing to give up to keep your blood pressure at a safe, healthy level?

3. *Resting pulse per minute.* How hard is your heart working for you right now? Is your resting pulse above 80? You should know that 70 beats per minute, and even 60, is quite possible. My average is 52. I know a 65-year-old who averages 42.

   Hold on—before you think the guy must be about to keel over, look at it from a physiological standpoint: His heart is working efficiently. In the course of a day, a week, or a year, it's beating far fewer times than yours. He achieved this by ensuring that each day he takes walks that last between 15 minutes and an hour.

4. *Hours of sleep nightly.* You know by now the paramount importance of sleep. One year or five years from now, how much do you want to be sleeping each night? It's up to you.

5. *Healthy foods regularly consumed.* You may not be able to eat the recommended three to five helpings of vegetables each day, or the two to three helpings of fruit, but you could probably add a lot more of both to your diet. You don't have to visit a health store to eat healthfully. You need only choose fresh foods from your traditional supermarket.

6. *Vitamins taken regularly.* If you're over 30, this grows in importance each day. Do you take a multivitamin? Do you take specific vitamins throughout the day to ensure peak performance? If you're in a highly stressful position, you probably need a good B-complex vitamin. Maybe you're not getting enough vitamin C. When's the last time you visited a nutritionist or dietitian and figured out what supplements would be best given your lifestyle and physiology?

7. *Great novels read.* To make the best yet to come, you can have goals beyond simply health and fitness. What great novels would you like to read, but year after year haven't begun? One option is that today most great novels are on cassette. Perhaps listening to them, rather than reading them, is your cup of tea. Either way, the choice—and the ability to get started—is yours. (Hint: Children love to be read to; it can be a rejuvenating treat for adults.)

A Stitch in Time

If you want to improve the quality of your life for the rest of your life, you can start with what you take out of the video store on your next trip.

8. *Classic or inspiring movies viewed.* Sure, it's easy enough to go down to the video store and rent the latest shoot 'em up or action thriller. Instead, what about a good biographical video? Or how about a historical novel on video? What about a documentary? At any given moment, you have a lot of alternatives in terms of what you're viewing.

9. *Family involvement.* Perhaps you're already good at this, but perhaps it's an area to revisit. Have you been to your son's Boy Scout troop meeting lately? Have you ever watched your daughter for a full soccer practice? Have you had a real family outing—not the kind where you go to a theme park, spend money, and have hectic fun, but where you bring a picnic basket, hike together, talk to each other, and spend the day in a quiet and enjoyable way?

A Complex World and More So

As you learned in Chapter 2, "Time Flies Whether You're Having Fun or Not," and Chapter 11, "Filing: Your Simple Salvation," population, information, media growth, too much paper, and an over-abundance of choices all converge to make it feel as if you have never had enough time. Realistically, these challenges will accelerate in the next decade.

You can count on complexity increasing. I see three possible scenarios: (1) Few people learn how to win back their time; (2) Some people learn how to win back their time; or (3) Most people learn how to win back their time.

1. *Few people learn how to win back their time.* What will society look like in this scenario? In the social environment, there will continue to be high stress, constant breakdowns, perhaps neglect of children, and people walking around in an overwhelmed state. In this scenario, more catastrophes will occur: train wrecks, plane crashes, auto mishaps.

   In the business environment, you will see more stress and burnout among professionals, increasing hostility, and more people walking around in microsleep. You will also see more cluttered desks and more people constantly playing catch-up. What's the typical individual's response in a society where everybody is on fast-forward and no one is in control of his or her time? More "me-first" attitudes, more investment in creature comforts that don't truly comfort, and more feelings of disenfranchisement. Not pleasant.

2. *Some people win back control of their time.* In the social environment, feeling overwhelmed is only intermittent. Breakdowns are seen as routine, but at least they're not constant.

   In the business environment, management training can alleviate some problems. What is the typical, individual response to being in a world where only some people are in control of their time (much like today)? Such people will choose fewer projects, but they'll be more important ones. People will be a little less stressed out because they'll understand what's going on. They'll try to find more enjoyment in leisure and clear their weekends of work.

3. *Most people win back their time.* Under such a favorable scenario, there will be a strong concentration on the family. More individuals will exhibit balance and control. There will even be a further development of the social graces.

   In the business environment, people will be able to have vacations and leisure time available on request. Businesses will stay lean, but only mean to the competition. Managers, from the top CEO down to the line supervisors, will be able to display confidence and compassion. They'll be able to respond to the requests and concerns of their employees—people will be of primary importance. Wages will actually increase. Efficiency and effectiveness will be the name of the game.

   What is the typical individual's response to existing in an environment where most people have control of their time? A "we-first" mindset is maintained amidst a quest for personal betterment. The individual pursues cultural as well as social endeavors, keeping an astute eye on the environment.

You can prevail under any scenario. Regardless of which scenario comes to pass, your ability to win back your time is up to you.

Conscious Choices

You can make choices, of course, about any aspect of your time and life, be they issues relating to work, change, technology, success, travel, health and well-being, relationships, marriage, or parenting. Affirmation techniques can be used to help reinforce those choices and turn them into reality.

Abundant research shows that after 21 days of repeating an affirmation to yourself, notable positive change occurs. Why? Your subconscious mind accepts the statements you give it repeatedly; it can't discern between what exists now and what you've chosen for your future! (Generally, the people who don't credit the power of affirmations have never used and trusted the process.)

As with any quest to reinforce the choices you make, write or type your decisions, and post them or record them on cassette and play them back. How many choices can you make in a sitting? There is no limit, although I'd suggest making no more than a dozen. Choose what feels right, and keep choosing. While you're waiting in a bank line, run through your choices. If you notice yourself wavering, recall the new behavior or feeling that you've chosen.

Some profound choices you can make are listed next. Read them all, and circle the ones that best meet your present needs. You may want to craft your own choices, using your own words. Keep reminding yourself of them for at least 21 days.

Aging and Well-Being:

➤ I choose to feel good about the age I am and relish the years I have left.

➤ I choose to face the future with confidence.

➤ I choose to adopt a healthy lifestyle.

Career Changes:

➤ I choose to feel good about my career move.

➤ I choose to be open to new ideas and information.

➤ I choose to apply the lessons from previous careers effectively in my new career.

Change in General:

➤ I choose to handle change with grace and ease.

➤ I choose to thrive on challenging situations.

➤ I choose to master changing technology in my field.

The Future:

➤ I choose to acknowledge that things will work out for the best.

➤ I choose to face the future boldly and decisively.

➤ I choose to arise each morning with great anticipation.

Opportunity:

➤ I choose to recognize and create opportunities.

➤ I choose to see each minute as new.

➤ I choose to be open to new avenues for prosperity.

Personal Development:

➤ I choose to be an active listener.

➤ I choose to personify grace and ease.

➤ I choose to acknowledge others often.

I find affirmations such as these useful as starting points, especially when I'm trying out a new idea that has always seemed out of reach before. To help fulfill an affirmation, ask yourself at the end of the 21 days, "What specific actions have I taken to follow through on this choice I have made?" Write down three specific instances.

A Stitch in Time

By choosing to feel worthy and complete, you automatically help redirect yourself and begin to accept that there is nothing you "must" do. Everything is based on your choice.

A Choice Worthy of All

An essential choice for nearly everyone is choosing to feel worthy and complete. This helps me to reduce anxiety, stay calm, and feel more relaxed. Depending on how long it's been since you've felt worthy and complete, you may have to reaffirm this choice for many days or weeks running. Nevertheless, keep at it.

If you choose to continue working on some task, even one assigned to you, you make that choice in the present moment, not in response to a prior agenda. A worthy and complete feeling yields a sense of inner harmony.

The Least You Need to Know

➤ Factors conspiring to make you feel time-pressed are likely to intensify in the coming years.

➤ While you'll get older and slower, the best is yet to come because you'll be able to draw upon your wisdom to steer your life faithfully in the desired direction.

➤ You can choose to see the totality and completion of your life up to this minute, anytime you want.

➤ You continually can make fundamental choices about where you want your life to go.

➤ The fundamental choices you can make regarding your time are, "I choose to feel good about how I spend my time," and, "I choose to easily have all the time I need to accomplish my goals and lead a balanced life."

Glossary

Contrarian   Somebody who opts to engage in activities at times and places when and where everybody else is *not* engaging in them.

Dynamic bargain   An agreement you make with yourself to assess what you've accomplished (and what more you want to accomplish) from time to time throughout the day, adjusting to new conditions as they emerge.

Faustian bargains   Shady deals, so named after a character the lead character in *Dr. Faustus*, by Christopher Marlow, who sold his eternal soul to the Devil for a better time on earth.

Hydration   When your body's tissues are sufficiently filled with water. To be dehydrated is to be parched.

Insidious   Something that is treacherous.

Leisure   That which is worth your time and attention, or that which is worth doing. Enjoying rewarding activity free from work and preoccupation with work.

Microsleep   A 5-to-10-second episode when your brain is effectively asleep while you are otherwise up and about. Microsleep can occur while you are working at your PC or driving a car.

Overchoice   The stress that comes from too many options, especially the "so-what?" variety.

Rapid eye movements (REM)   When sleeping, your eyes actually shift all over although your eyelids are closed; these movements and various levels of brain activity are essential to sound sleep.

Schlepping   A Yiddish word that means over-extending yourself, often in the context of accomplishing small tasks.

Seed work   Tasks you can easily assign to another because the downside risk if he or she botches the task is negligible.

Self-storage unit   A for-rent, garage-like space you can fill with any items you don't need too often.

Sound screen   An electronic device that creates a sound "barrier," which masks or mutes the effects of louder sound from beyond the barrier.

Spate   A large number or amount.

Telecommuting   Working outside the office (away from your employer's base of operations) and staying in touch with coworkers via electronics, such as a computer, fax, and phone.

Tickler files   A file system designed to give you a place to chronologically park items related to forthcoming issues and to remind you when you need to deal with such issues.

White noise   A non-invasive, non-disruptive sound (much like that of rushing water, a fan, or distant motor noise).

Bibliography

Arnold, David, Ph.D, and Gail Rutman, *Business on the Internet: The Concise Handbook* (DA & Associates, 1999).

Bates, Jefferson D., *Dictating Effectively: A Time Saving Manual* (Acropolis, 1981).

Biggs, Dick, *If Life Is a Balancing Act, Why Am I So Darn Clumsy?* (Chattahoochee Press, 1993).

Cameron, Julia, *The Artist's Way* (Tarcher, 1992).

Carr, David, *Time Narrative in History* (Indiana University Press, 1986).

Cathcart, Jim, *The Acorn Principle* (St. Martin's, 1999).

Choate, Pat, *Agents of Influence* (Knopf, 1990).

Coleman, Dr. Paul W., *The Forgiving Marriage* (Contemporary Books, 1990).

Connor, Richard, and Jeff Davidson, *Marketing Your Consulting & Professional Services*, 3rd edition (John Wiley, 1997).

Covey, Stephen, *The Seven Habits of Highly Effective Families* (Franklin/Covey, 1997).

Csikszentmihalyi, Mihaly, *Flow: The Psychology of Optimal Experience* (Harper, 1990).

Davidson, Jeff, *Breathing Space: Living and Working at a Comfortable Pace in a Sped-Up Society* (MasterMedia, 1991).

_____. *Marketing for the Home-based Business*, 2nd edition (Adams Media, 1999).

_____. *Marketing Your Career and Yourself* (Adams Media, 1999).

_____. *The Complete Idiot's Guide to Assertiveness* (Macmillan, 1997).

_____. *The Complete Idiot's Guide to Managing Stress*, 2nd edition (Macmillan, 1999).

_____. *The Complete Idiot's Guide to Reaching Your Goals* (Macmillan, 1997).

_____. *The Joy of Simple Living* (Rodale, 1999).

Diamond, Dr. John, *Your Body Doesn't Lie: How to Increase Your Life Energy Through Behavioral Kinesiology* (Warner, 1994).

Dominguez, Joe, and Vicki Robin, *Your Money or Your Life* (Viking, 1992).

Drucker, Peter, *The Effective Executive* (Harper & Row, 1967).

Dychtwald, Ken, Ph.D., *Age Wave* (Tarcher, 1989).

Faludi, Dr. Susan, *Backlash, The Undeclared War Against American Women* (Anchor, 1992).

Fanning, Tony, and Robin Fanning, *Get It All Done and Still Be Human* (Open Chain Publishing, 1990).

Farrell, Dr. Warren, *Why Men are the Way They Are* (McGraw-Hill, 1986).

Fisher, Jeffrey A., M.D., *RX 2000: Breakthroughs in Health, Medicine and Longevity by the Year 2000 and Beyond* (Simon & Schuster, 1994).

Friedan, Betty, *The Fountain of Age* (Simon & Schuster, 1993).

Fritz, Robert, *The Path of Least Resistance* (Fawcett Columbine, 1989).

Godfrey, N., *Money Doesn't Grow on Trees* (Fireside Books, 1994).

Grant, Lindsey, ed., *Elephants in the Volkswagen* (W. H. Freeman, 1991).

Gross, Irma and Mary Lewis, *Home Management* (out of print, 1938).

Jeffers, Susan, *Feel the Fear and Do It Anyway* (Harcourt, Brace & Jovanovich, 1987).

Johnson, Magic, *My Life* (Random House, 1992).

Kanter, Rosabeth Moss, *The Change Masters* (Simon & Schuster, 1983).

Kawasaki, Guy, *How to Drive the Competition Crazy* (Hyperion, 1995).

Kobliner, B., *Get a Financial Life* (Fireside Books, 1996).

Kostner, Dr. Jaclyn, *Virtual Leadership* (Warner, 1996).

Kutner, Lawrence, *Your School-Age Child* (Morrow, 1996).

Minkin, Barry Howard, *EconoQuake* (Prentice-Hall, 1993).

Moore-Ede, Martin, M.D., Ph.D., *The 24-Hour Society* (Addison-Wesley, 1993).

Osborn, Carol, *Enough Is Enough* (Putnam, 1986).

Peel, Kathy, *The Family Manager's Guide for Working Moms* (Ballantine, 1997).

Peters, K. Joan, *When Mothers Work: Loving Our Children Without Sacrificing Our Selves* (Addison-Wesley, 1997).

Postman, Neil, Ph.D., *Amusing Ourselves to Death* (Viking, 1985).

Postman, Neil, Ph.D., *Technopoly* (Knopf, 1992).

Proat, Frieda, *Creative Procrastination* (Harper & Row, 1980).

Rajineesh, Osho, *Don't Just Do Something, Sit There* (Maineesha, 1980).

Rifkin, Jeremy, *Time Wars* (Henry Holt, 1987).

Rose, Kenneth, *The Organic Clock* (Wiley, 1988).

Schor, Judith, *Consumerism* (Basic Books, 1993).

Scott, Dru, *How to Put More Time in Your Life* (Signet, 1980).

Sharp, Clifford, *The Economies of Time* (Oxford, 1981).

Shenkman, Richard, *Legends, Lies, and Cherished Myths of American History* (Morrow, 1989).

Smith, Marian, *In Today, Out Today* (Prentice Hall, 1982).

Stautberg, Susan S., and Marcia L. Worthing, *Balancing Act* (Avon, 1992).

Swenson, Richard A., *Margin: Restoring Emotional, Physical, Financial, and Time Reserves to Overloaded Lives* (Navpress, 1992).

Talley, Linda, *Business Finesse: Dealing with Sticky Situations in the Work Place for Managers* (Leadership University Press, 1998).

Taylor, Frederic, *The Principles of Scientific Management* (Harper & Row, 1911).

Toffler, Alvin, *Future Shock* (Random House, 1970).

Twitchell, James, *Carnival Culture* (Columbia University Press, 1992).

Wagner, Ronald L., and Engelmann, Eric, *The McGraw-Hill Internet Training Guide* (McGraw-Hill, 1996).

Waitely, Denis, *Timing is Everything* (Pocket Books, 1993).

Wills, Christopher, *The Run Away Brain: The Evolution of Human Uniqueness* (Harper Collins, 1993).

Articles (by date of article)

"Make Room for Dad," by Shari Roan, *Los Angeles Times*, November 3, 1991.

"In the Presence of Animals: Health Professionals No Longer Scoff at the Therapeutic Effects of Pets," *U.S. News & World Report*, February 24, 1992.

"Efficiency vs. Micromanaging," by Mark McCormack, *Milwaukee Journal Sentinel*, October 16, 1995.

"Time Crunch Marches On," *Pittsburgh Post-Gazette*, February 20, 1996.

"Children's Early Development Begins with Human Nurture," by Susan H. Thompson, *The Tampa Tribune*, April 28, 1997.

"Gone Ridin'," by David Sharp, *Bicycling*, June 1, 1997.

"The Secret Life of the Working Wife," by Linda Williamson, *The Toronto Sun*, August 22, 1997.

"Sabbatical is the Perk that Perks Up Faithful Employees," by Nick Ravo, *The San Diego Union-Tribune*, October 5, 1997.

"Scheduling with Software: Get Technical about Time-Management," by Sara Woodard, *The Times-Picayune*, October 9, 1997.

"Tech-Hip Teens Tell '007s' '121' Beeper Culture," by Isabelle de Pommereau, *Christian Science Moniter*, October 23, 1997.

"Home Work Lessons to be Learned by Both Child, Parents," by Anne Veigle, *The Washington Times*, October 28, 1997.

"Husband-and-Wife Teams Face Pressure at Home and Work," by Jeanne Hoban, *Crain's Cleveland Business*, December 8, 1997.

"'All Work and No Play' No Longer the American Way?" by Mary Leonard, *Star-Tribune Newspaper of the Twin Cities*, December 14, 1997.

"Where Are the Kids on Your 'To Do' List?" by Sandy Evans, *The Washington Post*, January 5, 1998.

"Is Parenthood Dampening Your Ardor?" by Barri Bronston, *Times-Picayune*, February 9, 1998.

"Strengthening Today's Families: A Challenge to Parks and Recreation," by Dennis K. Orthner, *Parks and Recreation*, March, 1998.

"Busy Moms Say They Can Have it All," by Ruby L. Bailey, *The Detroit News*, March 2, 1998.

"Pre-Teens, Parents Find Little Time for Talk," *PR Newswire*, March 19, 1998.

"'Habits' for Effective Families," by Nancy Kelleher, *The Boston Herald*, April 19, 1998.

"Powerful Hi-Tech Organiser," by Sam Cheong, *New Straits Times (Malaysia)*, April 27, 1998.

"Managing Technology," by Geoffrey Rowen, *The Globe and Mail*, May 20, 1998.

"Technology Crashing Around Us; You Won't Hear a Beep Out of Me," by Rob Morse, *The Arizona Republic*, May 22, 1998.

"Beeping and Nothingness," by Paul Vitello, *Newsday: Nassau and Suffolk*, May 24, 1998.

"Think Before You Send that E-mail," by Louise Kehoe, *Financial Times: London Edition*, May 30, 1998.

"Ignore E-mail at Your Peril," *The Dominion*, June 22, 1998.

"Leave it Out," by Peter Baker, *The Observer*, June 28, 1998.

"Time for Life: The Surprising Way Americans Use Their Time," by June Cotte, *Journal of Marketing*, July 1, 1998.

"E-mail a 'Blessing' for Businesses," by Stephanie Armour, *USA Today*, July 2, 1998.

"Think Fail-Safe," by Nikhil Hutheesing, *Forbes*, July 6, 1998.

"You've Got Mail, and Mail, and Mail..." by Tammy Reiss, *Business Week*, July 20, 1998.

"E-Phones Connect," by Suzanne Kantra Kirschner, *Popular Science*, August, 1998.

Index

U-V

W-Z